From Threatening Guerrillas to Forever Illegals

LATINX: THE FUTURE IS NOW

A series edited by Lorgia García-Peña and Nicole Guidotti-Hernández

Books in the Series

Marisel C. Moreno, *Undocumented Migration in Hispanophone Caribbean and Latinx Literature and Art*

Francisco J. Galarte, *Brown Trans Figurations: Rethinking Race, Gender, and Sexuality in Chicanx/Latinx Studies*

From Threatening Guerrillas to Forever Illegals

US CENTRAL AMERICANS AND THE CULTURAL POLITICS OF NON-BELONGING

Yajaira M. Padilla

University of Texas Press   *Austin*

Requests for permission to reproduce material from this work should be sent to:

> Permissions
> University of Texas Press
> P.O. Box 7819
> Austin, TX 78713-7819
> utpress.utexas.edu/rp-form

♾ The paper used in this book meets the minimum requirements of ANSI/NISO Z39.48-1992 (R1997) (Permanence of Paper).

LIBRARY OF CONGRESS CATALOGING-IN-PUBLICATION DATA

Names: Padilla, Yajaira M., author.
Title: From threatening guerrillas to forever illegals : US Central Americans and the cultural politics of non-belonging / Yajaira M. Padilla.
Description: First edition. | Austin : University of Texas Press, 2022. | Series: Latinx: the future is now | Includes bibliographical references and index.
Identifiers:
> LCCN 2021041579
> ISBN 978-1-4773-2526-1 (cloth)
> ISBN 978-1-4773-2527-8 (paperback)
> ISBN 978-1-4773-2528-5 (PDF)
> ISBN 978-1-4773-2529-2 (ePub)
Subjects: LCSH: Central Americans—United States. | Central Americans in motion pictures. | Central Americans—Press coverage—United States. | Central Americans—Legal status, laws, etc.—United States. | Immigrants in mass media. | Mass media and immigrants—United States. | Central American Americans. | Stereotypes (Social psychology) in mass media. | Central America—On television. | Central America—In popular culture.
Classification: LCC E184.C34 P33 2022 | DDC 305.868/728—dc23
LC record available at https://lccn.loc.gov/2021041579
doi:10.7560/325261

To Steven and our two Salvicanas, Sayra and Camila

Contents

Acknowledgments

*A*LTHOUGH I BEGAN TO EXPLORE MANY OF THE IDEAS for this project long before my visiting fellowship at Arizona State University's Institute for Humanities Research in spring 2012, it was my time there that helped me to truly visualize what this project could be and the purpose that it might serve. I recall that following my introductory presentation to the rest of the fellows on what would become this project, one of them asked a rather pointed question about why I felt it was important to write a book about yet another ethnic minority, such as US Central Americans, when the ethnic studies field was under attack. Indeed, just two years prior, the then governor of Arizona, Jan Brewer, had signed into law H.B. 2281, a bill written in reaction to the Mexican American studies program implemented in Tucson public schools that, broadly, prohibited the teaching of ethnic studies in public and charter schools in the state. Though perhaps a valid and relevant question, I could not help but feel at the time that I was being asked to justify more than my project, that I was also being asked to justify why US Central American studies mattered and, relatedly, why US Central Americans like myself mattered. This feeling derived from my own experiences growing up in Southern California, where I not only often had to explain to people that I was Salvadoran American, not Mexican/Chicanx, and why that distinction was important (to me). That experience is also one that I had during my undergraduate and graduate studies and have continued to encounter in my years as an academic. Admittedly, I cannot remember what answer I gave to the question, but the query and the feelings triggered have long stayed with me and given shape to this project. In many ways, this book is my answer to that fellow's initial question from the vantage point of critical scholarship (I've long since stopped feeling the need to justify why I identify as Salvadoran American and am proud of being so).

I would like to begin these acknowledgments, therefore, by thanking the Institute for Humanities Research at ASU (the faculty, staff, and other fellows) for providing me an opportunity to further develop this project and for challenging me. I would especially like to thank Sujey Vega, who, like myself, was also a visiting fellow that spring, and Lee Bebout. Their support of my work, kindness, and friendship, which endure to this day, made my time all the more pleasant in Arizona. Similarly, I would like to thank Jorge Pérez, with whom I was colleagues while we were both at the University of Kansas. Thank you, Jorge, for reading early drafts of articles that provided material for this book and for remaining a good friend and peer mentor throughout the years. I also owe a debt of gratitude to pioneering scholars such as Ana Patricia Rodríguez, Cecilia Menjívar, Leisy Abrego, and Arturo Arias, who, along with others, have established the field of US Central American studies and paved the way for scholars like myself. All of you have been supportive of me professionally and generous with your knowledge and time. Without your provocative work and commitment to the field, this project would not be possible. The same is true of the US Central American artists, poets, writers, and activists—both known and those who are yet to be—whose work and resilience inspire my research. Thank you to Nicole Guidotti-Hernández and Lorgia García Peña, for taking an interest in this project. I am so excited to be part of your newly launched series Latinx: The Future Is Now. At the University of Texas Press, I would also like to thank my editor, Kerry E. Webb, for being so welcoming when we first met and for seeing this project through from beginning to end. I am equally grateful to my anonymous reviewers for their critical eyes and suggestions for improving the manuscript.

At the University of Arkansas, my faculty home since 2013, I also have many people to thank. My colleagues and writing group partners, Robin Roberts, Susan Marren, Lissette Szwydky-Davis, and Constance Bailey, have been stalwart readers of multiple chapter drafts and pillars of support, encouraging me to keep going and finish this book even when the confidence and will to do so eluded me. All of us in this profession should have such a group of women in their corners. The Humanities Center at the University of Arkansas provided me with a subvention grant that helped defray the copyright cost of some of the images included in this book, for which I am also grateful. Outside of the university, I would like to thank my friend Jane Daniels, one of the most fascinating people I have ever met. Our shared conversations at the neighborhood Starbucks where we first encountered each other, and where I spent a lot of my time writing this book, were a welcome respite from what was often a lonely endeavor. In this regard, Alicia Yvonne Estrada and Maritza E. Cárdenas also merit special recognition and appreciation. More than just colleagues, you fierce *centroamericanas* have become true friends who have helped me both weather difficult situations and celebrate achievements in my personal and professional life with humor, humility, and compassion.

To my parents, Oscar and Alicia Padilla, and my siblings, Georgina, Lisa, and Oscar, and their families, I also want to say thank you. As complicated as all of our relationships can be, I am glad to be a part of this dynamic and growing family. And knowing that you are all there for me and love me despite the distance that separates us comforts me when I need it most. Last, but certainly not least, I would like to thank my daughters, Sayra and Camila, and my spouse, Steven. Sayri and Cami, you are what makes everything I do worth it. I am grateful for the unconditional love you give me, for the boundless excitement and smiles with which you greet me each morning and throughout the day, and for your patience with me, especially this past year, in which all of our lives were upended by the COVID-19 pandemic and I labored to finish this book. Steven, thank you for being the best coparent I could have asked for. You selflessly gave so much so that I could have the gift of time to complete this book, taking the lead with our girls, time and again, and ensuring that our household and family needs were met. Simply put, this book would not exist without you, and, more important, this family and my world do not function without you. Thank you for being who you are and for your unfailing love throughout this adventure of a life we have embarked on and continue to navigate together.

PORTIONS OF CHAPTER ONE FIRST APPEARED IN "CENTRAL American Non-belonging: Reading 'El Norte' in Cary Fukunaga's *Sin nombre*," from the edited anthology *The Latin American Road Movie* (Palgrave, 2016). An earlier version of chapter two appeared as the article "Domesticating Rosario: Conflicting Representations of the Latina Maid in U.S. Media," published in the *Arizona Journal of Hispanic Cultural Studies*. Finally, an earlier version of chapter five appeared as "Illegal Chickens: The Art of Branding Poultry in Central American L.A.," the last chapter of the edited volume *U.S. Central Americans: Reconstructing Memories, Struggles, and Communities of Resistance* (University of Arizona Press, 2017).

From Threatening Guerillas to Forever Illegals

Introduction

CENTRAL AMERICANS AMONG "US"

*I*N APRIL 2018, PRESIDENT DONALD J. TRUMP BEGAN tweeting about "caravans" of Central American migrants en route to the US-Mexico border, warning that they posed a grave threat to the national security of the United States. Trump's fixation on these "caravans," which largely comprised family units, women with children, and unaccompanied minors seeking asylum in Mexico and the United States, fanned the flames of what was one of his signature campaign promises and a central component of his anti-immigrant legislative agenda—the building of a literal wall on the US-Mexico border that, he initially claimed, Mexico would pay for.[1] Political fearmongering such as this is not a new occurrence. Central Americans have frequently been cast as unequivocal dangers to the nation's sovereignty and as one more example of the perceived ills wrought by Latin American (undocumented) immigration: crime, violence, disease, a drain on resources, and demographic changes that are contributing to the racial and cultural devolution of the country. During the 1980s and another notable conservative presidency, that of Ronald Reagan, Central Americans acquired a similar notoriety. This earlier period, which marked a key moment not only in US-Central American relations but also in the history of Central American immigration to the United States, shows Trump's portrayals of Central American "caravans" to be part of a longer trajectory of similarly problematic representations of Central America and its peoples. It also helps to foreground my main project here: interrogating the hegemonic ways in which Central Americans (in and outside of the isthmus) have been imagined in US political discourse, mainstream media, and cultural production over close to four decades, from the 1980s to 2020. This critical enterprise reveals not only the key bearing that such means of signifying US Central Americans has had and continues to have on the sense of and

1

state of belonging of these populations, but also the limits of narrowly conceived notions of Latin American immigration and Latinx communities in the United States.[2]

More than thirty years prior to Trump's tweet concerning Central American "caravans," President Ronald Reagan sounded a similar alarm during his 1984 address to the nation. Speaking of United States policy in Central America, Reagan warned against the imminent threat that the rise of communism in the region posed to the national security and economic prosperity of the United States and, more generally, to freedom in the Western Hemisphere. Reagan took particular aim at the Sandinista government in Nicaragua, which came to power in 1979, excoriating its "Communist reign of terror" as well as intentions to export that "terror to every other country in the region."[3] Reagan stipulated as a fact that the Sandinistas' most immediate target was El Salvador, an equally embattled country that would soon be communist unless the United States intervened. As a means of further substantiating the need for such efforts, Reagan emphasized the close proximity of Central America and, in particular, El Salvador to the United States, noting that "San Salvador is closer to Houston, Texas, than Houston is to Washington, DC." He also drew a sharp contrast between Nicaragua and El Salvador, making a case for the salvageability of the latter, whose government, according to Reagan, was an ally in the global fight against communism and whose people fundamentally loved freedom and peace. Thus, Reagan rationalized that US intervention in the region was more than just a strategic imperative; it was also a moral duty ("Address").

At the time of Reagan's address, Nicaragua, Guatemala, and El Salvador were all in the midst of civil or counterrevolutionary wars and had been for some time.[4] The Reagan administration was likewise already engaged in interventionist efforts in all three. Due to increasing reports regarding gross human rights violations by the Salvadoran government and more generalized fears that further intervention in El Salvador would lead to another Vietnam, the Reagan administration, however, faced significant opposition from politicians and a growing sector of the US public (Dunkerley 194–195). Engaged in a war of perceptions, Reagan wielded this address to support his policies. Key to his argument was the framing of Central America, on one hand, as a region teeming with unhinged subversives and, on the other, as on the cusp of democracy, with a general population desperately yearning for and deserving of it. What rendered this particular image of Central America so effective was not only its purposeful simplicity and Reagan's exploitation of Cold War tropes of communism as contagion but also the prejudicial assumptions of Central America as "backward," an area prone to banana republics and strong men that had yet to achieve the modern status of many of its Latin

American neighbors (Skidmore and Smith 321). As Reagan implied, this backwardness, coupled with the Soviet Union's aggressive courting of Latin American nations such as Cuba and Nicaragua, made Central America particularly susceptible to communist contamination. This perception of backwardness was also used to explain Central America's inability to govern itself and to achieve democracy without the economic and military aid of more advanced nations such as the United States.

Reagan was ultimately successful in lobbying Congress to continue to fund his administration's imperialist exploits in Central America. By 1985, economic aid to El Salvador alone totaled $744 million, adding to the $744 million the country had already received between 1981 and 1983 for "security" measures (Smith 35). By way of this address, Reagan also helped to concretize a particular vision of the isthmus and its inhabitants within the national imaginary, one that would work to the benefit of his administration's conservative, anti-immigrant domestic agenda. From the late 1970s to 1990, a period that corresponds roughly with the era of Central America's revolutions, the US Central American population more than tripled (increasing from 354,000 to 1,134,000), mainly as a consequence of the unprecedented influx of Guatemalan and Salvadoran refugees fleeing their countries of origin (O'Connor et al.). Upon arrival, the majority of these refugees encountered strong resistance to their claims for political asylum on the grounds that, according to the US government, they were not fleeing oppressive regimes but democratic states, a delusion clearly discernible in Reagan's address. Thus, and by contrast to Nicaraguans emigrating from a home country perceived as a communist stronghold under the Sandinistas, Guatemalans and Salvadorans were unlikely to be granted asylum. As has been reported, less than 3 percent of the claims filed by these refugee populations had been approved by 1984 (Gzesh).

To read such governmental maneuvers as merely a manifestation of the inherent contradictions of the Reagan administration's official stance on Central America would be to ignore that such efforts to systematically bar Central American immigrants from the nation also played out against the backdrop of a "changing America." The 1980s witnessed notable gains in minority civil rights and inclusion across a wide spectrum of institutions— the result of earlier civil rights struggles and feminist movements—as well as demographic shifts occasioned, in large part, by the increase in legal immigration from Asian, African, and Latin American countries in the wake of the Immigration and Nationality Act of 1965.[5] These social and political changes provoked racialized anxieties in a largely white-dominant majority that feared a hostile takeover of "their" country. These developments led to sustained efforts by conservatives, under the leadership of Reagan, to dismantle the welfare state by pushing for greater privatization and deregulation of the economy as well as attacks against affirmative action, bilingual and multicultural education, the reproductive rights of women, and the LGBTQ community as it wrestled with the devastation of the AIDS crisis. At the same time, the Right also targeted immigration, which they saw as likely to increase the number of people of color in the country and those people's political and social clout. Immigration from the southern border was of particular concern due not only to the proximity of Mexico to the United States and what was at the time a significant rise in undocumented migration from Mexico but also to predicted future increases in the Mexican American and US Latinx populations. The 1980s is, after all, often referred to as "the Decade of the Hispanic."

Considered in this light, the Reagan administration's discriminatory position with regard to Salvadoran and Guatemalan asylum seekers was as much about preventing more "brown" people from coming into the country as it was about helping to maintain the United States' standing as the leader of the "Free World" in the global fight against communism. It stands to reason, then, that Reagan's discursive rendering of Central Americans also served more than one purpose. As Stuart Hall reminds us, it is through the signifying practice of representation that "we give things meaning" ("Introduction" 3). And because "meanings also regulate and organize our conduct and practices [. . .] they are also what those who wish to govern and regulate the conduct and ideas of others seek to structure and shape" (4). Accordingly, Reagan's signification of Central Americans as strong men, violent subversives, and the like had the intended purpose and effect of transforming them into a multipronged menace to the nation. First and most obviously, Central Americans were potential carriers of communist contagion; second, they were Latin Americans (marginal ones, at that) whose addition to the growing immigrant presence in the United States was racially and politically dangerous. Inasmuch as this type of meaning-making or production of knowledge regarding Central Americans aided Reagan's focused efforts to influence congressional and public opinion, it also had devastating consequences for the civilians who were caught in the crossfire of US-funded civil wars and, relatedly, those who fled to the United States seeking refuge.

THIS BRIEF RECONSIDERATION OF REAGAN'S 1984 ADDRESS on Central America illustrates how the discursive renderings of US Central Americans as existential threats to the country (both ideological and biological) are intimately tied to the struggles waged by these populations against exclusion from US society as well as their prospects of becoming "real Americans." Hence, a fundamental premise of this critical inquiry is that dominant representations of US Central Americans constitute an unexplored yet valuable entry point into the cultural politics of *non-belonging* that undergird what can be conceived of as an emergent US Central American experience, one that begins with the Central American refugee crises of the 1980s. Although this experience is mostly limited to the specific histories of recent immigration and ethnic integration of Guatemalans, Hondurans, and Salvadorans, it is, as this study illuminates, a key and defining chapter in a larger narrative and history of the Central American presence in the United States.[6] As noted, US-based populations of Guatemalans and Salvadorans grew dramatically during the 1980s and continue to. So, too, has the population of Hondurans, which significantly increased in the aftermath of the wars.[7] These three groups comprise 86 percent of the overall US Central American population and have been the clear target of discriminatory immigration laws meant to bar or limit their settlement in the United States during and in the wake of civil wars (O'Connor et al.), and it is depictions of these populations that have dominated US Central American representation in mainstream media, political discourse, and cultural production of the last few decades.

Non-belonging is a concept that I offer and employ to register both the ways in which US Central Americans (immigrants and subsequent generations alike) have been constituted as Others who don't belong on a symbolic and material level, and the related means by which US Central Americans and others affirm, unsettle, and counteract this exclusionary condition. Such a condition, and sense, of marginalization, as I discuss in more detail in chapter one, has roots in Latin America's colonial legacy and Central America's peripheral status within Latin America proper. It is a condition nevertheless that becomes exacerbated, for many Central American immigrants, within the context of labor exploitation, social and racial stratification, and anti-immigrant policies and sentiments in the United States. Non-belonging likewise underscores the limits of narrowly conscripted notions and discourses of national affiliation based on citizenry, social and economic integration, and affect while also allowing for a broader understanding of the alternative forms of individual and communal belonging US Central Americans enact within the context of the diasporic and/or the transnational or transisthmian. These alternative forms, many of which exist in response to or are elaborated through a reworking of the very representations of US Central Americans problematized here, evoke notions of belonging as an instantiation of being as well as becoming or possibility.

Admittedly, much of the work undertaken here relates to the dimensions of this conceptual framework that contend with US Central American otherness and its effects. Although in the following chapters I recognize and explore to various degrees efforts by US Central Americans and others to refute and/or resist this systematic means of marginalization, I remain largely invested in elucidating the interrelated dynamics of the legal, economic, and social exclusion of US Central Americans and their mediated representations over the last four decades. This emphasis not only underscores the outsize impact that the multilayered disenfranchisement of US Central Americans has had on their integration as "Americans" but also constitutes a foundation for contemplating the more immediate and precarious social reality of many US Central Americans as the United States transitions away from the Trump administration and attempts to deal with the repercussions of its policies. That said, this study does not provide, nor does it pretend to be an exhaustive account of, all the myriad and imbricated ways that US Central Americans are signified as Others. This is due to practical considerations in delineating the length and scope of this study as well as the very nature of the representations central to this project.

As noted, these depictions are "hegemonic." In referring to them as such, I am channeling, in part, the notion of *hegemonic tropicalizations* set forth by Frances R. Aparicio and Susana Chávez-Silverman. This conceptualization refers to the means of troping, or of imbuing Latin America and its peoples, including immigrant populations, with specific attributes or traits in keeping with Western-based fictions of "Latin American and U.S. Latino identities and cultures" linked to the "tropics" (1). Because this troping transpires in a "privileged First World location" and aligns with the specific interests of structures of power, it is hegemonic (6). Although not all of Central America can be or should be subsumed under the banner of the "tropics," many of the representations focalized in this study tap into this understanding of the region. Certainly, Reagan's perverse description of Nicaragua's Sandinistas betrays "tropical anxieties" about the communist dangers that await in Central America's jungles. One can also make the case that depictions of political refugees do the same, as, in certain instances, they speak to the perceived dangers of what can happen when the Central American "tropics" exceed the boundaries of their geographic location and spill into or "invade" the United States.

Inherent to this means of troping, or giving rise to hegemonic depictions of US Central Americans, is a privileging of mestizo identities (of Indigenous and Anglo-European heritage) that likewise affirm gender and sexual norms. This is not surprising considering the long history in Hollywood and mainstream media of portraying US-born Latinx populations and, in particular, immigrants from Latin America as identifiably "brown" or as having what Clara E. Rodríguez emphasizes are "Latin looks." With few exceptions, this form of racialization is often accentuated via the added characterizations of these same populations as downtrodden simpletons or criminals belonging to the poor and/or working class. Such popular depictions of US Central Americans as primarily mestizo (alternately ladino),[8] however, are also consistent with racist discourses of *mestizaje* and national belonging in Central America proper and, more generally, Latin America. Cultivated and institutionalized by political elites and intellectuals in the late nineteenth to early twentieth century, the ideology of *mestizaje* romanticized Indigenous and Afro-descendent populations as relics of the past while promoting their "whitening" as a means of achieving racial homogeneity and modernizing nation-states. Although the perceived "primitivity" of both groups presented an obstacle to achieving the latter, the Indian occupied a privileged position as a national symbol given his native status, resulting in the Indo-European, or mestizo, racial vision of the Americas that remains prevalent today (Anderson and England 270). By racializing US Central Americans in this manner—as primarily *mestizo/ladino* or "brown"—these hegemonic depictions further marginalize or completely erase the existence and experiences of US Central Americans who also identify as Indigenous and/or Black.[9]

In similar fashion, the conventionally gendered and heteronormative vision offered by these dominant representations also tends to disregard the added complexities of women's experiences and to elide those of LGBTQ individuals. Mainstream depictions of Central American immigration, in particular, often posit male immigrants as having the most agency or potential for survival and success in the United States. Depictions of Central American asylum-seeking populations as defenseless victims likewise resort to these traditional views of gender and power relations, highlighting images of women and children and/or entire family units as a means of equating these groups with the feminine (a non-threatening position). Missing from these heteronormative views and accounts of (im)migration are those of LGBTQ individuals. Notably, and despite the amount of news media coverage devoted to Central American immigration since 2014—when a notable uptick in undocumented youth migration from the region once again garnered the attention of the mainstream media and the US government[10]—reports documenting the migratory reality of LGBTQ individuals in transit through Mexico and in detention centers in the United States remain scant. The same is true of accounts of Indigenous and Black Central American (im)migrants. Thus, even as they provide a key foundation for examining the cultural politics of non-belonging, hegemonic images of US Central Americans also impose certain constraints on this project, ones that are revisited in other parts of this book and further discussed in the conclusion.

Drawing on Stuart Hall's theories of representation, I analyze these dominant portrayals as part of an expanding regime of representation that fundamentally works to construe US Central Americans as unbelonging Others. The foundations of this regime are to be found in the prominent depictions of these populations engendered in the 1980s: the menacing guerrilla/military strongman of the Central American tropics and its correlative, the disenfranchised political refugee. Existing beyond these renditions are those of the Central American youth gang member, the maid (or *doméstica*), and what I term the *forever illegal*. A composite of sorts, this last figure speaks to newer waves of migrants from the region seeking better economic opportunities but also, and increasingly, refuge from similarly volatile conditions as their predecessors. The forever illegal likewise marks the enduring liminal legality or undocumented existence of a large majority of the US Central American population. These last manifestations are direct descendants of the former, having emerged in the consecutive decades of the 1990s and early 2000s, and brandishing a similar symbolic power and weight over the US public's perceptions of US Central Americans, particularly the undocumented. Although these figures bear the imprint of well-known clichés and stereotypes associated, more broadly, with the Latin American region, its peoples, and Latinx populations in the United States, they also remain bound to and are the byproduct of specific US Central American histories, geopolitical contexts, and immigrant realities. The trope of illegality, for example, has long been associated with "brown" bodies, especially those of Mexicans. Yet, as the Central American inflections of the forever illegal show, the means by which these racialized bodies come to be "illegal" and inhabit such a precarious condition are not all the same. The ways in which US Central Americans exist within and in relation to regimes of (im)migrant illegality is conditioned by their own particular nationalities and histories of immigrant reception in the United States.

I trace the emergence of this regime and its work of signification through a wide terrain of texts, including documentaries and fiction-based films, television series, online mainstream news and reporting, and street art about and by US Central Americans. In line with central tenets of cultural and media studies, these textual forms are mediating spaces through which individual and collective actors can be acted upon but are also capable of acquiring and exerting agency.[11] These texts are likewise connected by the intersecting discourses that permeate them. The same can be said of the other cultural works that are examined in this study with regard to shared political discourses linked to Latin American immigration as well as related discourses specific to Central America and its diaspora in the United States. Of equal importance is the fact that the majority of these texts are visual mediums, which plays a key role not only in the ways that US Central Americans are rendered within and through them but also in the types of meaning-making and racialized knowledges such portrayals afford. As Judith Butler maintains, seeing is also a form of reading and constituting, a modality of performativity by which something can be raced (quoted in Bell 170). These racialized knowledges help fuel broader narratives of US Central Americans as threatening and undesirable citizen-subjects of the nation.

The period covered in this study is bracketed by two conservative presidencies, that of Ronald Reagan (from 1981 to 1989) and that of Donald Trump (from 2017 to 2021). As was the case during the Reagan era, US Central Americans acquired a hypervisibility during the Trump presidency. Trump's use of undocumented migration as a political ploy, along with corresponding media coverage and related fictionalized accounts and documentaries focused on the same, once again thrust US Central Americans into the limelight and lodged them at the center of foreign policy and immigration debates.[12] Although hegemonic depictions of US Central Americans circulated throughout the four decades that separate these administrations, during both such depictions were especially prolific, fueling anti-immigrant sentiments and legislative efforts implemented in direct response to and disproportionately targeting undocumented Central American immigrants. These same representations also spurred advocacy and activism centered on immigrant and human rights. The symbolic currency of these portrayals, the degree to which they can affect public perception and governmental politics, was also greatest during these administrations. A significant case in point are the aforementioned "caravans" of Central American migrants that captured Trump's and the nation's attention in 2018.

Trump first referenced the "caravans" on April 1, 2018, in a tweet in which he also railed against the weak immigration laws of Democrats and a potential deal on DACA (Deferred Action for Childhood Arrivals), a program established via executive decision by his predecessor, Barack Obama, in 2012, which Trump similarly ended through executive action in 2017.[13] With two short phrases in the midst of these other attacks—"Getting more dangerous. 'Caravans' coming"—Trump painted an image of the Central American migrants en route as a multiplying and violent hoard on a collision course with the United States (quoted in Semple). This image belied the fact that these "caravans" were part of an organized effort by the immigrant rights organization Pueblo Sin Fronteras to help undocumented Central Americans migrate safely and seek asylum in Mexico and the United States and were not a new phenomenon. This was a calculated strategy employed by Trump in the months leading up to the midterm elections in November 2018. Channeling Reagan, Trump played into the racialized fears of terrorist attacks and demographic shifts of his Republican base, fears he continued to stoke with subsequent tweets in which he suggested that the "caravan" had been infiltrated by "Many Gang Members" and "some very bad people"[14] and with his controversial decision right before the elections to deploy 5,200 active duty troops to the southern border, adding to the 2,100 National Guard members who had already been mobilized. Despite some pushback within the mainstream media, Trump's theatrics of fear did impact public opinion concerning Central American migrants. As a Monmouth University poll from November revealed, more than half of those surveyed considered the migrant "caravan" as either a major (29 percent) or minor (24 percent) threat to the country ("Public Divided").

THE PARADOXES OF VISIBILITY

In disclosing the constructed nature of Central American other-ness and its effects, dominant representations of US Central Americans also provide a critical terrain. Traversing this terrain reveals the tangentiality of US Central American histories and im/migrant experiences within domi-nant conceptualizations of and discourses about Latin American immigra-tion in the United States. Trump's tweets about the migrant "caravans" exist within a historical and geopolitical vacuum, as does much of the reporting on this topic, confining this migrant reality to a presentist and US-based context that is disarticulated from the not-too-distant past of Central Amer-ican immigration and the related refugee crisis in the Reagan era. A similar moment occurred during and in the immediate aftermath of the Rodney King riots in the early 1990s, when many gang youth, particularly those affiliated with the Los Angeles–based Mara Salvatrucha (MS-13) and 18th Street Gang, were deported back to the region, where they now have a sig-nificant stronghold. As documented in academic scholarship and the news media, the United States facilitated the deportation to Central American countries—ones with crippled economies and little-to-no infrastructure fol-lowing decades of war—of the very gangs Trump decries and falsely claims originated in the region.[15] In effect, the United States has had a hand in the very gang-related crime and violence many Central American youth and family units have been attempting to escape through undocumented migra-tion, including group efforts such as migrant "caravans."

Moreover, and despite the noted Central American background of the migrants in such portrayals, this regional and ethnic-based distinction, like the stated histories of US intervention and immigrant regulation, has argu-ably failed to register within the greater national and popular imaginary of the United States. For all of their heightened visibility in key moments of immigration "crises" or "emergencies," US Central Americans remain paradoxically unseen or, more to the point, illegible. One main reason for this has been that US empire building, carried out since the nineteenth century in Central America, has often been undertaken in the guise of modernization and democracy. Indeed, as the title of Juan González's popular history of Latinos in the United States *Harvest of Empire* (2011) makes clear, most Americans fail to even conceive of the United States as an empire and therefore also fail to see Latin American immigration and the growing Latinx presence in the country as part of what it has reaped. Another equally pivotal reason is the fact that the means of portraying, addressing, and publicly legislating Latin American immigration in the United States has been and continues to be largely influenced by a myopic gaze on the US-Mexico border and Mexican (undocumented) immigration. Admittedly, there are well-established geographic, economic, and historical reasons for such myopia, reasons that I am not necessarily debating here. What I am calling into question, however, is the uncritical privileging of the US-Mexico boundary as the preeminent site of crossing and construction of migrant "illegality" for all who transgress it, and, along with this, the positing of Mexican immigration as the paradigm for all migratory movements that literally originate "south of the border."

Such a bias, whether effectuated consciously or unconsciously, is discernible in US political and popular discourse. Existing scholarship within media and cultural studies has done little to complicate or counteract this bias.[16] Leo Chavez's *Covering Immigration: Popular Images and the Politics of Nation* (2001) and *The Latino Threat: Constructing Immigrants, Citizens, and the Nation* (2008), Otto Santa Ana's *Brown Tide Rising: Metaphors of Latinos in Contemporary American Public Discourse* (2002), and, most recently, Leah Perry's *The Cultural Politics of U.S. Immigration: Gender, Race, and Media* (2016), among others, have been instrumental in shaping my approach to and thoughts regarding how US Central American immigration and US Central Americans have been discursively plotted within and outside the United States. These studies explore the visual rhetoric, cultural logics, and political implications of how Latin American immigration and Latinx populations, more broadly, have been portrayed in the media, political discourse, and popular culture from the passage of the 1965 Immigration and Reform Act to the early 2000s. My own critical inquiries draw on the conceptual frameworks and paradigms they offer but also add the relevance and specificity of US Central Americans within such frameworks and paradigms.

Case studies related to representations of Mexican (undocumented) immigration, the US-Mexico border, and Mexican Americans occupy a primary place in the majority of these studies. Chavez's *Covering Immigration* and Perry's *The Cultural Politics of U.S. Immigration*, which spend significant time contemplating the decade of the 1980s, also contend in nuanced ways with the case of Cuban immigrants and Puerto Ricans and, to a lesser extent, that of Asian immigration and Asian Americans. Absent in these studies, however, is any comparable exploration of Central American immigration and US Central Americans, which is all the more glaring in the aforementioned works focused specifically on the 1980s, when Central American revolutions and refugees acquired a high degree of visibility in the US political and popular imaginary. Central American immigration and US Central Americans are often relegated to passing references that acknowledge the presence of these communities as part of a growing Latinx population, but these studies do not deal with their unique histories and their potential significance to the broader conceptual frameworks they advance. Chavez's liminal incorporation of US Central American voices, for example, in *The Latino Threat* helps to further his argument regarding a "Latino Threat Narrative" in which all Latinx populations in the United States are posited as inassimilable illegal aliens that are an existential danger to US society. The fact, however, that this paradigm is developed largely in reference to the notion of Mexicans as the "quintessential illegal" and public discourses related to Mexicans and Mexican Americans as an invading force bent on taking back the US Southwest obscures any historical, sociopolitical, and ethnocultural nuance a supplemental Central American focus might afford (3). Ironically, in arguing against a dominant narrative that casts all Latinx populations as a threat, Chavez contributes to the continued interpolation of US Central Americans as Mexicans as well as to the illegibility of their experiences and voices.

By contemplating hegemonic representations of US Central Americans as critical incursions into a larger US Central American experience, I thus allow for the focalization of US Central American experiences of crossing and subjectivities that are, to a great extent, rendered illegible and of less critical import under an enduring "First World" gaze and by blanket notions of Latin American immigration and who and what are "illegal." Accordingly, I push back against the erasure of Central Americanness and its differences within regimenting public discourses and academic approaches to (im)migration related to Latinx peoples. Undocumented Central American migrants en route to the North traverse various national and political boundaries as well as social planes. Such crossings have yielded new amalgamations of power, including a US-Mexico multistate immigration regime and technologies of surveillance to help police, detain, and exploit Central American bodies as they move across those very boundaries and planes. The (im)migrant subjectivities forged within and in relation to these experiences of crossing are similarly multilayered, revealing the many ways in which transmigrating through Mexico—a dehumanizing and traumatic ordeal— leaves its own indelible imprint on the bodies and psyches of Central American (im)migrants, their sense of being undocumented and expendable, and the desperation as well as hopes for a better life that often propel these migrants to undergo such dangerous journeys in the first place. These US Central American (im)migrant subjectivities also beg related questions, which I contemplate in the conclusion: How does one speak of a US Central American borderlands subjectivity? And what, then, are the limits of paradigms and borderlands discourses premised primarily on Chicanx/Mexican American experiences in addressing such a query?

My argument in this book also complicates dominant conceptualizations and debates regarding Latin American immigration and insists on the need to reframe them altogether. The nuances of Central American border crossings and immigrant lives can be ascertained and addressed only by looking beyond the limits of the US-Mexico divide and its borderlands. It is not enough to only contend with the bilateral relationships of the United States and Mexico and the United States and Central America. We also need a complex understanding of multistate securitization, economic, and foreign policies as well as the added intersectional power dynamics, at various levels, that define Mexican and Central American relations dating back to the colonial period. Attention to such nuances is necessary for contemplating the subjectivities and lived experiences of US Central Americans. Such subjectivities and experiences likewise necessitate a wider lens than that which has been traditionally used to look at predominant models of Latin American immigration and Latinx communities. The diasporic roots; transnational proclivities; histories of US imperialism; multilingual, multiracial, and multiethnic make-up; and past and present immigrant realities of US Central American communities render insufficient nationalist paradigms such as those that have provided a foundation for the study of Mexican American/ Chicanx, Puerto Rican, and Cuban American culture, identity, group and communal politics, and US ethnic integration. Ultimately, and consistent with related scholarship by US Central American scholars working in a similar vein,[17] this study is both a renewed call to rethink and reconfigure Latinx studies and a testament to some of the ways that change is already underway.

Within the more specialized scope of what has been termed to varying degrees (US) Central American studies, work on US Central American cultural production has emerged as an early and strong focal point.[18] A quick overview of programming for major conferences in American studies, Latin American studies, and Latinx studies in the span of the last couple of years reveals, however, that explorations of the Central American diaspora as it is engaged in social media landscapes such as Twitter, Instagram, Snapchat, documentaries, music, and the like are also being undertaken. These represent exciting and new directions for the study of Central American populations in the United States. But such explorations centered on new visual mediums and critical spaces of possibility do not exist in a vacuum. US Central Americans have, for some time now, been a part of the US popular imaginary. This project, therefore, also represents a conscious effort to showcase what has come before as a means of bridging it with the now, helping to further flesh out an archive of visual studies regarding US Central Americans.

Chapter one, "Signifying US Central American Non-belonging," initiates and anchors this entire project. Whereas the first sections consist of a basic outline of the history of Central American immigration in the United States (1980s to 2020) and an explanation of the central tenets of non-belonging as a conceptual framework, in the final part of the chapter I provide a critical genealogy of the prevalent ways in which US Central Americans have been depicted in the US popular imaginary, beginning with the figure of the threatening guerrilla and ending with that of the forever illegal. This critical genealogy makes explicit the ways in which these depictions not only mark but are directly engaged in the cultural politics of non-belonging. Because of their signifying function, these hegemonic representations contribute to the othering of US Central Americans but also have the potential to render them in alternative ways.

The remaining chapters are loosely organized in keeping with this critical genealogy. In chapters two and three I examine to varying degrees depictions of US Central Americans as *domésticas* and gang members, outgrowths of earlier representations from the revolutionary period in Central America: the feminized political refugee and the threatening guerrilla/strongman. In chapters four and five I contend more specifically with representations of Central American immigrants as forever illegals. Although the actual or presumed undocumented status of US Central Americans also factors in the dominant renderings explored in previous chapters and informs this related trope, in these last chapters the condition of being "illegal" is front and center, helping to illuminate the geopolitical factors, multiple crossings, and governing structures that beget illegal US Central American subjects.

This chapter arrangement further emphasizes the ways in which these dominant depictions have through time contributed to a reifying narrative of US Central Americans as undesirable Others while still allowing for other possibilities, such as the elaboration of counternarratives of belonging or resistance. Indeed, the examples of counternarratives explored in this project were selected precisely because they work with and through these same prevalent images of US Central Americans, in particular that of the forever illegal. As such, these examples are drawn not solely from the work of US Central American cultural producers but also from that of others, including US and Mexican filmmakers.

In chapter two, "Domesticated Subject? The Salvadoran Maid in US Television and Film," I examine the depictions of *domésticas* such as Rosario in the hit sitcom *Will and Grace* and Dolores in the independent film *Dirt* (2004). Read against the backdrop of Hollywood portrayals of maids of color and post-1980s Central American (im)migration to the United States, representations of Salvadoran *domésticas* provide a site for exploring issues concerning Latinx visibility and invisibility within and out of the media spotlight, the exploitation and internationalization of the Latina workforce, and the construction of gendered US Central American subjectivities and desires for belonging that do not conform to hegemonic notions of immigrant assimilation. These depictions also speak to the ways in which Salvadoran/Latina immigrant laborers are absorbed into the nation through a colonizing process of domestication. Provisionally "included," these domesticated subjects remain subordinate to a system that exploits them while also helping to maintain the (neoliberal) status quo. Whereas Rosario's seemingly progressive representation serves to uphold this notion, that of Dolores does not, showcasing a Salvadoran woman who not only sees the process of domestication for what it is but also attempts to resist it.

In chapter three, "Lance Corporal José Gutiérrez and the Perils of Being a 'Good Immigrant,'" I interrogate further the neoliberal reality and logics that condition the representations of the Salvadoran *doméstica*. A case study of human-interest stories centered on José Gutiérrez, a "green card soldier" from Guatemala who was among the first to die in the Iraq War, brings into sharp relief a neoliberal approach to immigration that requires (male) undocumented youth from Central America be willing to die in order to belong. Gutiérrez's mediated representation as a "good" neoliberal immigrant subject likewise offers a means of understanding the predicament of youth asylum seekers in the Trump era. Like Gutiérrez, these newer arrivals are also required to subject themselves to death. However, their perceived or real association with MS-13 (a marker of their threatening nature and backwardness as Central Americans) makes their inclusion on the same neoliberal grounds of immigrant meritocracy and "goodness" a near impossibility.

Whereas in chapters two and three I contend with the stakes of nonbelonging for US Central Americans mostly within the context of the United States, chapter four, "Central American Crossings, Rightlessness, and Survival in Mexico's Border Passage," focalizes the process of US Central

American othering on the migrant trail. In this chapter I examine documentaries that chronicle the experiences of Central American transmigrants in Mexico, centering on the representational and affective politics of these films as well as their projection of Mexico as a "border passage." This vision of Mexico as both an extended border zone and a debasing passageway for Central American migrants underscores their rightlessness and transformation into human commodities en route to the United States. The latter is a result of the migration regulations and policing by an interstate US-Mexico border enforcement regime, global economic processes that engender and require cheap laborers, and a network of violent criminal entities for whom migrants are a lucrative source of income. Crucial to the human rights–based agenda of these films, this manifestation of Mexico also affords a broader understanding of how the ostracization of US Central Americans transpires across national borders.

Finally, in chapter five, "The Cachet of Illegal Chickens in Central American Los Angeles," I examine the politics of non-belonging in relation to three works by the self-proclaimed Guatemalan-Angeleno graffiti artist Cache. Recalling similar community-led efforts, Cache's pieces, consisting of a street mural and two related installations, challenge regimes of visibility and "illegality" that either occlude these populations and their transformative presence in Los Angeles or allow them to be seen only as criminalized illegals. Especially pertinent to the latter are Cache's installation pieces. Accentuated by the venues in which they are showcased, these works offer nuanced critiques of discriminatory immigration laws and proposed policies (Arizona's S.B. 1070 and the DREAM Act) while also gesturing toward the otherwise unseen realities of US Central American labor exploitation and gendered histories of immigration.

In the conclusion, "Seeing beyond the Dominant," I further contemplate the critical potential of non-belonging as a conceptual framework. Referencing works by US Central American diasporic cultural producers from newer generations who are active on social media helps to illuminate alternate forms of belonging that do not conform to or necessarily work through dominant tropes of US Central Americans and that bring to bear the perspectives of historically marginalized groups within these same populations. Additionally, I highlight the importance of regional perspectives and geographic space to the cultural politics of US Central American non-belonging through a discussion of how US Central American "border crossers" fruitfully complicate dominant/Chicanx-centric paradigms of the "borderlands" and "borderland subjectivities." Together, these means of "seeing beyond the dominant" offer additional areas of exploration for understanding an evolving US Central American experience and its non-belonging dimensions.

CHAPTER ONE

Signifying US Central American Non-belonging

D EPICTED AS THREATENING GUERRILLAS, DOMESTIC workers, MS-13 "gang-bangers," and, more broadly, forever illegals, these portrayals have populated political discourse, film and television, the news media, and literary works for nearly four decades and created hegemonic representations of US Central Americans. As a key foundation for this project, in this chapter I illuminate (1) the interlinked and enduring ways in which such depictions have signified and continue to signify US Central American populations, and (2) the critical possibilities and implications of these very significations related to what I call non-belonging. Discussed in more detail below, non-belonging is a term and conceptual approximation that encompasses the ways in which US Central Americans come to be and exist as Others in the United States based on citizenship status, race and ethnicity, class, gender, and sexuality, as well as their efforts to contest this same exclusionary condition. This tension between how US Central Americans are figuratively and materially deemed to not belong and how and through what means they envision themselves as belonging is at the core of a US Central American experience that has taken shape in the years since the 1980s. As I argue, the noted hegemonic depictions of US Central Americans provide an avenue for both discerning and actively engaging with the cultural politics of non-belonging that undergird this emergent experience.

An initial overview of Central American immigration history in the United States from the 1980s through the second decade of the 2000s helps to ground my broader argument regarding hegemonic depictions of US Central Americans and, relatedly, my conceptualization of non-belonging. Thereafter, I engage in a lengthier discussion of non-belonging as a "working paradigm," placing it in the broader context of existing frameworks that have been advanced by other scholars to account for the marginalization of US Central American populations. The critical genealogy that follows, of the aforementioned manifestations of US Central Americans as threatening guerrillas, political refugees, *domésticas*, MS-13 "gangbangers," and forever illegals, shows how these portrayals have likewise played a key role in the fashioning of US Central Americans as undesirable citizen-subjects. Although much of this genealogical discussion revolves around this particular function of these portrayals, the possibilities they also hold for challenging US Central American exclusion are likewise addressed.

ON NON-BELONGING

The Central American refugee crisis of the 1980s drastically changed what had been the pattern of Central American-US migration up to that point, and it laid the foundation for the US Central American communities that exist and continue to grow today in urban centers such as Los Angeles; San Francisco; the Washington, DC, area: Houston, and Miami.[1] This moment similarly constitutes a pivotal originating point for the legal, social, and economic battles that vast members of these more established communities, as well as those belonging to newer communities in the Midwest and the US South, continue to face. As noted in the introduction, Reagan's interventionist efforts in Central America influenced and negatively impacted the prospects of political asylum for the majority of the Salvadoran and Guatemalan refugees who sought safe harbor in the United States during the 1980s. At the same time, pursuing legal residency through some other means was made extremely difficult for these immigrants. Legislation such as the 1986 Immigration Reform and Control Act (IRCA), otherwise known as Reagan's "amnesty" law, was applicable only to immigrants who met certain standards *and* who arrived prior to 1982, excluding more than half of the Guatemalan and Salvadoran population, which arrived afterward (Menjívar, "Liminal Legality" 1012).[2] Related immigration measures gave way to similar uneven opportunities and results. As Cecilia Menjívar notes, in 1992, following intense lobbying by immigration groups, the US government began granting Temporary Protected Status (TPS) to Salvadorans who had arrived prior to 1990 ("Liminal Legality" 1013). The program was afforded to Salvadorans, giving them a provisional reprieve from deportation due to the violent conflict in El Salvador and their inability to return, but Guatemalan refugees were not provided the same opportunity.

In the decades since the 1980s, subsequent waves of migration from the isthmus have continued to foster the expansion of US Central American communities. Census data suggests that from 1980 to 2017, this population grew tenfold, from 354,000 to 3,527,000, with about half of the foreign-born individuals belonging to this group arriving after the year 2000 (O'Connor et al.). Consequently, Central Americans now compose one of the largest immigrant groups from Latin America residing in the United States, second only to Mexicans.[3] The majority of these post-conflict arrivals have continued to hail from El Salvador, Guatemala, and increasingly Honduras. Between 2007 and 2015, the increase in immigrants from these three countries outpaced that of all the other foreign-born populations combined, rising by 25 percent versus 10 percent, respectively (Cohn et al., *Rise* 4). At the same time, the number of Mexican immigrants declined (4). Migration from these three countries, commonly referred to as the "Northern Triangle" of Central America, has been motivated by a combination of factors, including ongoing political and economic instability, poverty, systemic violence and corruption, food insecurity, family unification (as in the case of increasing numbers of unaccompanied migrant youths), and natural disasters, among others.[4] Notably, estimates from the Pew Research Center suggest that 55 percent of these immigrants from El Salvador, Guatemala, and Honduras are also unauthorized (Cohn et al., *Rise* 5).[5] Moreover, by comparison to the overall foreign and native-born population, these immigrant groups tend to be less educated, be less proficient in English, have lower incomes, and be more likely to live in poverty (O'Connor et al.).

Like those of the Central American refugees before them who were fleeing wars, the prospects of attaining legal permanent residency have been just as dim, if not more so, for these newer arrivals. Broad legislative measures focused on immigration, such as the 1996 Illegal Immigration Reform and Immigrant Responsibility Act (IIRIRA), have included more stringent rules and requirements for noncitizens applying for legal permanent residency and more funding for border security and physical barriers, and they increased the parameters of what are considered deportable offenses. In the specific case of the Nicaraguan Adjustment and Central American Relief Act (NACARA), which was passed in 1997 and was, among other things, seemingly meant to address the issue of Central American asylum seekers whose claims had been previously denied, the pathway to legality remained an expensive and taxing ordeal. Like TPS, NACARA status did not extend to all Central American refugees nor benefit those who did qualify for it equally. Nicaraguans, along with Cubans and refugees from the former Soviet Union, who were also beneficiaries of the law, could request a "cancellation of removal" and have their status changed to that of legal permanent residents without being subjected to a case-by-case court hearing, while the Salvadoran and Guatemalan refugees who were eligible for some of the law's basic benefits (including obtaining a work permit) could not and still cannot (Menjívar, "Liminal Legality" 1014). In the wake of 9/11, as the US government has set its sights increasingly on border security and counterterrorism initiatives, already limited laws such as NACARA have become more restrictive, and efforts to develop and pass wide-scale immigration reform on the level of IRCA and IIRIRA have stalled.

The election of President Donald Trump in 2016 took what was an already grim situation for many US Central Americans in terms of their potential to become fully integrated members of US society and made it even more difficult. Certainly, the case can be made that under the Trump administration Central American immigrants faced a context of arrival whose hostility rivaled that of the Reagan years. Building, in some cases, on practices established during Barack Obama's presidency (2008–2016),[6] the Trump administration took significant measures to curtail the inflow of undocumented Central American immigrants, which, since 2011, has increasingly included family units and unaccompanied youth (O'Connor et al.). In 2017, the administration discontinued the Central American Minors (CAM) program, which allowed parents living in the United States to request refugee status for their children or relatives living in El Salvador, Guatemala, or Honduras.[7] Then, in 2018, it adopted a controversial "zero tolerance" policy that resulted, among other things, in the forced separation of nearly 5,400 children from their parents at the US-Mexico border.[8] In keeping with this same policy, the administration sought greater legislative power to hold these immigrant families and unaccompanied minors in detention indefinitely, to deny all detainees due process by fast-tracking deportations and bypassing immigration hearings, and to make it nearly impossible for these immigrants to seek asylum in the United States. In June 2018, Attorney General Jeff Sessions announced, for instance, that cases based on domestic abuse and gang-related violence—two of the key reasons many of these undocumented Central American immigrants list for fleeing from their home countries—would no longer be considered grounds for seeking asylum in the United States (Kopan). This shift in asylum policy was followed in 2019 by the implementation of two other restrictive measures meant to impede undocumented migrants from seeking asylum at the US-Mexico border: the Migration Protection Protocols (or "Remain in Mexico" program) and the "Third-Country Asylum Rule." Whereas the first measure requires that asylum seekers remain in Mexico while their case is adjudicated, the second mandates that they must apply for asylum in a country they travel through before seeking it in the United States.[9] The outbreak of COVID-19, which was declared a global pandemic by the World Health Organization in early 2020, led to related measures by the Trump administration to further block the entry of these asylum seekers, including closing the US-Mexico and US-Canadian borders to all nonessential travel beginning in March 2020. As part of this same effort "to limit the spread of the virus" to and within the United States, immigration proceedings for asylum seekers forced to wait in Mexico were suspended indefinitely, and US Customs and Border Protection Agency officers were empowered to immediately turn away any immigrant caught crossing the border unauthorized, returning them either to the country from which they had entered or deporting them back to their country of origin.[10]

Such actions to block undocumented Central Americans from coming into the United States through the legal means of asylum coupled with similarly alarming efforts to disenfranchise and eventually expunge from the country portions of the US Central American population shielded under DACA and TPS. Recipients from El Salvador, Guatemala, and Honduras rank within the top five of all DACA populations, with the most recent data available from US Citizenship and Immigration Services showing that approximately 24,660 Salvadorans, 16,770 Guatemalans, and 15,420 Hondurans are currently protected under the program ("Approximate Active DACA Recipients"). The Trump administration's decision to rescind DACA in 2017 threatened the livelihoods and futures not only of these recipients but also of their families, including their US-born children and spouses.[11] The administration's related move in late 2019 to terminate the Temporary Protected Status of just over 250,000 Central Americans, some of which had resided in the country for more than twenty years, similarly put at risk the socioeconomic existence and emotional well-being of these immigrants and their families (Cohn et al., *Many Immigrants*).[12]

This synopsis evinces the extent to which foreign and domestic policies have contributed to the legal and civic disenfranchisement of large sectors of the US Central American population over the last forty years. Indeed, as this overview stresses, US Central Americans are or have been routinely subject to multiple forms of "legal violence," a type of aggression that, according to Cecilia Menjívar and Leisy Abrego, is "embedded in legal practices, sanctioned, actively implemented through formal procedures, and legitimized" (1387). Inherent in this type of systemic oppression is a view of US Central Americans as undesirable citizen-subjects, as individuals who are not worthy and do not belong in the country, which is reified via the passing and implementation of the noted policies and laws. This matrix of damaging government-based policies does not, however, account for all the dominant means through which US Central Americans come to be deemed as Others. The analysis I undertake in this project suggests that exclusionary ideals and discourses of American national belonging and identity, which are given meaning and promulgated, in large part, through cultural representation, are likewise implicated in this process. The same can be said of global structures of dominance such as what Aníbal Quijano defines as the "coloniality of power" and, relatedly, what Arturo Arias and Claudia Milian proffer as the "coloniality of diaspora."

The coloniality of power, as conceptualized by Quijano, is a system of power rooted in the social classification and integration of colonized subjects into the modern capitalist system based on race that was implemented under European colonial rule. Speaking about the colonization of the Americas, Quijano posits that this racialized means of establishing and codifying social relations gave rise to "new historical identities," that of "Indians, blacks, and mestizos," while also redefining existing identities that until then had been mainly associated with geographic origin or country of origin such as Spanish, Portuguese, and European, linking these to whiteness (534). This notion of race "grant[ed] legitimacy to the relations of domination imposed by the conquest," deeming colonized peoples as racially and culturally inferior and European colonizers as racially and culturally superior. This racist hierarchy similarly informed the forms of labor control and divisions of the colonial period. "Whiter" individuals had more economic power and prospects, and thus competitive advantages in the emergent global capitalist system, while those who were "darker" became a critical source of exploitable and unwaged labor, ensuring their continued subjugation and disenfranchisement. Indigenous groups were subjected to a form of unpaid serfdom that provided them with neither protection nor land (as was the case with feudal serfdom in Europe), and Black populations from Africa were literally enslaved (538–539).

According to Quijano, this system of power, enacted on a global scale by European colonizers, transformed Europe into the center of economic power and knowledge production at the time and laid the groundwork for future paradigms and relations of power. He notes, for example, the constitution of modern nation-states in Latin America in the mid- to late nineteenth century, which was a process premised on Eurocentric views. Latin American countries sought to emulate the European model, engaging in violent efforts to culturally and racially "homogenize" their heterogeneous populations through means such as the mass genocide of Indigenous groups and the systematic marginalization of Black peoples. Indeed, this quest for homogeneity is also behind the dominant and exclusionary discourses of *mestizaje* in Latin America referenced earlier. Thus, despite the end of European colonialism, Quijano maintains that the Eurocentric model of the coloniality of power continues to dominate and operate.

Drawing on this concept, Arias and Milian contend that the violent abjection of Central Americans in the United States is largely due not only to the coloniality of power but also to what they term the coloniality of diaspora, a system in which "ethnoracial and historical traits bind people to a colonizing past" (140). In other words, colonized peoples such as Central Americans, whose marginalization is a product of the coloniality of power, carry their ethnic, racial, cultural, and economic stratification with them into their new diasporic realities. Certainly, it is no coincidence that the Central American refugees who arrived in the United States in the 1980s from El Salvador and Guatemala were largely *mestizo/ladino* or Indigenous and increasingly from poor, rural, or working-class backgrounds. These marginalized civilian populations bore the brunt of the violence and repression during the civil wars in their native countries and, in the case of the Maya in Guatemala, were systematically targeted for elimination. It is also not surprising that in the years since this initial period, the demographic makeup of Central Americans migrating to the United States has changed little. These populations, with the addition of those hailing from Honduras, including Afro-descendant groups like the Garifuna, continue to be among the most vulnerable and affected by ongoing violence, socioeconomic and political instability, and climate change.[13]

Within the context of the United States, US Central Americans continue to occupy an inferior status because they not only are of Latin American descent but also hail from one of the least "developed" regions in Latin America. This presumed inferiority is further compounded for many US Central Americans by the political and socioeconomic realities of being undocumented and/or foreign, classifications that mark them as criminally and morally suspect, and as perpetual outsiders. Many of them also must contend with psychological scars accrued during and in the aftermath of civil wars and as a result of dehumanizing journeys through Mexico as well as forced family separations. Being classified as "Hispanics" or "Latinos" contributes yet another layer to this process of othering for Central American immigrants, especially for those who also identify as Indigenous and/or Black. These racialized pan-ethnic labels tend to reinforce a notion of all Latinx populations as Spanish speakers, as mestizos/ladinos (or "brown"), and, in the case of "Hispanic," as linked to European ancestry. Hence, the imposition of these terms on groups such as the Maya or Garifuna represents another form of forced homogenization that once again contributes to the erasure of their communities and culture, only this time within the multiethnic landscape of the United States. Such an imposition likewise obfuscates the added racism such populations face within the Latinx community itself, a racism informed by the logics of white supremacy as developed and instituted in the colonial contexts of North America and Latin America.

As a working paradigm, non-belonging can register as well as provide a platform from which to further interrogate these added dimensions of US Central American exclusion. Not the least of these is the pronounced nature, and to a certain extent the inescapability, of this state of being, which the prefix "non-" linguistically underscores. According to dictionary.com, "non-" is "a prefix meaning 'not,' freely used as an English formative, usually with a simple negative force as implying mere negation or absence of something (rather than the opposite or reverse of it, as often expressed by un-)." In keeping with the semantic difference noted in this definition between the related prefixes "non-" and "un-," non-belonging denotes a condition of *not* belonging, of existing outside of the realm of (national) belonging because of the inherent insufficiencies many US Central Americans are perceived to have and the exclusionary socioeconomic and political structures of power that fuel and benefit from such perceptions. Although existing in a state of non-belonging does not necessarily preclude any and all forms of belonging or inclusion, many US Central Americans cannot easily transition out of or reverse this state of being, as the term "unbelonging" might imply.

A pivotal scene from one of the most well-known and enduring representations of the Central American refugee experience, Gregory Nava's epic *El Norte* (1983), helps to illustrate these ideas. Nava's film relates the poetically tragic story of Maya siblings Enrique and Rosa Xuncax, who are forced to flee their native Guatemala following the persecution and murder of their parents by government forces. Having escaped the violence of civil war and also survived dangerous crossings through Mexico, once in the promised land of "the North," the siblings must contend with a disillusioning and an alienating existence as undocumented immigrants and exploitable laborers. In the film's culminating scene, Rosa succumbs to the typhus she contracted from sewer rats while crossing clandestinely into the United States. Lying in a darkened hospital room with her brother at her side, Rosa laments a migratory experience and immigrant reality characterized by persecution, discrimination, and dislocation. Being Mayans made them enemies of the state in their war-torn homeland. Mexico, a country of transit, was not only poor but also similarly unwelcoming of Central Americans and *indios*. And in the United States, they were confronted with the sad realization that the American Dream they so vehemently sought was out of reach for disenfranchised peoples like them who, as was also the case in Guatemala, were seen only as *brazos*, or arms for labor.

Rosa's deathbed observations—in essence, a recap of the film's plot—offer a strategic mapping of how Central Americans like her and Enrique

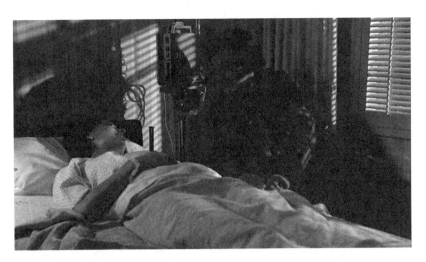

1.1. *Rosa's death scene in* El Norte.

are rendered unbelonging Others within the context of the national and the diasporic. The Guatemalan state's violent repression of Mayan communities during its thirty-six-year-long civil war, the cause of the siblings' initial displacement, is, to a large extent, a manifestation of the coloniality of power. Perceived to be inferior in all respects, racially, socially, and culturally, Indigenous populations, as was noted earlier, became the logical targets of a genocidal campaign operating under the official cover of fighting the spread of communism in the region.[14] Calling to mind Arias and Milian's notion of the coloniality of diaspora, this state of abjection is a condition that persists for the siblings and is reified with each leg of their journey. They are rejected in Mexico and relegated to the margins of society in the United States for being undocumented, Central American, and, most important, Indigenous. Indeed, as Alicia Estrada's discussion of *El Norte* suggests, Enrique and Rosa undergo a process of de-Mayanization throughout their journey. In essence, they must traverse various "cultural and social *ladino*" planes on their way to becoming Latinx and modern "American" subjects in the United States ("Decolonizing Maya Border Crossings" 183). It is this necessary loss of their indigeneity, the most "lacking" aspect of the siblings' identity, that the film ultimately underscores and, as Estrada also argues, problematically affirms via its Western gaze.

In Rosa's case, there is also the question of her gender, which in the film limits both her ability to be independent from her brother and her employment possibilities (working in a factory or as a maid in a private home). Rosa's gender also connects her more directly to her Maya culture

| *Signifying US Central American Non-belonging*

and identity. Of the two siblings, it is she who is cast as the standard bearer of Maya traditions and family values, continually reminding Enrique of both and, by the film's end, constituting his only remaining link to Guatemala. Of the two, Rosa is also, however, the one who struggles the most to assimilate and who does not survive their life in "the North." As such, a case can be made that Rosa's more pronounced Mayanness, as tied to gender, makes her transition into modernity and US society more difficult, even impossible, by contrast to her brother. Through her laments upon dying, Rosa thus articulates more than just her feelings of loss and alienation. She also speaks to the systems of power and the migratory displacements that, coupled with her and Enrique's positionality as outsiders in both Guatemala and the United States, have likewise contributed to their enduring otherness.

It is these complexities regarding the realities of US Central American exclusion that are encapsulated by the conceptual framework of nonbelonging. Such an emphasis, however, does not necessarily preclude other critical possibilities. Non-belonging, as intimated by the hyphen that likewise distances the negative prefix "non-" from the stand-alone term "belonging," also foregrounds the aspirations for and claims of belonging of US Central Americans. As shown in *El Norte*, many of these visions of a better future and social integration in the United States are wedded to conscripted and inherently contradictory ideals of immigrant assimilation such as that of the American Dream. Imposed "from above," this ideal continues to occupy a vital place in Central American (im)migrant imaginaries. Documentaries of Central American transmigration through Mexico (discussed in chapter four) reveal time and again that for undocumented Central Americans who are risking their lives to get to the United States, achieving economic success by US standards is equated not only with financial security for themselves and their families but also with the acquisition of social currency as "Americans," meaning inclusion. Autobiographical works such as *An American Dream* by Raul Mendez-Hernandez (2014), *Full of Heart: My Story of Survival, Strength, and Spirit* by J. R. Martínez and Alexandra Rockey Fleming (2012), and *December Sky: Beyond My Undocumented Life* by Evelyn Cortez-Davis (2003) evince similar American Dream–based ideals and aspirations.

In keeping with elements of traditional ethnic autobiographies that affirm the mythos of the United States as a "melting pot," these narratives relate the personal struggles with adversity of the authors as well as their success in the United States. Both Mendez-Hernandez and Cortez-Davis, for instance, write about their experiences as youths in war-torn El Salvador and as undocumented immigrants fighting to make their American dreams a reality. Whereas in Mendez-Hernandez's narrative this dream manifests in more abstract terms, as a goal that motivates him to survive a harrowing journey through Mexico and persevere until arriving in the United States, Cortez-Davis tells of how she accomplished her dream by obtaining a college education and the legal standing that allowed her to move "beyond [her] undocumented life," as the subtitle of her autobiography suggests. Not being an immigrant himself, Martínez's *Full of Heart* varies from these other accounts, centering primarily on his struggles and rise to national fame following the traumatic bodily injuries he suffered while serving in the Iraq War. Nevertheless, his account of his mother's experiences as an undocumented immigrant from El Salvador raising him alone in the US South does recall the narratives of Mendez-Hernandez and Davis-Cortez and affirms the same assimilationist message. Tellingly, in acknowledging that his mother's tribulations and sacrifices, including her decision to stay in the United States to raise him despite having two other children in El Salvador, are what enabled him to have a better life, Martínez also posits himself and his triumphs as the fulfillment of his mother's American dream (235).

Such ideals and hopes are, of course, linked to deep-seated discourses of immigration and nation in the United States, ones rendered problematic by the reality and presence of the very (im)migrants who hold such notions and expectations. In her analysis of *Time* magazine's 1985 special issue *Immigrants: The Changing Face of America*, Lauren Berlant maintains that the seemingly pro-immigrant discourse that permeates the issue functions as "a central technology for the reproduction of patriotic nationalism" (*Queen of America* 195). It does so "not just because the immigrant is seen as without a nation or resources and thus as deserving of pity or contempt, but because the immigrant is defined as *someone who desires America*" (195; emphasis in original). Given this logic, America is upheld as a nation to be loved and coveted by immigrants, who, if good to America, will be loved in return (196). At the heart of such affective constructions of the immigrant as a desiring subject and, by the same token, of America as an object of desire, are notions of belonging. The ideal immigrant is one whose love for America drives her to want to eschew her foreignness in order to be American, who wishes to become "one of us." As Berlant also notes, however, such sentiments are laced with nativist anxieties about being economically and culturally overrun by foreign Others (196). Wanting to belong, then, can be a double-edged sword for immigrants. If your desire is too great (meaning, there are too many of you) and/or that desire is not reciprocated (meaning, you are not the right kind of immigrant), then you are rendered a threat to those who do belong.

By the same token, non-belonging also offers the possibility of discerning and further understanding forms of belonging enacted by US Central Americans that do not subscribe to these exclusionary ideals and discourses.

These alternative efforts stress diasporic and/or transnational affiliations that unsettle hegemonic notions of American national belonging. The communal spaces of knowledge and resistance created via social media hashtags such as #CentAmStudies and #CentralAmericanTwitter are a prime example. In a reflection piece published in *Latino Studies* in 2017, Leisy J. Abrego notes the pivotal role #CentAmStudies has played in generating greater awareness of Central American studies beyond academia and as an avenue for 1.5- and second-generation US Central Americans to collectively reflect on what "[they] think it means to be Central American" (97). Discussions initiated using #CentAmStudies spurred by current events affecting US Central Americans and their diverse histories, identities, cultures, and political views allow for needed connections among a group that does not see itself reflected in "classrooms, work sites, neighborhoods, and mainstream media" (97). As such, the articulations of community fostered by #CentAmStudies, ones rooted in a sense of and notions of Central Americanness, constitute a challenge not only to the dominant ethos of immigrant/minority group assimilation in the United States that stands for belonging but also to the marginalization and broader lack of representation of US Central Americans.

The hashtag #CentralAmericanTwitter constitutes a similar space of community-making and opposition. Although launched in 2014, the hashtag did not gain significant prominence until 2017, one year into the Trump presidency, when Zaira Miluska, an Afro-Salvadoran American launched the Twitter account @CentralAmericanBeauty, showcasing the beauty of the Central American region and people.[15] Freddy Jesse Izaguirre writes in an article on the online platform *Medium* that in the midst of the onslaught of news media coverage of migrant caravans and the Trump administration's cruel immigration policies, the hashtag created a conversation that provided a needed respite, a place where Central American diasporic subjects could not only find others like them but also see their cultures and countries of origin reflected in a different light. Being able to share, among other things, memes, recipes, music playlists, book recommendations, scholarly works, art, news, politics, and their personal lives was and continues to be a lifeline for people, like Izaguirre, hoping to survive the "war on migrants" (Izaguirre). As it has evolved and facilitated greater visibility for Indigenous, Afrodescendent, and LGBTQ groups, #CentralAmericanTwitter has also given rise to needed critiques of the homophobia, sexism, and racism that persist in the (US) Central American community, both off- and online. To date, #CentralAmericanTwitter continues to operate in much the same way: as an avenue for its followers and participants to find and grow community, to assert and contest identities (self-defined or imposed "from above"), and, in the process, to engender counternarratives of what it means to belong as Central Americans in the United States and other parts of the world.

Ultimately, then, via non-belonging, I am invested in looking at the US Central American experience through the (dis)juncture of not belonging and belonging. Informing this theorization are analogous paradigms such as that of "non-existence" proffered by sociocultural anthropologist Susan Bibler Coutin and that of (Central American-American) "invisibility" advanced by cultural critic Arturo Arias. In *Legalizing Moves: Salvadoran Immigrants' Struggles for U.S. Residency*, Coutin defines the concept of "nonexistence" as a state experienced by individuals who are legal nonsubjects, such as undocumented Salvadoran immigrants who reside in the United States but who do not have a legal presence or Salvadoran nationals whose citizenship-based rights and humanity are nevertheless violated in their countries of origin (27). Coutin notes that, like existence, nonexistence also has gradations, can take multiple forms, and is not always all encompassing or complete. Individuals can thus move in and out of existence and experience it in differing ways (27). Non-belonging operates in a similar way, in the sense that the notion of not belonging that it speaks to is, in essence, a deeply rooted and persistent state that Central Americans experience in and outside of their nations of origin, but one that also remains multifaceted and does not completely negate the possibility of belonging. Indeed, as I have been arguing, the forms of belonging that US Central Americans enact are ones precisely forged from within their state of exclusion and status as undesirable Others. Moreover, such efforts can take various shapes—not all of them contestatory—and achieve different levels of inclusion.

Conceptually speaking, non-belonging also echoes central tenets of Arias's notion of "invisibility," a means of accounting for what he describes as the "nonrecognition," the "sense of nonbelonging" and "of nonbeing" that Central Americans experience in and outside of their nations of origin. This invisibility is a consequence of what Arias argues is, on one hand, the construction of "a Latino identity through the abjection and erasure of the Central American" and, on the other, the silencing by US Central Americans of past histories of war, oppression, and equally traumatic border crossings (*Taking Their Word* 186). Part of this silencing entails assuming Latinx identities, such as Mexican American, as a matter of self-preservation. All of these constitute, for Arias, a negation of Central American identity that has resulted in the inability of US Central Americans to establish an identity politics that would allow them to emerge and be recognized in the United States (213). The nomenclature of "Central American-American" that Arias likewise proposes speaks both to this marginalization of Central Americans within the Latinx matrix of the United States and of Latin America proper, and to their nonidentity. As Arias explains, "'Central American-American' underlines the fact that it is an identity that is not one, for it cannot be unequivocally designated either as 'Latino' or as 'Latin American,' but is outside those two signifiers from the very start" (204).

Like the systemic exclusion of US Central Americans encapsulated by non-belonging, the invisibility of which Arias speaks is also a condition "first imposed on [Central Americans] in their countries of origin" and then "carried over" into the United States (186). The fact that, as Arias claims, US Central Americans have as yet been unable to establish an identity politics of their own and thus have remained invisible leaves little room, however, for contemplating ways in which these populations nevertheless assert their presence outside of these parameters. Non-belonging, by contrast, does allow for the latter, as the forms of belonging that US Central Americans articulate also register their presence and indicate modes of visibility that are defined not solely in terms of the (Latinx) identity politics Arias privileges. My broader argument concerning how dominant representations of US Central Americans, especially ones in visual mediums, factor in these politics of non-belonging similarly complicates this notion of invisibility. US Central Americans still need more cultural and political representation, yet they are not entirely hidden from view. Dominant depictions of US Central Americans have become more pervasive in news media, films, and literature in recent decades, affording them a paradoxical visibility that allows them to be "seen" but that does not necessarily render them or their (im)migrant experiences legible. And while these same portrayals still contribute primarily to the marginalization of US Central Americans, they also provide an avenue for contesting it.

FROM THREATENING GUERILLAS TO FOREVER ILLEGALS

As the critical genealogy outlined in this section suggests, hegemonic representations of guerrillas, war-torn refugees, domestic workers, gang youth, and, more broadly, forever illegals confer upon US Central Americans different meanings in line with the given historical context and discourses within and through which they have flourished. They also, however, consistently affirm the idea that Central American immigrants (and subsequent US-born generations) are objectionable citizen-subjects. The basis of this objectionability is the presumed threat these populations pose to the national security and body politic of the nation as well as the related sense that US Central Americans do not belong in the United States or, in the meritocratic logic of neoliberalism, do not deserve to be here and are incapable of being "Americans." Traditional signifiers of immigrant abjection such as an objectionable race, gender, sexuality, class, and, in the majority of cases, lack of citizenship status render US Central Americans as such. So, too, does the link of US Central Americans to the isthmian region and its perceived "backwardness."

Capable of individually and collectively signifying US Central Americans as unbelonging subjects, this group of linked depictions can be construed as part of an expanding "regime of representation," as posited by Stuart Hall in "The Spectacle of the 'Other.'" Speaking in relation to popular images of Black athletes, Hall explains that even though depictions of these athletes can be interpreted in multiple ways, these images nevertheless "say something" about the difference and otherness of said individuals (230). What is communicated about this difference and otherness corresponds with racialized and essentialist discourses (as in the case of stereotypes) and is amplified through intertextuality with other images. The "whole repertoire of [such] imagery and visual effects" in a given historical moment is consequently a "*regime of representation*" (232; emphasis in original). It is through such regimes that racialized knowledge about the real and symbolic bodies of the Other is produced and, as Hall further adds, becomes naturalized through the circulation of power (259–261).[16] Accordingly, the dominant portrayals of US Central Americans in question operate as a regime of representation that has worked to primarily signify and magnify the difference and otherness of Central American populations in the United States. The resulting view of US Central Americans as undesirable and as not belonging within the confines of the nation has been legitimized through the strategic deployment and circulation of these same representations by the US government, the media, and the film and publishing industries, among others. Legitimized as such, this knowledge has had and continues to have a direct bearing on the livelihoods of US Central Americans. In short, this seeming "truth" is a form of symbolic violence directly tied to the systematic efforts to legally, culturally, and financially disenfranchise US Central Americans discussed in the previous section.

Christian Smith notes that the US media's preoccupation with Central America exploded during Reagan's presidency, producing an average of 550 television news stories on Nicaragua and El Salvador alone in each of his eight years in office (89–90). Special reports, which aired on all the major broadcasting networks, aimed to provide audiences with a more nuanced view of the Central American civil conflicts, including the armed Left and its cause. Such reporting nevertheless fell short of its goal due to, among other things, the fact that most of the US public lacked not only the interest but also the knowledge necessary to fully grasp the sociopolitical reality being depicted (237–238). These same media accounts were likewise little match for the renditions of the conflicts found on the big screen. Along with their broader popular appeal and reach, blockbuster films such as John Milius's *Red Dawn* (1984), Roger Spottiswoode's *Under Fire* (1983), and Oliver Stone's *Salvador* (1987) offered US audiences action-packed plotlines that echoed, in some instances, Reagan's hawkish take on the Central American communist peril and, in all cases, his patronizing view of the region's broader populace. Recalling nineteenth-century visions that imagined the isthmian tropics as a site of unforeseen dangers for US interlopers,[17] these films left little doubt as to the related and seemingly imminent threats that Central America's revolutions posed to the United States, threats encapsulated in the singular figure of the armed guerilla.

The right-wing cult classic *Red Dawn* envisions a world in which most of Europe and Latin America have been overtaken by militant Leftists and the United States has been left alone to stand against the forces of "evil." Both El Salvador and Honduras have fallen to communism (as Reagan predicted would happen if the United States did not intervene in Central America). Meanwhile, Mexico has devolved into revolution, clearing the path for a literal infiltration of the United States from "south of the border" by an alliance of Russian, Cuban, and Nicaraguan soldiers. It is up to a small group of mostly Anglo teenagers in a small Colorado town to survive that attack and escape from being captured. Notably, and by contrast to the Cubans, who are led and encapsulated by the film's main antagonist, Colonel Ernesto Bella (Ron O'Neal), the Nicaraguan Sandinistas are indistinguishable from each other and lack any depth. Aside from the minor character of the Nicaraguan captain (Judd Omen), the Sandinistas factor as a faceless hoard. This dehumanizing characterization is notable given the heightened anxieties about demographic changes and the growth of the undocumented/Latinx populations during this same period. As previously mentioned, among these populations were also Salvadoran and Guatemalan political refugees, who were emigrating en masse to the country and whom the Reagan administration sought to bar from claiming asylum. In keeping with the conservative ideology of the time, the Central American guerrilla, as depicted in this film, clearly incarnates the perceived dangers of US Central Americans as ideological and biological threats to the nation.

Spottiswoode's *Under Fire* and Stone's *Salvador*, two films meant to be critical of the Reagan administration's interventionist efforts in Central America, did little to unsettle this prevalent image of the isthmian region as a "hotbed" of communist contagion and of the imperiling Central American guerrilla.[18] Both films follow the experiences of white US journalists,

1.2. *James Woods in* Salvador.

played by Nick Nolte (*Under Fire*) and James Woods (*Salvador*), who contend with personal and ethical dilemmas while reporting from the front lines in Nicaragua and El Salvador. As Neil Larsen astutely observes, in these films Central America appears as an ahistorical and primitive place where violence is endemic and disarticulated from any links to US imperialism or the structural inequalities and systemic oppression that led to the Nicaraguan and Salvadoran armed revolutions (44–45). Depictions of the people who inhabit this region follow suit. When not helpless victims (and would-be refugees), Central Americans factor as either military strongmen or equally misguided and primal revolutionaries. Blurring the lines that would otherwise separate these last two figures underscores the fact that from an outsider's (American) perspective these types of men amount to the same thing. Ultimately, what renders these brutes so dangerous (to the protagonists and the United States) is not their authoritarian or communist leanings, but rather their consistently violent and backward natures. By depicting Central America as anachronistic, as Larsen contends, these films render the region and its peoples as outside of the linear progression of civilization and modernity. Arguably, it is these same brutes who factor as US-invading Sandinistas in *Red Dawn*.

Supplementing these hegemonic depictions of menacing guerrillas were those of Central American political refugees. Along with notable representations in films (*El Norte*), television, and news media, the figure of the Central American refugee was also prevalent in a wide range of literary texts. Bestsellers such as Barbara Kingsolver's *The Bean Trees* (1988), as well as works by Chicana writers including Ana Castillo's *Sapogonia* (1990),

Graciela Limón's *In Search of Bernabé* (1993), and Demetria Martínez's *Mother Tongue* (1994), are prominent examples. These fictionalized accounts were written with the aim of bringing broader awareness to the sociopolitical reality in Central America, its refugees, and the hostile context of arrival they faced once in the United States. These texts reflected and can be seen as part of the broader activism of the Central American Solidarity movement of the time, a widespread campaign against US intervention in Central America that galvanized large sectors of the religious community as well as the political Left in the United States.[19] The Central American characters portrayed in these texts are often embedded in primary or secondary plotlines involving an integral element, known as the Sanctuary movement, of this wider campaign. A response to the systematic denial of asylum to Salvadoran and Guatemalan refugees under the Reagan administration, this effort likewise entailed the operation of an "underground railroad" to help clandestinely transport refugees to the United States and provide them with safe haven.

Like the portrayals of menacing guerrillas, the depictions of Central American refugees in such texts are limiting and problematic. In addition to a tendency to idealize or romanticize the figure of the refugee, these narratives render such characters in traditionally gendered and normative terms. Whereas male refugees are often former political or social activists whose public exploits and past traumas deem them heroic, sensitive, and at times noble, female refugees are generally depicted as helpless victims with little or no agency. They are posited as collateral damage for the political endeavors of men (their husbands, their brothers, their sons, a patriarchal and oppressive state, etc.). Relatedly, male refugees often factor as revolutionary Latin lovers that elicit the romantic affections of Anglo and Chicana protagonists alike. They are men in need of (sexual) love to heal their psychological and emotional traumas, who are worthy of sympathy and understanding rather than fear and rejection. Their female counterparts, by contrast, tend to incarnate suffering mothers or martyrs whose pain and loss (often of a child) is all-consuming and defining. This is the case of the Guatemalan couple, Estevan and Esperanza, in Kingsolver's *The Bean Trees*. Their backstory, consisting of Estevan's activism as a union leader and the kidnapping of their young daughter by government forces, fuels an image of Estevan as a tragic and selfless hero with whom the main protagonist, Taylor Greer, falls in love. However, in Esperanza's case, this same backdrop serves mostly to accentuate her status as an afflicted and inconsolable mother whose loss is so painful that she attempts to take her own life.

These representations of Central American refugees also remain uncritically beholden to the First World perspectives and privileges of the authors and their American protagonists. This limited vision is evident even in the depictions afforded by Chicana authors, whose claims to solidarity with the Central American peoples were also premised on a shared sense of oppression and anti-imperialist struggles as fellow Latinxs. In the case of Limón and Martínez, their firsthand experiences in Central America or as part of the Sanctuary movement were also a factor. As Ana Patricia Rodríguez first noted in her essay "The Fiction of Solidarity: Transfronterista Feminisms and Anti-imperialist Struggles in Central American Transnational Narratives," the solidarity enacted in and through the aforementioned Chicana-authored texts is a "fiction" precisely because the authors fail to recognize "that solidarity is not transparent or innocent, but rather critically shaped by borders, power, and unequal hierarchical relationships, even within Latina/o feminist communities" (221). Hence, as Rodríguez convincingly claims in a related discussion, it is "Chicana/o histories, subjects, and protagonists" who are really at the center of Chicanx solidarity narratives (*Dividing the Isthmus* 154). The Central American immigrant subjectivities and the plight that these narratives sought to highlight in the first place are consequently obscured or appropriated. The same can be said of Kingsolver's novel, in which Estevan and Esperanza's storyline serves first and foremost as a catalyst for the protagonist's individual and sociopolitical maturation.

One can further make the case that in their attempts to render Central American refugees victims worthy of sympathy and safe haven, these authors also show these same individuals to be ill-equipped to adapt and thrive in the United States. The character of Esperanza and her attempted suicide in Kingsolver's novel speak to this, as does the portrayal of José Luis Romero, a Salvadoran refugee and key figure in Martínez's *Mother Tongue*. The Chicana protagonist, Mary, falls in love with José Luis as a consequence of her involvement in the Sanctuary movement. Having been subjected to torture because of his political activism in El Salvador, José Luis's traumas prove too much for the relationship and for Mary's love to heal, resulting in José Luis leaving, presumably to return to El Salvador, and being heard of again only decades later when he writes Mary a letter from Canada. Mary, on the other hand, is left on her own to raise the child they conceived together, doing so successfully. Although the relationship between Mary and José Luis is fraught for several reasons other than his psychological and emotional wounds, including Mary's idealization of him and her inability to allow his trauma to be his own, this end to their story is significant in that it posits Mary as the more resilient of the two. It is she who can carry on into the future by raising their son, whereas José Luis cannot exist within the United States and must literally escape once again (although it is back to

El Salvador). It likewise bears mentioning that in related representations of Central American refugees, this inability to cope and survive in the United States is marked by the actual death of the characters and/or made more acute by their lack of modernity. Recall Rosa's portrayal and demise in *El Norte*.

Thus, although they do not render US Central Americans in overtly threatening ways, these portrayals of refugees add to the sense that these populations do not belong and cannot "make it" in the United States, thereby also reinforcing their undesirability as potential citizen-subjects. This is troubling not only because these prevalent depictions of Central American refugees and their implications are cultivated in narratives intended to be more empathetic and inclusive of this group, but also because of the neoliberal turn in immigration policy taking place at the time. As Leah Perry contends, the Reagan era marked the beginning of a decided shift from a view of the United States as a "nation of immigrants" that welcomed and aided newcomers to that of a country in the throes of an "immigration emergency" in which what mattered most was individual responsibility and immigrant merit (3–5). Indeed, the eligibility requirements for IRCA, as well as its passage in 1986, made clear that moving forward, any legalization and the degree to which immigrants would be welcomed into the country would depend largely on their ability to prove their moral worthiness and their socioeconomic value to US society.[20] In essence, narratives that imagined Central American refugees in ways that underscored their failure to transcend their seeming "brokenness" and "backwardness" cast these populations as incompatible with the emerging neoliberal paradigm of immigrant desirability and inclusion.

Despite the end of the Cold War and the era of Central American revolutions, such means of portraying and signifying US Central Americans have not ceased. In the three decades since, the image of the Central American male guerrilla has given way to a newer, albeit just as sinister, manifestation: the Central American gang youth, often belonging to the infamous Mara Salvatrucha, or MS-13. Similarly, traces of the Central American political refugee can be gleaned in the figure of the immigrant *doméstica*, which has also increasingly been depicted as Salvadoran. Often, there is even a direct conflation of these two figures, as in Limón's novel *In Search of Bernabé* and the films *El Norte*, *My Family/Mi Familia* (1995), and *The End of Violence* (1997). In all these works, the character, and the literal body, of the *doméstica* is rendered both the object and the intersectional site of multiple forms of physical, symbolic, and legal violence. These newer manifestations speak to the added nuances of a Central American immigrant reality that is moving or attempting to transcend the period of revolutionary upheaval in the isthmus. Nevertheless, these portrayals also continue to evoke, either explicitly or indirectly, dominant images of US Central Americans from the past. What is more, they remain wedded to and rehash the same problematic discourses regarding US Central Americans as a racialized menace, as hapless victims, and, in general, as deficient because of their national or regional origins. As part of the same regime of representation, these more contemporary depictions, which are just as symbolically potent, continue to constitute US Central Americans as unworthy subjects who cannot belong.

An episode from the freshman season of the hit television series *Bones*, which aired on Fox from 2005 to 2017, helps to elucidate the latter. In the episode "The Woman in the Garden," the investigative team of Dr. Temperance "Bones" Brennan (Emily Deschanel), a forensic anthropologist, and FBI Special Agent Seeley Booth (David Boreanaz) must solve the mystery of an exhumed cadaver discovered in the trunk of a car during a traffic stop in "Little El Salvador," a predominantly Salvadoran immigrant neighborhood in the Washington, DC, area. The car in question was being driven by a member of a notorious Salvadoran street gang known as the Mara Muerte (Death Gang). As Brennan and Booth discover, the cadaver belongs to a young Salvadoran woman named María, who had been employed as a maid in the home of a prominent US senator. The gang member behind the wheel turns out to be the victim's brother, José, who also worked for the senator. Given the undocumented status of José and his wife, he had chosen to bury his sister (and their father, who had died of natural causes a few months prior) on his own. When he was caught, José was in the process of moving the bodies of his sister and father from the community garden where he had originally buried both to another clandestine grave site on the senator's property. As is revealed at the end of the episode, his sister's murderer is the house manager, who is also Salvadoran and who during a heated argument had caused María to sustain a traumatic injury to her head, from which she later died.

In this episode of *Bones*, the Mara Muerte is a clear stand-in for MS-13. The gang functions as an obvious red herring, one meant to distract viewers as they, along with the lead investigators, attempt to unravel the mystery at hand. The gang's villainy is brought to bear in stereotypical fashion with sinister tattooed figures, repeatedly referenced as "gangbangers" or "killers," who are shown to ruthlessly prey upon and victimize the Salvadoran immigrant community to which they, too, belong. This portrayal of the gang and its modus operandi provides the basis for the parallel that is likewise drawn in the episode between the Mara Muerte and the state-funded death squads that terrorized and tortured Salvadoran nationals during the country's civil war. Tellingly, it is Brennan who most effectively underscores and solidifies this connection for viewers. Following a physical altercation with the leader of the gang's DC unit, Brennan states to her coworker that she has dealt with people like him before, individuals "who get what they want through fear—gangbangers, members of death squads." In what amounts to another First World appropriation of the experiences of actual political refugees and torture survivors from Central America, Brennan then goes on to recount her own terrifying experience in El Salvador while helping to identify victims of the death squads in Milagro de la Paz. This village, coincidentally, is also where the murder victim, María, and her family hail from. As Brennan intimates, her work made her a target of federal authorities, leading to her imprisonment in a clandestine cell for three days, during which she was subjected to mental and physical abuse by a man who could have been "a cop or a soldier; it's hard to tell."

Brennan's account solidifies for viewers the interchangeability of Mara Muerte gangbangers and death squad operatives, as both are seemingly products of a Salvadoran country that is characterized by lawlessness and a deeply rooted savagery. At no point in this account, or the episode, are any specifics given about the Salvadoran civil war, its causes, or its duration to help viewers contextualize the existence of the death squads that Brennan alludes to throughout and the violence they perpetrated against the Salvadoran people (and her). Similarly, there is no mention of the dynamics that led to the establishment of gangs such as MS-13 (in the United States, not El Salvador) and their spread across borders and throughout Central America. Lacking any such information, viewers are left to conclude that the malevolence and violence that renders Mara Muerte members akin to their death squad brethren is innate rather than a consequence of socialization, among other historical and political factors. The show thus offers an image of Salvadoran gang members that is not unlike that of the menacing guerrillas and, relatedly, the brute strongmen of the 1980s whose violent natures and deficient ethnic and cultural origins were key aspects of what made them such threatening figures. The fact that the Mara Muerte is correlated with death squads and not specifically armed revolutionaries is beside the point because in the show these two entities are treated in similar ways and evoke related anxieties for the US public. The death squads are also a violent threat to the social order and, as Brennan's personal ordeal underscores, a danger to US citizens. So, too, is the Mara Muerte.

In the same way that in this episode the Mara Muerte is suggested to be an extension of Salvadoran death squads, the Salvadoran immigrants targeted by the gang are likened to refugees of war. Although Maria's murder does not occur at the hands of the gang per se, she remains a part of this same persecuted and largely undocumented immigrant community, as does her brother, José, whose membership in the gang was, as viewers learn, a means of protecting his family. Along with procuring fake papers from the gang for María, José's gang status affords him protection for his undocumented wife and their US-born son. Brennan and Boothe's involvement in his sister's murder case, however, make him the target of the gang as well, who ensures his silence by beating and threatening his life. In this sense, then, José is represented as different from the other cold-blooded and criminal members. Just as important, María and José's father is identified by Brennan as a possible torture victim, making him an actual political refugee. The show attempts to further complicate this representation of María, José, and the broader Salvadoran immigrant community as pseudo-refugees by also noting their status as undocumented laborers, whose lives matter little to wealthy employers like the US senator and his family. Throughout the episode, the senator and his wife remain conveniently oblivious to who their employees are and what type of work they perform for their benefit. As a key scene with José's wife highlights, these immigrants likewise contend with the added fear of being deported back to a country as "barbaric" as what Brennan describes. When Boothe threatens José's wife with deportation and separation from her son if she refuses to cooperate with his and Brennan's investigation, Brennan asks him to stop, explaining, "She's lived with terror and intimidation her whole life [in El Salvador]."

Posited as would-be and/or actual refugees, María, José, and the broader US Salvadoran community are reduced to mere victims of the Mara Muerte as well of global capitalism and a broken immigration system. Moreover, they appear just as helpless and unassimilable as Central American refugees fleeing wars were often imagined to be during the 1980s. María's murder does more than simply underscore her marginality and expendability as an undocumented domestic worker. Her demise also denies her a future in the United States, marking her lack of belonging and literal exclusion from the country. José's fate at the close of the episode affirms a similar notion. Considering Brennan's repeated observations about the dangers of El Salvador and the fact that the Mara Muerte has José in its crosshairs, José would seem to have a potential case for seeking asylum or some form of witness protection. Yet, at the close of the episode, he and his family are slated for immediate deportation back to El Salvador, a move that, like his sister's death, signals his own expulsion from and inability to belong in the United States. One can argue that among the reasons why José must likewise be expelled are his undocumented status and his gang membership. Regardless of his unselfish motivations for joining the Mara Muerte, these are unsurmountable factors that make him unworthy of being allowed to stay in the United States and that do not portend a "successful" cultural, social, and economic integration into American society.

Contemporaneous with these representations of US Central Americans as gangbangers and disenfranchised *domésticas* is that of the forever illegal, a nomenclature inspired by famed poet Roque Dalton's characterization of his Salvadoran compatriots as "los eternos indocumentados" (the eternally undocumented).[21] Also part of the noted regime of representation, this tropological manifestation is brought to bear in images of unauthorized Central American men, women, unaccompanied youth, and family units, who are often shown en masse and in dire circumstances (i.e., in detention centers, as part of migrant "caravans," riding atop cargo trains through Mexico, seeking asylum at US ports of entry, or stranded and desperate in Mexico). Such representations underscore the "illegality" of the Central American subjects in question and actively participate in its construction. As Nicholas De Genova contends, migrant "illegality" is a product as much of legal discourses and statutes as of spectacles of border enforcement and policing, which are rendered in images and through other visual discourses (1181). Defined, first and foremost, by their illegality, these portrayals of Central Americans as forever illegals have the effect of also rendering them a people without a past or a future, a people who have always been and will forever be "illegals."

Although not unique to the Trump era, these representations of Central Americans became especially prolific and ubiquitous during it. One reason for this was the Trump administration's anti-immigrant efforts and the precarious realities for Central American asylum seekers that accelerated these efforts. These depictions also have a powerful symbolic currency. On one hand, these renderings can inspire sympathy for and galvanize sectors of the US public on behalf of undocumented Central Americans and their plight. On the other hand, these same renderings can be used to affirm racist and xenophobic notions about the looming threat that these same populations pose to the national and economic security of the United States. One notable instance is a widely circulated photograph in the mainstream news media taken in 2018 of a Honduran woman and her five-year-old twin daughters fleeing tear gas near the border wall in Tijuana, Mexico. Identified by reporters as María Lila Meza Castro, the woman in the photograph and her five children (only two of which appeared in the photograph) were among a group of Central American migrants who had been barred from seeking asylum in the United States for weeks and forced to wait in Mexico. The US Border Patrol responded to a collective effort by the frustrated group of migrants to access the ports of entry and enter the country through other means by attacking the group with tear gas and rubber bullets. Like similar images of Central American children who were held in cages, who were separated from their parents at the US-Mexico border, or who drowned alongside their parents while attempting to cross the Rio Grande, this photograph, taken by Reuter's photographer Kim Kyung-Hun, also stoked public outrage.

In the image, Castro appears mid-flight, frantically dragging her meagerly clothed daughters, Saira and Cheili, alongside her. Clad only in T-shirts and pull-up diapers, one of the girls wears flip-flops while the other lacks shoes entirely. Castro wears a T-shirt that prominently displays the characters from the Disney movie *Frozen*, an ironic detail often noted in articles concerning the tear gassing incident. Near the frightened family lies a cannister of tear gas from which white smoke rises, and beyond that are other migrants also running or standing in groups, as if just realizing what is occurring around them. Many of these clusters of migrants remain near the red border gate and barbed wire fencing that can be seen in the background. Writing for *The Intercept*, Natasha Lennard suggests that what made the photograph disturbing to so many people was not the fact that the use of violence against immigrants at the border or of tear gas against disenfranchised and minority groups by the US government were new occurrences, but rather that "visual representations of [such] violence at the border have proven rare." Lennard likewise observed that for all its potential to fuel public condemnation of the Trump administration's actions against Central American asylum seekers, the photograph could just as easily be seen as playing into the narrative pushed by the administration of the US-Mexico border as an "immigrant 'crisis' zone" that requires militarized intervention and tighter regulations.

This interpretive and symbolic fluidity makes such representations of US Central Americans as forever illegals reminiscent of those of war-torn refugees in the 1980s. Prominent depictions of Salvadoran and Guatemalan asylum seekers revolved around similar notions of them as victims of US immigration and foreign policies and, alternately, as demographic and national security threats to the country. Notably, visual representations of these same political refugees by sympathetic US activists tended to also emphasize women and children, not unlike the photograph of Castro and her young daughters (and countless others).[22] The intended result of such a strategic move was the generalized feminization and infantilization of these refugee populations to make them less threatening (De La Cruz 1109). Akin to the literary portrayals of Central American refugees explored earlier in this chapter, such visual renderings robbed asylum seekers of any agency and called into question their ability to thrive in the United States.

The figure of the forever illegal similarly evokes this idea of victimization and dependency, with one added nuance. The "illegality" that is front and center in this representation of US Central Americans occludes their histories and experiences as undocumented immigrants. Few, if any, of the news reports that featured Castro's image, for example, referenced her story of migration. Other than note that she was hoping to reach her husband in Louisiana (Gutiérrez and Siemaszko), these media accounts did not address what she had endured while en route to the United States with her five children or while forced to wait in Mexico at a makeshift camp for asylum seekers. Nor was there any mention of the reasons that drove her to leave Honduras. Unlike in the 1980s, reporting about the current reality on the ground in Central America driving these new waves of refugees is scant. For undocumented immigrants like Castro, however, it is this recognition of the dangerous conditions they are fleeing that is critical to their claims for asylum and to their being seen as more than just "illegals" invading the country.

CONTESTING US CENTRAL AMERICAN UNBELONGING

Over the last four decades, these hegemonic means of imagining US Central Americans in the US popular imaginary have worked to deem them undesirable Others who not only do not belong but also are *incapable* of belonging. Yet, as Hall likewise notes in "The Spectacle of the 'Other,'" the meanings ascribed to something via representation cannot be fixed, though that is precisely what representation attempts to do (270). Prevalent and privileged forms of meaning can still be unsettled and reappropriated to produce alternate meanings, a process Hall refers to as trans-coding (270). It follows, then, that these same representations of US Central Americans can also function as discursive sites of negotiation through which to contest prevalent notions of US Central American marginalization and its material effects.

Javier Zamora's poem "Second Attempt Crossing" helps to substantiate this point. It is part of Zamora's poetry collection *Unaccompanied* (2017), which draws on, among other things, his experiences as an undocumented and unaccompanied youth who migrated to the United States when he was nine years old. The poem recalls an instance during the speaker's migrant journey when "La Migra" unexpectedly descended upon the group of migrants with which he was traveling, prompting them to frantically scatter in different directions. One of the migrants, named "Chino," to whom the poem is dedicated, used his body to shield the speaker from the blows of the immigration officers who captured them. The speaker expresses regret at never having thanked "Beautiful *Chino*" for his actions, then proceeds to reveal who this individual was in the final verses: a former member of MS-13 who was fleeing the gang and who, even after they had parted ways once in the United States, continued to call the speaker twice a month until his former gang found him. As such, the last verses of the poem also constitute a tender tribute and farewell to someone the speaker viewed as a protector. The poet writes,

> farewell your tattooed chest: the M,
> the S, the 13. Farewell
> the phone number you gave me
> when you went east to Virginia,
> and I went west to San Francisco. [. . .] Farewell
> your brown arms that shielded me then,
> that shield me now, from La Migra. (9–10)

Zamora's endearing and nuanced portrait of Chino stands in sharp contrast to the dominant image of the threatening and violent MS-13 gang member cultivated in mainstream media and used so effectively by the Trump administration to push its hard-line agenda on immigration. Rendered through the eyes of the poem's speaker and a fellow unaccompanied minor, Chino is not a monster. He is "beautiful," a caring individual who looked after the speaker during and after their migratory journey, even though he, too, was a frightened youth traveling alone in search of refuge in the United States. By representing Chino in this manner, the poet offers a counternarrative to the dominant and often vacuous depictions of Central American subjects as forever illegals. The victimization of unaccompanied youth such as the speaker and Chino is not the prime focus of this poem; rather, it is the significant and lasting bond forged between them in the midst of their otherwise alienating existence. This instantiation of belonging enacted by two Central American migrant subjects presumed to be undesirable works to both humanize them and make their realities more legible.

It is this means of signifying US Central American non-belonging—both its exclusionary realities and inclusionary possibilities—that the remainder of this book further tracks, beginning with the next chapter. Like Zamora's image of Chino, the portrayal of the protagonist of *Dirt*, Dolores, brings to bear the duality of signification through representation. Although Dolores's representation underscores a process of "domestication" that ensures the continued invisibility and exploitation of Salvadoran *domésticas*, it also offers an alternative reading of this trope. Not only does Dolores find a community among a diverse group of immigrant coworkers, some of whom are also undocumented, but she also strives to maintain her Salvadoran national identity and connection to her cultural roots. It is precisely these efforts to foment and maintain a sense of belonging from "within the margins" that allow her to partly stave off her exclusionary status as a US Central American Other.

CHAPTER TWO

Domesticated Subject?

THE SALVADORAN MAID IN US TELEVISION AND FILM

*L*IKE OTHER TELEVISION SITCOMS FROM THE 1990S AND early 2000s, NBC's hit series *Will and Grace* was revived decades later, in its case in 2017. During its original eight-season run (1998–2006), the show was a staple of NBC's Thursday night lineup and Nielsen's list of the top twenty television series. It was also the recipient of numerous Emmy, Golden Globe, SAG, and GLAAD (Gay and Lesbian Alliance against Defamation) awards. When the show first aired, it was lauded as a groundbreaking series for its portrayal of openly gay leads, which was a departure from previous depictions of LGBTQ people as primarily peripheral and nonexistent characters (Gay and Lesbian Alliance against Defamation). The main cast of the show consists of Will Truman (Eric McCormack), a gay lawyer who shares an apartment with Grace Adler (Debra Messing), a straight interior designer and his best friend; Jack McFarland (Sean Hayes), Will's flamboyant gay friend; and Karen Walker (Megan Mullally), a married wealthy socialite whose sexuality is ambiguous and who works as Grace's receptionist. Outside of its four white leads, the show also features Rosario Salazar, Karen Walker's sassy Salvadoran maid, played by Shelley Morrison (née Rachel Mitrani), an actress of Spanish-Jewish descent. Though this was originally slated to be a limited role, the comedic fireworks between Karen and Rosario, as well as fan enthusiasm for Rosario's character, led to Morrison becoming a permanent member of the cast.[1] With the exception of Morrison, who had retired from acting, all of the show's original cast members returned to reprise their roles in the show's revival run (2017–2020).[2]

Though absent from the reboot of *Will and Grace*, Rosario's character plays a key role in an election-themed webisode, "Vote Honey," that went viral and aired on NBC in September 2016.[3] Morrison even makes a brief cameo at the end of the special, whose popularity influenced the network's decision to revive the series. Several of the jokes featured in the special revolve around Rosario, alluding to her Salvadoran ethnicity as well as then-presidential candidate Trump's derogatory statements regarding Mexican immigrants and his campaign promise to build a border wall. For example, at one point in the episode, Grace asks Karen how she can support Trump and be his friend given his rhetoric about Mexicans and Karen's relationship with Rosario. After Will reminds Grace that Rosario is in fact from El Salvador, not Mexico, Grace replies, "What's the difference?" as the audience laughs on cue. To fans of the series, this is a familiar joke. In the show's first run, Karen often refers to Rosario as Mexican, only to have Rosario or another main character correct her in the same way that Will corrects Grace. Meant to poke fun at Grace's and Karen's ignorance despite their professed concern for Rosario, this joke nevertheless raises a central question: Is Rosario's Salvadoran identity as inconsequential as the show makes it out to be? This chapter constitutes a critical response to the seemingly innocuous nature of Rosario's Salvadoranness and the larger query it inspires. I take a nuanced and critical look at representations of the immigrant and ethnically specific Salvadoran maid, or *doméstica*, focusing on the portrayals of Rosario in *Will and Grace* and Dolores in Nancy Savoca's lesser-known independent film *Dirt* (2004).

As the popularity of Rosario's character underscores, the Latina/Latin American immigrant maid and/or nanny has become a staple in contemporary US television and film. Although predominantly a minor or secondary character, as is the case in movies such as *Down and Out in Beverly Hills* (1986), *As Good as It Gets* (1997), and *Babel* (2006), the maid character has also been elevated to protagonist in feature films such as *Maid in Manhattan* (2002), starring Jennifer Lopez, and James L. Brooks's dramedy *Spanglish* (2004), featuring Spanish actress Paz Vega. More recently, in the critically acclaimed whodunit *Knives Out* (2019), Cuban actress Ana de Armas plays a nurse/caretaker in the spirit of the Latina maid. The growing visibility of this figure has been in keeping with demographic changes occasioned by increased immigration from Latin America after 1965, adding to the exponential growth of the overall Latinx population in the United States, and what has been an accompanying Latinx boom in Hollywood and the music industry since at least the 1990s. Still, cultural analyses of portrayals of the Latina maid within the current context of transnational immigration from Latin America to the United States remain scant,[4] with the notable exception of Irene Mata's *Domestic Disturbances: Re-imagining Narratives of Gender, Labor, and Immigration* (2014). Equally scarce are studies of US Central Americans within the specific scope of film and visual media, especially ones that engage with the experiences of women and issues related to the construction of gendered identities and subjectivities.[5]

This exploration of contemporary depictions of Salvadoran *domésticas* combines a focus on both of these lacking areas. Doing so facilitates, on a broader level, a contemplation of the ways in which the US media contributes to the (in)visibility of Latinx peoples while also participating in what Lisa Lowe has suggested is "the construction of the nation as a simulacrum of inclusiveness" (5). The thinly veiled attempts to imbue the figure of the Latina maid with more nuance in *Maid in Manhattan* and *Spanglish* do little to hide the fact that both films are still, at their core, reiterations of the narrative of the American Dream.[6] Part of this contemplation includes the related issues of immigrant subjectivities, transnational Latinx identities, the "browning" and feminization of international labor, and US dominance. In addition to underlining the heterogeneity of a Latina immigrant workforce mobilized by global and political processes, my explicit focus on Salvadoran maids further enables an exploration of these stated concerns and issues from the vantage point of US Central American experiences and perspectives that have been underexamined or ignored. Included in the latter is the process of forging US Central American identities that are reflective of both US and transnational ties. Such identities are informed by notions of belonging and not belonging and, as this analysis also shows, constitute a means of mitigating and/or resisting the exclusionary status of being a "domesticated" foreign Other.

THE SALVADORAN *DOMÉSTICA* IN CONTEXT

My reading of the Salvadoran *doméstica*, as envisioned in US television and film of the late twentieth and early twenty-first centuries, is informed by my understanding of the figure of the Latina maid as part of a more generalized stereotyping of women of color as servants, particularly African American women as "mammies" or "Black domestics," and as a result of specific historical and geopolitical factors. Scholars such as Charles Ramírez Berg and Clara E. Rodríguez have drawn attention to the different stereotypes of Latina women that have been engendered in Hollywood. Among these are those of the Latina "spitfire," the hypersexualized temptress or harlot, the female clown, the "dark lady," and the no longer prevalent "good girl/Madonna" incarnated by María of *West Side Story* (1961) fame.[7]

For the most part, these stereotypical portrayals envisioned Latina women as also having heavy accents and being racially "brown" or *mestizas*, as epitomized by Natalie Wood's portrayal of María in *West Side Story*, for which she literally wore brownface.

Other representations, such as that of the domestic servant or cleaning lady, junkie, single mother, and exploited worker or victim, are stereotypical images, as Angharad N. Valdivia suggests, shared with other women of color (92). The mammy figure, for instance, of the Old South and so prevalent in the advertising imagery of the postbellum United States comes to mind.[8] Just as I am arguing that the Latina maid and its Salvadoran variant can be viewed as a signifier of affirmations as well as contestations with regard to US hegemony, assimilation, immigration, and Latinx identities, Morgan posits that the mammy stereotype can be similarly understood as a "messenger" (88). In addition to construing her continued service to a white household as a "reunifying gesture toward North-South reconciliation," Morgan contends that the mammy also "became a defender of class privilege and the status quo . . . offer[ing] a ready solution not only to the problem of how to assimilate former slaves into contemporary society but also to the challenge of how to keep the middle-class Euro-American woman in her ladylike role of home administrator" (88). The recurring image of the Latina maid, thus, overlaps with the representation of the African American domestic servant not just in its depiction of a stereotypical ethnic and racialized workforce (in the case of Latin American women immigrants, also one that is foreign), but also in its ability to convey a "message" that upholds white privilege and that acts as a "solution" for how to incorporate (in a nonthreatening manner) a foreign supply of labor on which US society depends.

The fact that in recent years the maid on screen has also become an immigrant, as suggested by the appearance of the Salvadoran *doméstica*, can be explained, to a certain extent, by significant global sociopolitical and economic developments. As Pierrette Hondagneu-Sotelo notes, by the 1970s the percentage of African American women working as domestic servants began to decline. Women in the profession became older, while younger and more politicized generations of African American women began to reject such positions "imbued with servitude and racial subordination" (16). Mary Romero's work on Mexican American and Chicana domestic servants in the Southwest also notes that many of these women, especially Chicanas, tend to leave their occupations for office jobs or factory jobs that "do not demand the same level of deference and servility" (90). The voids left by these groups of women have been increasingly filled by foreign-born Latinas (Hondagneu-Sotelo 17), part of the newer waves of Latin American immigrants to come to the United States in the 1970s, '80s, and '90s.

With regard to Central American women, it is important to note that even prior to this period of immigration, a significant precedent had already been set by Salvadoran women who had been contributing to the labor market in East Coast cities such as Washington, DC, since the 1960s, recruited to work as domestic servants by diplomatic families and employees of US government agencies (Repak 77). For the groups of Central American female migrants that came after them, many of whom fled economic strife and the civil wars waged in Guatemala, El Salvador, and Nicaragua throughout the 1970s and 1980s, work as caretakers, nannies, and maids was and continues to be a viable and attractive option given the undocumented status of many. Women from El Salvador and Guatemala comprise a large segment of the Latina labor force in the private sector of many urban areas, in some cases even more so than Mexican women, according to studies by Zentgraf (77) and Hondagneu-Sotelo (8).

Narrowly rendered portraits of the racialized or ethnic maid in US television and film have paralleled many of these social and economic developments. While by the 1960s representations of the African American house servant were all but eradicated,[9] the image of the Latina servant continued to subsist and proliferate.[10] Added to the aforementioned filmic examples are a series of television shows, including the short-lived *I Married Dora* (1987), featuring an undocumented housekeeper facing deportation who marries her Anglo employer; sitcoms such as *Dharma and Greg* (1997–2002), *Veronica's Closet* (1997–2000), and *My Name Is Earl* (2005); and the dramedy with a telenovela flair *Devious Maids* (2013–2016), the brainchild of the Mexican American actress Eva Longoria. Although the stated or presumed ethnicity of the *doméstica* tends to be Mexican in most of these venues, the maid, nanny, or cleaning lady featured has increasingly become Central American, and in many instances is a Salvadoran immigrant. In fact, the lead character, Dora Calderon (played by Elizabeth Peña), in *I Married Dora* is from El Salvador. This shift is in keeping with the migratory patterns of the last forty years as well as the broader observations made in chapter one concerning the increased visibility afforded to US Central Americans during the 1980s. Recall such depictions in Gregory Nava's films *El Norte* and *My Family/Mi Familia*, as well as in Wim Wenders's *The End of Violence*, in which the figure of the political refugee is conflated with that of the *doméstica*. Beyond these are portrayals of the Salvadoran maid such as those in the teen comedy *Clueless* (1995) and in less commercial dramas such as Todd Solondz's *Storytelling* (2001), in addition to those explored here: Rosario in *Will and Grace* and Dolores in *Dirt*.

Looking at the contrasting portrayals of the Latina/Salvadoran maid through this alternate lens of historical contextualization and Hollywood's prevalent typecasting of women of color as domestic servants and subordinate Others imbues this figure with layers of connotative meaning and critical functions related to more general questions of Latina immigrant labor and marginalization in the United States, as well as to the particulars of US Central American gendered subjectivities and emerging Latinx identities. Elucidating how the representations in question (those of Rosario and Dolores) mediate and negotiate these discourses requires a fundamental understanding of what Ramírez Berg contends is the ideological function of stereotypes. Referencing the work of Richard Dryer, Ramírez Berg posits that in addition to being ahistorical and homogenizing, stereotypes are ideological in that they not only maintain the status quo by demonstrating why the "in-group" is in power and why the "out-group" is not but also define the Other. Stereotypes identify the contours by which this out-group is to be known and situated in dominant discourse, as is the case with the stereotypes of Latinxs as Latin lovers, dark ladies, bandits, and the like, which "defines them first and foremost outside of the mainstream" (22). As Ramírez Berg further elaborates, "The stereotypical definition of Others, therefore has powerful ideological consequences, simultaneously marginalizing Them and establishing and maintaining an explicit Us-Them boundary" (22).

The stereotypical image of the Salvadoran maid, however, is also complicated by her identification not just on the basis of her ethnicity and assumed subservient nature, which, like limiting depictions of Latinx individuals more generally, mark her automatically as "foreign," but also by the fact that she is part of an immigrant labor force. Additionally, her "desirability" is premised not on some perceived notion of Latina sexuality, such as in the portrayals by Jennifer Lopez and Paz Vega, but rather on her ability as a worker. Hence, building upon Ramírez Berg's conceptualization of Latinx stereotypes, I argue that because the Salvadoran *doméstica* is explicitly constituted as an immigrant laborer on which the United States depends, the way in which this foreign Other is situated within dominant discourse is through a process of "domestication." Non-belonging is implicated in this process, given that domestication can also be seen as providing the Salvadoran immigrant women subjected to it with the veneer of inclusion while still reinscribing their undesirability and marginalization.

In her piece "Manifest Domesticity," Amy Kaplan calls attention to the points of convergence between nineteenth-century notions of domesticity in US women's literature and the imperialist discourse of Manifest Destiny. According to Kaplan, the links between the domestic and the imperial project of civilizing are visible when we think of domesticity not as a "static condition" but as "a process of domestication, which entails conquering and taming the wild, the natural, and the alien" both at home and abroad (480).

A convergence existed, therefore, between women's projects of domestication, which included domesticating both their slaves and their unruly children, and US colonization of the foreign Other. Viewed through this conceptual lens, the Salvadoran immigrant who is pictured serving and working in the home of her employer, and whose migration to the North has been instigated in large part by US free market policies and intervention in Latin America, is also rendered a "domesticated" Other. As such, she reinforces and perpetuates a colonial mindset within the current context of Latin American immigration to the United States and gendered international labor. Her stereotypical portrayal is also suggestive of the need to domesticate all foreign subjects, those alien elements who reside in the United States and are integral to the US economy, but who must, nevertheless, remain inferior.

Domesticating the Salvadoran immigrant entails a necessary disavowal of the past. Key historical realities such as those related to traumatic border crossings and an equally distressing past of civil war are glossed over in favor of a more immediate immigrant reality that focalizes immigrant life in the United States. For many Salvadorans, however, it is difficult to forget the civil conflict that ravaged their country from 1980 to 1992 and was a key impetus for their emigration out of El Salvador. Referenced in my discussion of Reagan's 1984 congressional address on Central America, this was a war in which the United States factored considerably, sending millions of dollars in foreign aid to help support El Salvador's oppressive military government in their fight against the "communist threat." The involvement of the United States in El Salvador, similarly, impacted the context of arrival of many Salvadoran immigrants who were denied asylum precisely because they were not deemed political refugees whose lives were threatened in their country of origin. All of this played a role in the social and economic stratification experienced by the vast majority of these same Salvadoran refugees once in the country. Underplaying the historical parallels between the "domestication" of El Salvador and its migrants by the United States facilitates a less critical and, therefore, more "consumable" and placated representation of the Latina foreign laborer.

This notion of domestication informs and is a central thread of the following analysis of the conflicting representations of the Salvadoran maid characters Rosario and Dolores. While both characters are examples of media depictions of foreign-born domestic laborers, each gives way to a different understanding of the socioeconomic reality of Latina servitude. On the prime-time show *Will and Grace*, Rosario is a highly visible portrayal of the figure of the Salvadoran *doméstica*. However, this rendering fails to call into question the stereotype of Latina servants. While it can be argued

that this representation is also a result of the conventions used within situational comedy and must be considered as such, it nevertheless promotes
an image of the Salvadoran maid as a domesticated foreign Other that does
not undermine the status quo upheld in the show.[11] Indeed, and despite
the celebrated progressivism of *Will and Grace*, as critics have observed, the
show fails to "represent a challenge to the dominant norms of US culture"
in terms of sexuality (Battles and Hilton-Morrow 102).[12] When read against
the backdrop of the Clinton administration's embrace of neoliberalist ideologies and policies touted as race and gender neutral, one can likewise make
the case that the show evinces and promotes a similarly problematic "color-
blindness" that believes itself to be antiracist and antisexist.[13] Speaking to this
last point, network executives at NBC argued that the *Will and Grace* revival
would be successful, in large part, because audiences in the Trump era were
"wistful for the Bill Clinton 1990s" (Barnes). This celebratory view of the
Clinton years, which the show is clearly meant to evoke and channel, belies
the actual state of affairs and disenfranchisement of many underrepresented
communities during the stated era (and now).

By contrast, Dolores's depiction in the independent film *Dirt* undermines
both the more generalized stereotype of the Latina maid and the notion of
domestication. Positioning Dolores's viewpoint and experiences as those of an
undocumented immigrant in a multi-Latinx New York allows her a critical
visibility and historical depth unlike those of Rosario. Through Dolores's eyes
viewers are privy to the extent to which class, race, and legal status condition
her working environment and relationship with her employers, making discernible the unequal power relations that are largely brushed aside on *Will
and Grace*. In other words, *Dirt* examines the dark underside of the neoliberal
view of progressivism and prosperity celebrated on the show. Relatedly, the
depiction of Dolores affords a broader conceptualization of transnational Salvadoran and Latinx identities and immigrant subjectivities shaped by alternate notions of national and cultural belonging that do not affirm the ideal of
the American Dream. In this sense, then, Dolores's representation sets its own
parameters for understanding her life as an undocumented domestic servant
and thus also defines the terms by which she is viewed.

"OUTING" THE MAID ON *WILL AND GRACE*

The character Rosario first made her appearance on the hit sitcom
Will and Grace at the end of the show's first season. Far from being meek or
completely subservient, this Salvadoran maid was sarcastic and poignantly
blunt, a quality that at first glance imbues her character with a certain sense

2.1. *Rosario and Karen in* Will and Grace. *NBC/ NBC Universal via Getty Images.*

of critical agency. In Rosario's debut episode, "The Object of My Rejection," Karen takes Rosario to meet Will, hoping to get legal advice about how to prevent Rosario's impending deportation. Will suggests that Rosario marry Jack to acquire her legal citizenship. Consequently, the episode ends with Jack and Rosario walking down the aisle in a comical farce made all the more humorous by Jack's overt gayness.[14] Tellingly, when Rosario first appears on screen, she is dressed in a prototypical maid's uniform: a light blue and standard silhouette with white cuffs and a white apron, complemented by a simple red jacket or windbreaker. When Karen asks Rosario to take a seat in Will's office, she not only coaxes Rosario by patting one of the chairs but also speaks to her as if she were incapable of understanding English: "Come on, honey . . . sit-o down-o. Try not to talk-o." In an unexpected outburst (because it is in English, albeit heavily accented), Rosario quickly counters by directing herself to Will and stating, "You see how she talks to me? I speak English, okay?" With this one remark, Rosario not only drops a comedic blow but also calls attention to the patronizing and erroneous assumptions adopted by many Anglos that (1) immigrants cannot speak English and (2) that not speaking English is suggestive of a lack of intelligence, as evidenced by Karen's deliberately slow and enunciated speech.

Although in this first encounter Rosario's Salvadoran background is not immediately espoused, there are a significant number of markers meant to set her apart as a Latina immigrant Other as well as to inscribe her role as the maid. For one, the entire subplot revolves around Rosario's defining characteristic as an undocumented immigrant, emphasized all the more by her heavy accent and "brown" features (though, notably, these are not those of the sexualized Latina beauty). Two, the uniform that Rosario dons the first time she is introduced on the show and in which she will be continuously seen, leaves no doubt about what Rosario's occupation is nor about what class or social position she occupies in comparison to her employer and Will. In effect, Rosario's uniform acts as what Hall terms an encoded televisual sign that on one level is meant to communicate her status as an employee and on another level defines her as a "domesticated" Other.

At first glance, such a blatant stereotype of the Latina *doméstica* seems to suggest that Rosario's depiction is, in fact, a parody, which, according to the Oxford English Dictionary, can be defined as "an imitation of a work more or less closely modeled on the original, but so turned as to produce a ridiculous effect" (qtd. in Hutcheon 32). In this sense, Rosario's racialized ethnicity, undocumented status, accent, and wardrobe are *meant* to produce a hyperbolized image of the foreign domestic, an imitation with the potential to also be critical of the very object or subject it is modeled after. Even her full name, Rosario Inez Consuelo Yolanda Salazar, composed of four different and overtly Hispanic first names, seems to contribute to the construction of this parodistic representation. Yet for all its critical possibilities, Rosario as a parody of the Latina maid remains problematic. In *A Theory of Parody*, Linda Hutcheon argues that beyond the definition of parody as opposition or contrast (with the connotation of ridicule), the term can also be understood as "repetition with difference" (32). This difference or distance between the original and the imitation is signaled by irony. And while this irony can be "playful" and "critically constructive," it can also be "belittling" and "destructive" (32). To a certain extent, the representation of Rosario is a double-edged sword. On the one hand, it can call into question through ridicule certain forms of oppression and exploitation. On the other hand, however, it also runs the risk of reaffirming the same stereotypes it emulates as well as the discourses it seeks to destabilize.

One relationship in which these destructive aspects of Rosario's portrayal are most discernible is the one between Rosario and her employer, Karen, itself another parody of Scarlet O'Hara's relationship to her "mammy," the central difference being that the African American servant has been replaced by a Salvadoran immigrant. During episode 12 of the show's second season, "He's Come Undone," Karen barges into Jack and Rosario's room late at night and orders Rosario to get up from bed to make some cocktails for her guests. When Jack admonishes Karen for overworking his new wife, Karen responds by taunting Jack: "Well, well. Look at you. Sticking up for your Mexican mama, huh? You like that?" Rosario then interjects, "I told you, lady, I'm from El Salvador." Here again, the show's parodistic depiction of Rosario lends itself to interpretation as a critical commentary regarding the exploitative conditions under which many live-in *domésticas* work. As Hondagneu-Sotelo's study reveals, often employers of live-in maids and nannies expect them to be on call twenty-four hours a day precisely because they reside within their homes and there is no clear division between work and nonwork hours (32). Through the use of comedy, this scene not only engages this form of abuse but also seems to be criticizing it.

By the same token, Rosario's affirmation that she is Salvadoran also *seems* to call attention to Karen's ignorance (and perhaps that of the audience) regarding the heterogeneity of Latin American immigrants and colonial-based hierarchies within Latin America and Latinx communities in the United States (i.e., the perceived inferiority of Central Americans vis-à-vis Mexicans and the "Mexicanization" of US Central Americans).[15] However, despite the emphasis on Rosario's Salvadoranness, it is apparent from Karen's quick dismissal of Rosario's declaration of identity and the latter's continued need to restate it that, outside of signaling an ethnicity that is non-Mexican, it is of little consequence. As was the case in the 2016 election special, no real understanding of what it means to be a Salvadoran immigrant, including specific histories of US political and economic intervention, (unauthorized) border crossings, and experiences with US regimes of "illegality," is provided or entertained. Rosario's inclusion and visibility, thus, depends on the occlusion of this contextual information as well as her reification as a foreign and ethnic Other. She remains as such even while appearing alongside another marginalized group, gay men, who in this case are also Anglo and privileged—a point to which I will return. This notion is further underscored by the fact that Rosario is one of only a few recurring characters of color to be featured on the show and the only one to consistently appear alongside the otherwise all-Anglo cast; this is all the more striking given that the show is set in New York, a racially and ethnically diverse urban setting.[16]

In the same episode, there is another scene in which Jack helps Karen and Rosario resolve their pending argument regarding Karen's mistreatment and exploitation of Rosario. The three have the following conversation in the small linen closet where Rosario is ironing napkins while Jack looks on:

JACK. We had a little talk, and Karen has decided that from now on, she's gonna treat you, my wild Latin rose, like a decent human being.

ROSARIO. Is that true?

KAREN. Yeah, honey.

ROSARIO. Then I quit.

JACK and KAREN [both]. What?!

ROSARIO. I didn't sign on to work for a decent human being. I signed on to work with Miss Karen.

Ensuing afterward is one of the signature trademarks of Karen and Rosario's rapport with each other: an explosive outburst in which each of their voices overlaps the other to the point of incoherence, followed by each one professing their love for the other. Karen tells Rosario that it is good to have her back, while Rosario begs of Karen, "Oh, don't ever leave me, cupcake." The scene is then neatly tied up with Jack's words: "Well, I guess everybody's happy. . . . I forgot that even though harsh words are exchanged sometimes, underneath it all is love."

This unique triangulation between Rosario, Karen, and their mediator, Jack, merits further deconstruction, as it helps to elucidate Rosario's subservience to both. Much of what makes this scenario and the interactions between these three figures humorous is its campiness. Jack's sham marriage to Rosario is funny precisely because of his flamboyance and because she does not exude any of the prototypical sexuality expected of Latinas on screen. It is this levity that makes what could otherwise be seen as a critique of "straight marriage" and an act of fraud inoffensive to mainstream audiences. After all, Jack and Rosario's nuptials are still an illegal means of circumventing US immigration law so that she can stay in the country, a notable fact considering the passage of key immigration reforms during the show's run, including the 1996 IIRIRA, which included more stringent rules and policies for legalizing one's immigrant status.[17] Jack's ability to be "one of the girls" also allows him to partake in and highlight the homosocial nature and underlying queerness of Rosario's and Karen's relationship.[18] Karen, like Jack, has a "campy disposition," one that is manifested in her embrace and celebration of excess as well as her "flagrant sexuality" (Cooper 518–519). Moreover, her sexual identity remains unfixed on the show (519). She flirts indiscriminately with men and women alike, most often and playfully with Jack but also with Rosario, who responds in kind through the use of endearing phrases (e.g., "Oh, don't ever leave me, cupcake").

Still, as Richard Dyer observes, camp is "deeply ambiguous" (51). For all its fun and wit, camp can also obscure and prevent needed interrogations of issues such as male chauvinism and sexism that are present in the LGBTQ+ community (50–51). To this, we could add racism and classism. When Jack calls Rosario a "wild Latin rose," he evokes stereotypes of Latina wanton sexuality and exoticness from a position of power as a man who, despite his sexuality, is white and a native-born US citizen. The potentially transgressive nature of his campiness changes neither his status nor Rosario's (although she has through her marriage with Jack secured a pathway to citizenship). In this way, such an interaction and use of camp fails to effectively challenge the hierarchies embedded and affirmed through such stereotyping.

A similar dynamic defines Karen and Rosario's interactions and long-standing relationship. According to the official website dedicated to the show during its original eight-season run, Karen and Rosario have a "reciprocal condescending relationship," that masks the fact that they "truly care for one another."[19] This interpretation of Karen and Rosario's relationship as "reciprocal" holds true only if one ignores the class and ethnic/racial differences that mark it and that Karen's performance of camp also fails to nullify. This performance, like that of Jack's, makes Karen's whiteness and privilege all the more obvious, and with it Rosario's subservience. Recall that Rosario makes it explicitly clear that despite her employer's "excess," and perhaps because of it, she prefers to work for "Miss Karen" rather than for someone who will treat her humanely.

Consequently, what is projected in this interaction is an image not of a "feisty" Salvadoran immigrant maid—recalling that of the Latina "spitfire"— who breaks the mold, but of one who is ultimately "tamed" back into her rightful place and likes it. Rosario's unwavering affection for and continued desire to work for Karen are a disturbing indication of how this Salvadoran immigrant has been successfully interpolated as a domestic servant and in the process has also become a "domesticated" Other who upholds the neoliberalist status quo. Although her Salvadoran ethnicity and existence as part of an immigrant workforce are acknowledged, her domesticated status robs her of any real agency or historical depth and, hence, continues to keep *her* in the closet.

DOLORES AND *DIRT*: "THIS IS NO J-LO FANTASY"

Nancy Savoca's independent film *Dirt* draws a portrait of the Salvadoran *doméstica* radically different from that of Rosario on *Will and Grace*. Previous to the film's airing on the prime cable channel *Showtime*, *Dirt* appeared in select and limited engagements, the majority of them film festivals. It won various awards and nominations, including the Best Film award at the El Cojo Festival in Madrid, the Best Director award at the Los Angeles International Latino Film Festival, and a nomination for Best Long-form Teleplay from the Writer's Guild of America. The movie tells the story of Dolores del Rosario (Julieta Ortiz), an undocumented Salvadoran immigrant who earns a living cleaning the homes of the affluent in Manhattan's Upper East Side. This character-driven story line and portrayal is in keeping with Savoca's feminist voice and previous depictions of ethnic women, mainly Italian Americans and Latinas.[20] At the same time, it also speaks to what Chris Holmlund notes is a key trait of independent cinema: the ability to express "outsider perspectives" typically ignored by major Hollywood studios (1).

Each day, Dolores faces a similar routine: she rides the subway into the city to perform her job as an invisible worker in a world of luxury that stands in vast contrast to her own one-bedroom apartment in a multi-Latinx neighborhood in Queens. She shares her living space with her husband, Rodolfo, and her teenage son, Rudy, who are also undocumented. With her husband out of work, Dolores must struggle even harder to survive, as she is not only supporting her family but also sending money back home to El Salvador to finance the construction of a house she hopes to inhabit with her family in the near future. Dolores's life seems to gradually unravel as the plot progresses. She loses two of her higher paying jobs; is cursed by La Loca, who lives in the apartment below; and finally is forced to deal with the sudden death of her husband, who is killed while working on a recently acquired construction job. With the help of a benevolent employer and friends, Dolores collects enough money to take her husband's body back to El Salvador. However, after burying her husband and realizing that there is no future for her or her son in El Salvador, Dolores decides to return to the United States, where there is always an endless supply of work—an endless supply of dirt to clean.

Dolores's depiction in *Dirt* undermines limiting portrayals of Latina servitude while also contesting the notion of "domestication" that makes Rosario a likable but unaffecting representation. As one of the film's favorable reviews suggests, "This is no J-Lo fantasy" (Scheib). In other words, *Dirt* does not pretend to be a Cinderella story (as in the case of *Maid in Manhattan*) that calls attention to issues of racial, gender, and class inequality only to sideline them for the sake of a happy ending. This is made clear from the beginning of the film. In the opening scene Dolores is pictured emerging from a crowded subway exit in Manhattan, wearing a mid-knee-length skirt, a jacket, and (as is revealed later) a mass-produced T-shirt with the words "New York" printed across the front in patriotic red, white, and blue colors. While she does not wear a tailored uniform, Dolores's clothing nevertheless

2.2. *Dolores and Mrs. Ortega in* Dirt.

indicates her working-class and immigrant status. The notion of national and local belonging evoked on her shirt, via the city's name and its colors, ironically, is premised on the negation of immigrant experiences like her own. Moreover, this same cheap, mass-produced T-shirt also astutely calls to mind the gendering of another form of immigrant labor: the maquiladora industry.

As happens throughout the film, in this initial scene the camera focuses on Dolores's facial expression, capturing its mixture of frustration and determination. While illuminating and emphasizing her perspective, this cinematic close-up creates a sense of intimacy between the viewer and Dolores. It is this exploration of Dolores's experiences and view "from below" that adds depth to her image as a Latina maid and similarly underscores one of the film's strongest themes, that of invisibility. Often, Dolores finds herself alone, cleaning what seem to be the virtually sterile and uninhabited apartments of her mostly Anglo employers. She seldom sees them, following the orders they leave for her in handwritten notes on the dining room table. At other times, however, as is the case with the Ortegas, the only upper-class Latinx family she works for, Dolores is forced to interact with them. Ironically, it is at these times that Dolores's invisibility is most pronounced.

One such instance involves a scene in which Dolores is asked by Mrs. Ortega to clean her bathroom while she is getting ready for work in the morning. When Dolores greets Mrs. Ortega in Spanish, Mrs. Ortega insists that Dolores speak English to her, claiming that Dolores needs to "practice." This opening exchange occurs as Dolores stands in the doorway, watching

Mrs. Ortega blow-dry her hair in front of the bathroom mirror wearing only a bra and a pencil skirt. Shot from a low angle, the camera looks over Dolores's shoulder, showing us what she sees: Mrs. Ortega, absorbed in her own image in the mirror, speaking to Dolores without moving her gaze away from her own reflection. In what follows, the two women engage in a cursory conversation in which Mrs. Ortega does most of the talking and Dolores continues to clean. Close-ups are shown of Dolores's application of cleaning products on the bathtub and toilet while Mrs. Ortega is heard in the background talking about her aspirations to be a congresswoman and how worried she is about her son. When Dolores interjects that she, too, knows about adolescents, Mrs. Ortega ignores the remark. This entire exchange is carried out without either woman ever looking at the other; when the camera does provide a close-up of Dolores's face, it is by way of a frame-within-a-frame shot, emphasizing her reflection in a mirror above the toilet.

Although both women are Latinas, their differences due to class and citizenship status are clearly marked in this pivotal scene. Dolores's subordination to Mrs. Ortega is visually rendered by the lowly position Dolores occupies on the screen, literally scrubbing the "dirt" while Mrs. Ortega stands above her, and by the fact that Dolores is never really in Mrs. Ortega's field of vision; that is, Mrs. Ortega does not see or acknowledge Dolores even though she is apparently speaking to her. In addition to her economic wealth, Mrs. Ortega's decision to run for Congress also provides her with significant political clout and visibility in the media, a complete inversion of Dolores's situation as an undocumented and poor woman. Mrs. Ortega represents a privileged and dominant viewpoint, although she is not Anglo and has, to a certain extent, internalized the colonial mindset. She believes in drawing an important distinction between herself and the immigrant help and has adopted an assimilationist discourse, as exemplified by her insistence that Dolores speak English. Moreover, in a later scene, Mrs. Ortega sends her husband to fire Dolores because she is scared that she will lose the election if people find out she employs undocumented immigrants. As her husband informs Dolores, Mrs. Ortega has taken a "harsh stance against illegals in the city."

Of note here is that this exchange between Dolores and Mrs. Ortega is not filtered through Mrs. Ortega's dominant viewpoint, but rather Dolores's. In this sense, Dolores's representation as the Salvadoran *doméstica* is not enforcing the status quo, but rather challenging it by revealing its oppressive underside. In an attempt to convince Mr. Ortega to let her keep her job, Dolores emphasizes her ability to be discreet, evidenced by the fact that she has never said anything and has lived in the country for twelve years without anyone knowing. Ultimately, as she claims, "I am invisible." Dolores's naming of her own condition is the most critical commentary of all; she verbalizes the very premise on which her relationship with her employers depends and that they need to ignore in order to feel better about themselves and maintain the position of power they hold. Unlike the comic escape of *Will and Grace*, this reality cannot be laughed away, and it is for this reason that Mrs. Ortega cannot fire Dolores herself and must send her husband to do it. Furthermore, given the circumstances and perspective, it is difficult to reduce Dolores to a one-dimensional stereotype or marginal character whose background and struggles are of no consequence.

Dolores's relationship with the Ortegas stands apart not only because it underscores the class dynamics and differences related to legal status that mark the Latinx experience but also because it is unlike any exchanges she has with other Latinx individuals and immigrants in the film. In the building complex in which the Ortegas live, Dolores works alongside an ethnically and racially diverse group of employees, including Gerald from Jamaica, who runs the service elevator; Mona, an Afro-Latina from the Dominican Republic who is a cleaning lady and nanny; Mike, the doorman from Italy; and Flaherty, the building handyman and supervisor, whose Irish background connotes the experience of earlier waves of Irish immigrants in New York at the turn of the century. At home, Dolores is also surrounded by a predominantly working-class Latinx community with a strong Puerto Rican presence. This multi-Latinx focus calls to mind Frances Aparicio's critical reconceptualization of the term "Latinidad," especially in what refers to Latino images in media and popular culture. Instead of positing *Latinidad* from the dominant viewpoint imposed from the outside, as a notion that makes Latinxs homogeneous and more digestible for Anglo audiences, Aparicio argues that *Latinidad* needs to be understood as a "concept that allows us to explore moments of convergences and divergences in the formation of Latino/a (post) colonial subjectivities and in hybrid cultural expressions among various Latino national groups" ("Jennifer" 93). Understood as such, *Latinidad* provides a way of constructing "interlatino knowledge" (94), a type of knowledge based on the recognition of both differences and affinities between Latinx groups, thus subverting the homogenizing function of Latinx stereotypes precisely by emphasizing and revealing heterogeneity.

In *Dirt*, this "interlatino" understanding is produced in several ways, beginning with the representation of a Latina maid who is Salvadoran (being played by a Mexican actress) and the myriad shared stories and encounters among different Latinx groups the film showcases as part of Dolores's social and economic context.[21] Dolores and Mona's relationship is particularly revealing in this regard. Speaking to each other in Spanish or Spanglish in the basement laundry room provides an important outlet for Dolores and Mona, as they get a chance to not only figuratively air their employer's dirty laundry but also discuss their own complaints regarding their jobs. When Dolores informs Mona about her upcoming interview with another prospective employer, Mona, speaking over a mound of Mrs. Ortega's dirty undergarments, responds, "Poor Dolores. Your clients are the worst. They're always checking up with you, trying to see if they catch you make a mistake, to see if you are a criminal. But what can you do? It's a job, no?" Aside from their position as maids, Dolores and Mona also share a solidarity based on their undocumented status. After Dolores is fired by the Ortegas, Mona, who, along with the other employees, is relating her experience of migration, reveals that she crossed the US-Mexico border hidden in a fruit truck, unlike many Dominicans, who enter by way of Puerto Rico. It is at this point, too, that Dolores has her own flashback of the precarious journey across borders she undertook with her son, an experience that nearly cost both their lives. The camera pans to a scene of Dolores traveling alone with her son in the back of a semitruck with little ventilation. A desperate Dolores lifts the face of her barely conscious son close to the only window available, hoping he will not die. Later, as Dolores travels home she recalls another memory of carrying her son in the desert while other migrants scramble around her trying to seek shelter from bright lights, presumably those belonging to the border patrol.

In this depiction of Salvadoran undocumented immigration, it is the harrowing experience of border crossing that takes precedence over that of El Salvador's civil war. In speaking to the particulars of this experience, Savoca calls attention to yet another reality that largely goes unaccounted for, that of undocumented Central American migrant women traveling alone or with children. Although images of women and children have increasingly factored in representations of US Central Americans as forever illegals and have been strategically employed in the US media, these women's accounts as migrating mothers remain on the periphery of US debates and discussions about undocumented (im)migration, in scholarship, and in cultural representation (Padilla, "Migrant Marías" 102, 105). The women who undertake such journeys and whose lives as immigrants in the United States are impacted by the psychological and physical traumas they endure likewise contribute to this silence. Often, these women are unable to voice and/or contend with their traumas (105). Notably, in this scene with Mona and the rest of the building's immigrant employees, Dolores does not share her personal experience, choosing instead to remain quiet even as viewing audiences relive it with her.

This emphasis on Dolores's migratory experience at the US-Mexico border does not mean, however, that the topic of the Salvadoran civil conflict is elided in the film. Though it is subtle, the war does have a presence. During a job interview, Mrs. Cambridge, a rich and elderly socialite, ushers Dolores into her photo gallery. Most of the photos hanging on the walls capture images of Mrs. Cambridge with high-profile figures such as Hillary Clinton and Barbara Bush, except for a select few that register the faces of people suffering in different parts of the world. Commenting on this section of "inspiring" photographs taken by her son Jack, Mrs. Cambridge ponders aloud, "I think that our country is only now beginning to understand such tragedy. Don't you, Dolores?" After a brief silence, Mrs. Cambridge asks Dolores what country she is from and, following Dolores's answer, Mrs. Cambridge states, "Well, you understand tragedy, don't you?" This question, which is left unanswered, calls attention to the specter of war that also forms part of the Salvadoran immigrant reality. Even though within the more recent waves of migration from El Salvador the violence of the war has factored less, it persists as a key historical aspect of Dolores's Salvadoran background and foregrounds the new forms of persecution and "tragedy" immigrants such as Dolores suffer because they are undocumented.

Being undocumented may be a predicament shared by Dolores and other characters such as Mona, but it is also one of the key elements, aside from nationality, that divides the working-class Latinx groups in the film. La Loca, for example, who lives below Dolores and whose presumed background is Puerto Rican, makes a living by renting out apartment space to recently arrived undocumented workers, crowding them into one bedroom. Like Dolores's former employer, Mrs. Ortega, La Loca uses the privileges of her citizenship status (if not necessarily her class) to exploit those who are unauthorized. La Loca does so, however, without the burden of feigning shame or caring what others think. Indeed, in the film it is rumored that it was La Loca who called the INS on Dolores's husband, Rodolfo, causing him to lose his job in a local restaurant. Yet, divisions such as these based on citizenship are not always abusive or cause for tension. When Rodolfo dies, it is his Puerto Rican coworker, Mario, who raises funds to help Dolores with funeral expenses, and even La Loca offers her condolences. Thus, the film also showcases instances of Latinx unity in the face of certain types of oppression and loss.

Encompassed in these portrayals of Latinx intersections, which are part of Dolores's representation, is also a notable reflection concerning Salvadoran American and Latinx identities defined by immigrant and transnational ties and alternate notions of belonging. One of Dolores's and Rodolfo's hopes is to finish building their house in El Salvador so that they can return to settle there and make a living by opening a small grocery store. Hence, despite the fact that Dolores and Rodolfo are determined to prosper in the

United States, their goal is not necessarily to stay in the country, but to return "home" one day. Such visions for the future and longing to go back to El Salvador problematize the traditional narrative of immigrant assimilation, epitomized by the notion of the American Dream. Neither Dolores or her husband desire to be "Americans" or to fully integrate into US society. Through transnational enterprises such as the sending back of remittances and investing in property in El Salvador, Dolores and Rodolfo endeavor to live out a different dream. It is one largely motivated by their sense of national and cultural belonging to El Salvador rather than to the United States, where they exist as part of a disenfranchised Latinx workforce and community. Even at the end of the film, when Dolores chooses to return to the United States with her son, Rudy, after burying Rodolfo in El Salvador, she does so not out of a sense of personal desire or drive, but for practical reasons and because of her son. With Rodolfo gone, the wish of returning is no longer the same for Dolores, nor is it financially viable. Moreover, unlike her and Rodolfo, their son has grown up mostly in the United States and among a diverse group of Latinx peers. Rudy does not wish to stay in El Salvador nor feel that it is *his* home.

Echoing Mata's discussion of Latina counternarratives of domestic labor and immigration in the United States, Dolores's portrayal and this added transnational dimension to her story thus "disrupt[s] and displace[s] notions of national belonging while offering [a] realistic narrativ[e] of labor and mobility" (58). In so doing, Dolores's depiction does not afford an image of an easily "domesticated" or incorporated subject who affirms dominant and oppressive views, or who is content with serving and being subservient to her mistress. If anything, this representation of Dolores underscores her ability to define herself not only by way of her hard labor but also through her refusal to completely forfeit her cultural ties and Salvadoran national identity. Therefore, what makes this depiction of the Salvadoran *doméstica* so relevant and poignant is not the fact that it shows the character of the maid completely transgressing her status as a foreign immigrant Other. Rather, it is that the depiction shows the maid's awareness of her Othering and her efforts to resist this process of marginalization in spite of it all.

BEING SALVADORAN MATTERS

In an *LA Weekly* interview, the late Chicana actress Lupe Ontiveros revealed that she estimated having played the role of the maid in both theater and film some three hundred times (Lewis). Ontiveros's claim speaks to the core of this analysis, for while the maid seems to be everywhere, at least as a secondary character or as a marginalized Other, her personal story is rarely scripted or engaged. Nor are we privy to the historical context of immigration and US dominance that conditions her citizenship and employment status in the United States. The critical look at the Salvadoran *doméstica* in this chapter has attempted to bring into focus precisely this missing background and the narratives that would provide us with a more nuanced reading of this Latina figure. As such, it is possible to see the ways in which the divergent portrayals of the Salvadoran maids Rosario and Dolores underline key issues concerning stereotypical images of Latina women, a gendered immigrant labor force that is a significant element of the US economy, and transnational Salvadoran/Latinx identities.

Fundamental to understanding these representations is their ideological construction as images that either affirm the notion of a domesticated foreign Other (capable of being integrated into US society, all the while upholding dominant hierarchies and unequal practices) or subvert such a view and interpretation of Salvadoran/Latina immigrants and communities. Despite appearing on a television sitcom lauded for being (neo)liberal and inclusive, Rosario's representation on *Will and Grace*, like that of the other characters featured on the show, fails to challenge an oppressive status quo. Instead of undermining one-dimensional and limited views of Latina servitude and agency, Rosario's depiction falls in line with other problematic stereotypes of women of color. Her status as an immigrant and a maid upholds the image of the domesticated foreign Other. Relatedly, her noted Salvadoran ethnicity never functions as anything more than the basis of a joke.

The portrait of Dolores in *Dirt* elaborates a more judicious representation of the social reality of Salvadoran maids. Dolores's portrayal does not function as a stereotype and renders these marginalized workers visible while also revealing and contesting many of the hegemonic economic and social structures that keep these workers exploited. This depiction is similarly poignant given the broader questions it raises in terms of *Latinidad*, the elusive ideal of the American Dream, and Salvadoran American subjectivities. Inherent to these queries are also notions of non-belonging. Dolores's insistence on holding on to her Salvadoran ties and cultural sensibilities, even within the purview of her multi-Latinx reality in the United States, constitutes an articulation of belonging that does not conform to the traditional narrative of immigrant assimilation. Ultimately, Dolores's characterization shows to what extent and why being a Salvadoran and immigrant *doméstica* can and does matter.

CHAPTER THREE

Lance Corporal José Gutiérrez and the Perils of Being a "Good Immigrant"

ONE OF THE FIRST SOLDIERS TO DIE IN THE US-LED invasion of Iraq in 2003 was Marine Lance Corporal José Gutiérrez. His death made headlines because of his standing not only as one of the earliest casualties of the war but also as a so-called green card soldier. A native of Guatemala, Gutiérrez migrated to the United States as a teenager in the 1990s and, following his high school graduation, enlisted in the US Marines under an immigrant recruitment program that afforded him a pathway to citizenship in exchange for his successful military service. Prompted by his death and that of other "green card" soldiers,[1] Congress passed the Armed Forces Naturalization Act of 2003 (H.R. 1954), which, among other things, expedited the process of awarding posthumous citizenship to immigrant soldiers who died in combat and extended those same benefits of citizenship to the families and children of the deceased.[2]

The political discourse surrounding the passage of this legislation, along with mainstream media accounts, blogs, and online military tribute sites, was instrumental in crafting a dominant image of Gutiérrez as an American hero, and relatedly as an "exceptional" Latino or Latin American immigrant. The particulars of his life as an orphan in Guatemala, his history of unauthorized border crossings, and his fraudulent means of acquiring a green card prior to enlisting were all recast within a familiar narrative: the epic tale of an immigrant whose greatest desire was to be an American, pursuing that dream against all odds and at all costs. The fact that Gutiérrez did not achieve that goal until after his death made his story all the more tragic and inspiring, and served to further entrench it in the US popular imaginary. Indeed, in the more than fifteen years since Gutiérrez's passing, this particular representation of his American life and death remains prevalent and even has been strategically recalled within the context of debates spurred by Trump's anti-immigrant and racist rhetoric.[3]

Discussions of Gutiérrez have not been limited to mainstream media accounts and politics, however. Along with Heidi Specogna's documentary *The Short Life of José Antonio Gutiérrez* (2006), which questions the assimilationist bent of other media accounts, Gutiérrez's case appears in scholarship that critiques the targeted recruitment of Latinx youth into the US military. As Hector Amaya posits, what initially appears as hagiography is a form of violence perpetrated against fallen green card soldiers through the bestowing of posthumous citizenship. Granting posthumous citizenship is, according to Amaya, not only a fundamentally illiberal act because the deceased are not able to consent to their naturalization but also a "practice consistent with U.S. imperialism" ("Dying American" 7–8). In her discussion regarding dominant notions of *Latinidad* and Indigenous identities, Alicia Estrada underscores yet another form of violence perpetrated against Gutiérrez in prevalent media representations: the erasure of his Maya ancestry ("Latinidad" 148). Notably, with the exception of Estrada's preliminary observations, this aspect of Gutiérrez's identity has also been largely overlooked in the scholarship about him.

Lisa Marie Cacho's allusion to Gutiérrez's story in *Social Death: Racialized Rightlessness and the Criminalization of the Unprotected* provides the basis for a slightly different theoretical inquiry. As Cacho contends, the visibility afforded to Gutiérrez as a green card soldier and as a fallen American hero in the national media signaled the potential recoverability and deservingness of undocumented Latinx subjects, who, like him, pledged their allegiance to the United States and decried the terrorism perpetrated by other brown bodies (i.e., Arab and Muslim immigrants). Cacho explains that in the immediate aftermath of 9/11, "illegality" was grafted onto Arab and Muslim immigrants who were viewed as foreign terrorists. During this time, the focus of the media shifted momentarily away from undocumented Latin American immigrants, who were displaced as the most immediate threat facing the United States. This shift created an opportunity for these same undocumented populations, otherwise considered *"ineligible for personhood,"* or, as Cacho explains, individuals "subjected to laws but refused the legal means to contest those laws as well as denied both the political legitimacy and morally credibility necessary to question them" (6), to be recuperated as deserving of legal status and the very personhood denied them. Such recuperation was achieved through acts of docile patriotism like the military service and death of Gutiérrez (109).

In conversation with these scholars and their critical approaches to Gutiérrez's case, in this chapter I take a closer look at the mainstream telling of his story, focusing specifically on a human interest article titled "Death of a Dream" that was published in the *Los Angeles Times* soon after Gutiérrez's reported death in Iraq. Featured in Gutiérrez's "hometown" newspaper, "Death of a Dream" provides an extensive overview of Gutiérrez's life from his early childhood in Guatemala to his death and funeral as a US marine. As a human interest story, this account relies on a human-interest frame that "places the emphasis on the personal and emotional side of an event, issue or problem" and presents the news "in a narrative format that focuses on how issues affect particular people" (Steimel 224).[4] Despite, and perhaps because of, the fact that this privileging of the personal and cultivation of the emotive often comes at the cost of communicating specific information about broader policy issues and concerns, the human-interest frame remains one of the most widely used in news media. Not surprisingly, it is also a frame that has been shown to influence both social and government policies such as those related to immigration.[5]

These characteristics make narratives such as "Death of a Dream" a key mediating space for exploring how US Central Americans have been and continue to be signified in the US popular imaginary and, relatedly, the material effects of such significations. In this instance, "Death of a Dream" provides readers with a personalized account of Gutiérrez's story that fundamentally renders him a "good immigrant" consistent with neoliberal logic and that, relatedly, elides or dismisses key aspects of Gutiérrez's immigrant reality and Guatemalan background. This problematic depiction, however, also evinces the high costs of being "good" and of inclusion for Gutiérrez and, by the same token, for more recent male youth arrivals from Central America. In effect, for these undocumented adolescents, belonging requires nothing short of their willful subjection to multiple forms of death.

Congruent with this focus, the first two sections of this chapter explore Gutiérrez's portrayal in the article as a good neoliberal immigrant subject, one whose legal and social belonging in the United States is largely determined by his deservingness. Gutiérrez's status as a US marine and death in Iraq, aspects of his story and immigrant subjectivity that are clearly privileged in "Death of a Dream," play a critical role in this construction. So, too, does his reality as an orphan in Guatemala, another dimension of his story that has remained largely unexplored in scholarship about him. Gutiérrez's orphanhood is attributed to the lack of a viable family unit capable of nurturing him into adulthood as well as to a Guatemalan nation and, by extension, isthmian region that similarly cannot care for its citizen-children. Within the article, Gutiérrez is thus constituted as a true "orphan of Central America." Painting such a portrait of Gutiérrez and his life prior to migrating to the United States helps to make his reality as an undocumented youth from Central America more palatable to a US audience. At the same time, it also renders forgivable his immigrant transgressions, offenses such as being "illegal" and what many would perceive as "manipulating the system." Both of these transgressions would otherwise deem Gutiérrez a "bad immigrant" or unworthy under the same neoliberal paradigm of immigration.

This representation of Gutiérrez as an orphan, however, can also be construed as a disavowal of his Guatemalanness and all that it implies, including histories of US intervention in the country as well as of unauthorized journeys and border crossings through Mexico and into the United States. Depicting Gutiérrez in this manner is a means of doing away with all the factors that make him unassimilable, a point further supported by the fact that the article also completely elides his Maya ancestry despite referencing facets of his life where this aspect of his identity would have been paramount. As such, his orphanhood can also be understood as a form of metaphorical death, one that is just as necessary for his ascension into the ranks of worthy immigrants and American patriots as is his physical death on the battlefield. Therefore, it is only by subjecting himself to these literal and figurative forms of death that Gutiérrez can be included and be perceived by others as belonging in his "adopted country." This process of abjection is what the article ultimately makes discernible and effectively affirms for readers. One need not look any further than the article's main title, "Death of a Dream," which bereaves the loss of the American Dream Gutiérrez achieved precisely through his own demise. The title of a *Time* magazine article published just three days after "Death of a Dream" puts it more bluntly: "In Death, a Marine Gets His Life Wish"—his "life wish" being to be an American citizen (Crittle). Underlying the sentiments expressed in these titles is Gutiérrez's presumed disposition to give up his (Guatemalan) life for one in the United States.

Arguably, these same expectations are required of the Central American undocumented male youth who have continued to migrate to the United States since Gutiérrez's death. But the ability of these newer arrivals to be recuperated as "good immigrants" is not necessarily the same due to how these adolescents have been associated with and defined by their Central Americanness. Along with a hostile US political and social climate in which the lines between "good" and "bad" immigrants continue to be increasingly blurred, these youth have had to contend with public discourses and gendered media representations that consistently align them with transnational criminal gangs such as MS-13. Similar to Salvadoran and Guatemalan refugees deemed communist subversives during the 1980s, the Central American origins of these juveniles has become more focalized and all the more damning. The impossibility of being divorced from their Central Americanness, especially during the Trump era, has consequently rendered these youth consummate "bad immigrants," criminal foes who are morally and financially unworthy of legal inclusion and of no value to US society.

Such notions are also borne out in human interest stories such as "A Betrayal," a *ProPublica* article published in 2018 that I examine in the final section of this chapter. A Pulitzer Prize–winning piece, "A Betrayal" centers on the plight of an undocumented Salvadoran youth referred to as "Henry," who became an FBI informant as a means of escaping his MS-13 gang affiliation. Placing the article's representation of Henry as a deserving asylum seeker in dialogue with that of Gutiérrez in "Death of a Dream" illuminates the ways in which hegemonic depictions of the latter foreground the necropolitics that undergird the very means of belonging generally afforded to male undocumented youth from Central America under neoliberalism. The fact that undocumented immigrant youth like Gutiérrez, who are targeted for recruitment into the US military, and those who have been and are currently being held in detention at the US-Mexico border and elsewhere are required to willfully subject themselves both literally and symbolically to death is an exercise in necropower. This form of sovereignty, premised on notions of "who matters and who does not, who is *disposable* and who is not," is a principle means by which the United States safeguards its national security in times of ongoing "crises," be it an overseas war in the Middle East or one unfolding at the US-Mexico border (Mbembe 27).

This analysis also shows, however, how depictions of Gutiérrez represent a linchpin in the continuum that exists between earlier portrayals of Central Americans as menacing guerrillas or subversives at the height of the revolutionary period and more recent depictions of them as gang youth or terrorists. Although hailed as a "good immigrant" and American war hero in the US popular imaginary, Gutiérrez's sublimated Central Americanness and previously undocumented status could have just as easily designated him a similar threat as the youth who have been unequivocally deemed malevolent members of MS-13 by Trump and his allies. Certainly, the Trump administration had little qualms about deporting US military heroes like Gutiérrez.[6] Gutiérrez therefore occupies a middle ground between these equally disconcerting depictions that posit Central Americans as existential dangers to the United States while also revealing the high stakes of belonging. Compared to the "domestication" expected of (Salvadoran) female immigrants discussed in chapter one, the price of nominal and conditional inclusion for male undocumented youth from the region is just as consequential and, perhaps, more lethal.

"Death of a Dream" was published on March 25, 2003, just four days after Gutiérrez died in combat. It was the first of four such human interest stories about local Latino soldiers that the *Los Angeles Times* ran as part of the series Green Card Marines, a topic of interest in a state with a large Latinx community whose youth have been increasingly targeted for recruitment and enlistment in the armed forces.[7] A tribute, the article offers a literal re-membering of Gutiérrez's life, beginning with an account of the familial and economic hardships he faced as a young boy in Guatemala, resulting in his being orphaned; his decision to migrate undocumented to the United States and struggles to adapt to his new environment; his enlistment in the US Marine Corps; and finally a rendering of his death and much publicized burial in Guatemala. Helping to piece together this life story are carefully selected fragments taken from letters written by Gutiérrez to his only surviving sister, Engracia; his poems; and interviews with individuals who knew him both in Guatemala and in the United States (social workers, unofficial caretakers, foster parents, and siblings). Notably, and despite the nuances afforded concerning Gutiérrez's story, such as the fact that he was killed by friendly fire, the article remains at its core a teleological narrative of immigrant assimilation that celebrates his Americanness and, by extension, that of the targeted readership. In other words, "Death of a Dream" is what Hector Amaya refers to as a "biography of patriotism," one invested in "giving meaning" to the life and death of immigrant servicemen like Gutiérrez so as to "preserve the nation" through the continued affirmation of exclusionary public discourses of American nationalism, exceptionalism, and ideal citizenship ("Latino Immigrants" 242).

Critical to this version of Gutiérrez's story and its powerful ideological sway is his representation in the article as a "good immigrant" according to neoliberal standards. It is Gutiérrez's designation as such that ultimately facilitates his Americanness and all that it signifies. As Christina Gerken details in *Model Immigrants and Undesirable Aliens: The Cost of Immigration Reform in the 1990s*, legislation such as the 1996 Illegal Immigration Reform and Immigrant Responsibility Act (IIRIRA), as well as related welfare and anti-terrorism policies that also significantly impacted immigrants,[8] was instrumental in institutionalizing a new neoliberal approach to US immigration policy and discourse. Intended to transition the US immigration system into a market-like structure, such measures transformed the granting of legal entry into the United States into a commodity that immigrants had to show they merited by following certain rules, accepting personal responsibility, and proving that they would not be a financial burden or criminal threat (38). What became most relevant to evaluating immigrant status and legal inclusion was thus how well individuals met certain legal, moral, and financial expectations of what it meant to be an American citizen, as defined by the government and embraced by the public at large, expectations that ultimately did and continue to uphold white privilege, traditional family values, and the (hetero)normative status quo. Moreover, because such legislative measures were also fundamentally meant to combat the problem of illegal immigration, this emphasis on immigrant merit was also overtly tied to perceptions of immigrant "illegality," or whether or not a person came to the country the "right way," and what that revealed about their moral character.

Gutiérrez's representation in "Death of a Dream" conforms to these neoliberal standards of immigrant "goodness" and desirability, proving to readers that he not only meets the stated expectations but is also truly exceptional. Thus, it is Gutiérrez's youthful potential and military status and death that are underscored the most. Observations by Gutiérrez's former foster parents included in the article reference, for example, his overprotective nature, his helpfulness around the house, and the tender ways in which he interacted with younger foster children. Many of these same individuals also allude to Gutiérrez's drive, stressing his "street smarts" as well as devotion to schoolwork, sports, and learning English. Relatedly, social workers are quoted as finding "his grades remarkable for someone who was still learning English" and perceiving him to have an "aura about him" (Arax et al.). Their words offer a nod to Gutiérrez's promise and all around "specialness," which is echoed by the article's authors, who likewise describe Gutiérrez as "memorable" both in and outside of school. Such observations and authorial insights are consistent with similar statements made by caretakers who knew Gutiérrez in Guatemala. Collectively, these reflections help to make the case for Gutiérrez's immigrant worthiness under neoliberalism by highlighting his responsible and family-oriented disposition, his individual drive and self-motivation, and his innate decency.

Adding significantly to this portrait of immigrant merit is the article's discussion of Gutiérrez's motivations for joining the US armed forces. According to his sister Engracia, Gutiérrez "enlisted out of gratitude to the United States for having given him a second chance" (Arax et al.). Echoed by others in comparable news accounts about Gutiérrez,[9] this notion concerning Gutiérrez's patriotic sense of gratitude for his "adopted country" is one of the more steadfast claims about his story in the mainstream media. Underlying claims such as these are presumptions regarding Gutiérrez's loyalty to and preference for the United States over Guatemala. Along with signaling his successful assimilation, these presumptions reify notions of American nationalism and superiority on the world stage. For these reasons, and despite the fact that the article notes that Gutiérrez was also motivated by practical needs to pursue enlistment (such as financial stability and funding to continue his education), this particular view of his fateful decision carries the most weight. In effect, this interpretation resonates more with the general readership and its sense of what it should or does mean to be American, all the while offering further evidence of Gutiérrez's deservingness as an immigrant.

Gutiérrez's general standing as a US marine and the article's portrayal of him as a fallen hero have the same effect. As Piotr M. Szpunar notes, the military idea, or "the symbol of a unified, coherent force," is not only "central to the myth of American exceptionalism," whose basic premise is that America is different and superior to other nations, but also a principal means of disseminating such a myth (183). Slogans used in military recruitment efforts, such as the long-standing marine mantra "The Few, the Proud, the Marines," are a prime example of this exceptionalism, as they speak to the "exceptional and unified character of the military" (187). Tellingly, these same notions regarding the superiority of the United States and its military are reiterated by Gutiérrez in a letter penned to his sister days before he was deployed to Iraq. Gutiérrez writes, "We [the Marines] are the best-known armed force in the world" and likewise notes, "Just mentioning the word 'Marines' brings tranquility, because people know it is safe" (Arax et al.). The effect of including these carefully selected quotes from Gutiérrez's letter in the article is twofold. One, his statements evince his seeming internalization of US exceptionality and his transformation into an embodied mouthpiece for the same ideology. Two, Gutiérrez's "specialness" or remarkability (in this case by association) is once again underscored. Counting himself among the ranks of such a superior security force in the service of the greater good such as the US Marine Corps, and being proud of doing so, confers upon Gutiérrez a similar exceptional status, one crystallized by his "ultimate sacrifice."

Interestingly, "Death of a Dream" highlights the tragedy of how Gutiérrez died and the seeming attempt by the US military to initially cover it up more than his actual demise on the battlefield. According to the article, it was not until several weeks after his sister Engracia was first notified of his death by US officials that she actually learned that Gutiérrez had been killed by "friendly fire." This information came by way of a condolence letter from the Marine Corps (Arax et al.). In response to the news and lack of specifics, Engracia is quoted as saying, "I still can't believe he was killed by one of his fellow soldiers. [. . .] I just find that hard to accept. I know it won't bring my brother back to life, but I want to know what happened to him" (Arax et al.). This implied critique of the US military's lack of transparency regarding Gutiérrez's death and the added injurious consequences for his sister are followed by a similarly unfavorable description of Gutiérrez's funeral services in Guatemala City (held after his funeral services in the United States) as "gaudy" and impersonal, and courtesy of the US government (Arax et al.). Such nuanced comments and criticisms add depth to Gutiérrez's story. And, in keeping with the particulars of the article's human-interest frame, these same efforts to add granularity to the narrative also render Gutiérrez's immigrant saga more compelling and entertaining for readers. Ultimately, though, these elements fail to meaningfully unsettle Gutiérrez's military-based exceptionality and iconic stature as a fallen American war hero.

A large reason for this are the photographs used to visually frame this story. The images included of Gutiérrez dressed in his formal Marine uniform and of his funeral, among others, have their own framing effects and ideological pull, ones related to yet also separate from that of the article's written text. Speaking on the key role that visuals play in framing news stories, Brantner et al. note that "images serve as entrance stimuli into news stories and increase the probability that a news story gets further attention" (526). Images can also transmit human emotions more directly than text (527). Relatedly, research by Paul Messaris and Linus Abraham shows that visuals are "effective tools for framing and articulating ideological messages" (220). This is due to the "special qualities" that visuals possess, which include iconicity (the "notion that picture perception is based on similarity or analogy"), indexicality (images are seen as "direct pointers" of reality, rather than representations), and syntactic implicitness (propositions made via images are "more reliant on the viewer's ability to make intuitive sense of implicit meanings on the basis of contextual and other cues") (216–219). Such qualities have the effect of making images appear more authentic and natural, rendering viewers less aware of the framing process and the ideological messaging being transmitted to them. Moreover, because of this lack of readerly awareness, images can also more easily convey controversial views (such as racist ones) that readers might otherwise reject or take issue with were these views communicated verbally (225).

Factoring prominently on the first page of the article (in both the print and online versions) is the aforementioned photograph of Gutiérrez donning his dress uniform.[10] This standard graduation portrait taken of Gutiérrez following his completion of basic training is the single most enduring and prevalent image of him in news media and the US popular imaginary. It also factors prominently in more critical takes on Gutiérrez's life, such as the aforementioned documentary *The Short Life of José Antonio Gutiérrez*. In the photo, Gutiérrez stares stoically at the camera, conveying both a sense of bravado and the seriousness of his soldier's commitment to the United States. Indeed, as the article mentions, Gutiérrez sent a copy of this

3.1. *Gutiérrez's marine graduation photograph from* The Short Life of José Antonio Gutiérrez.

same photograph to Engracia with a letter stating, "Feel proud to have a brother who is very intelligent and very valiant, because from today on my life is no longer mine, it has entered the realm of mystery, because I don't know what's going to happen" (Arax et al.). Having this be the first image of Gutiérrez that readers see colors their perception of him as an immigrant and the accompanying narrative about his life. This portrait reifies the neoliberal view of the "good immigrant." And, as with Gutiérrez's "biography of patriotism," it engages readers in a process of identification with him that is also conditioned by the discourses of American nationalism, patriotism, and ideal citizenship. Also playing a role in this process is the enduring romanticization of the (fallen) soldier in American culture, particularly that of the "simple, heroic, and humble American GI" of wars past (Huebner 18). Gutiérrez may not have been US-born, but as his successful immigrant trajectory and Marine Corps uniform suggests, he was American-made.

The final visual included in the article, a photograph of Gutiérrez's funeral, similarly underscores his soldierly sacrifice and interpolation as an American. The photograph consists of a high-angle shot of Gutiérrez's casket, enveloped in an American flag as is custom for fallen soldiers, being ushered down the central aisle of a large and crowded church in Lomita, California, by fellow US marines. Whereas the initial "face-to-face" encounter

3.2. *Memorial service for José Gutiérrez after he was killed in Iraq. Pool/Getty Images News via Getty Images.*

with Gutiérrez's portrait invited readers into his story, this last image creates a sense of distance, allowing readers to "zoom out" of the narrative. Inasmuch as this literal view from above affords a more expansive panorama of the funeral, it also visually underscores the magnitude of Gutiérrez's heroism. Readers are witness to the "ultimate sacrifice" that Gutiérrez made for the United States, one being honored by the spectacle of the hero's funeral depicted. But they are also reminded of Gutiérrez's similarly valiant efforts to succeed in America despite the hardships he faced in his native Guatemala. The signification of these mutually constitutive acts of heroism in this photograph, not to mention the symbolic weight of the image of the fallen soldier in US culture, solidifies Gutiérrez's standing as an American war hero. The narrative may complicate such a notion via the aforementioned critiques of the US military's lack of transparency concerning Gutiérrez's death and his funeral services in Guatemala (Arax et al.). However, the ability of this photograph to mobilize and affirm the American sensibilities of

US readers proves to be much more powerful, affirming yet again an uncritical vision of the "good immigrant."

Images such as Gutiérrez's military graduation portrait contribute in other ways to his broader representation as a good neoliberal immigrant subject. On full display in Gutiérrez's portrait is not only his status as a newly minted US marine and all that it implies but also his phenotypical "brownness," or Latinoness. This visual marker of racialized and ethnic difference would under many other circumstances contribute to Gutiérrez's marginalization in US society, especially given his previously undisclosed undocumented status. However, within the context of the article's representation of him as a "good immigrant," one can argue that this is not necessarily the case given how neoliberal multiculturalism seeks to neutralize and repurpose such differences for its own benefit. As Maher and Elias detail, "NLMC (neoliberal multiculturalism) embraces actors' racial and cultural differences provided these differences can be transformed into market assets nonthreatening to existing hierarchies" (230). The objective of this is to encourage the rise of a "few minority individuals," and use those same exceptions as a means of "justify[ing] the continued subjugation of most minorities" (230). In portraying Gutiérrez as a deserving immigrant, the article likewise renders him the type of minority exception lauded by neoliberal multiculturalism. His exultation on the page maintains "existing hierarchies" based on ethnicity, race, gender, sexuality, class, and citizenship status while also obscuring the very structures of power responsible for those same hierarchies.

Viewed through this lens, Gutiérrez's Latinoness is an acceptable, or at the very least tolerable, "asset" that makes him all the more appealing as a minority exception. In embracing this aspect of Gutiérrez's identity, whether consciously or unconsciously, readers once again succumb to and validate certain myths about the United States and reaffirm Gutiérrez's status as the quintessential "good immigrant." In the process of doing so, readers also elide realities such as the problematic recruiting of (undocumented) youth like Gutiérrez in the first place and the equally unsettling efforts and means of granting these same youth posthumous citizenship (as Amaya discusses). The depiction of Gutiérrez's orphaned life in Guatemala in "Death of a Dream," examined in the following section, also helps cement Gutiérrez's overall standing as a good neoliberal Latino/immigrant subject. However, by contrast to the nonthreatening Latinoness communicated by way of Gutiérrez's visual image, his specified Guatemalan origins and cultural affiliation do not inspire the same level of acceptability. As the portrayal of Gutiérrez's orphanhood suggests, these are elements of his life from which he can and must be divorced so that he can be brought into the fold of the American family.

Subsumed within the larger narrative of Gutiérrez's deservingness in "Death of a Dream" are his immigrant transgressions: his juvenile delinquency in Guatemala, his multiple unauthorized attempts to cross the border, and the fact that once he did make it into the United States undocumented, he lied about his age, thereby circumventing the deportation process and securing an avenue for asylum and, eventually, a green card. All of these offenses are ones that would signify Gutiérrez as a "bad immigrant" in keeping with the neoliberal notions of immigrant meritocracy at play in the article. However, as the initiating sentence of Gutiérrez's story suggests, these are offenses that readers should excuse: "After all he had seen, Jose Antonio Gutierrez might have been forgiven for telling the lie" (Arax et al.). Although this sentence explicitly references the lie Gutiérrez fabricated about his age, claiming to be sixteen when in reality he was twenty-two, the authorial sentiment expressed extends to all of Gutiérrez's infractions (legal or otherwise). Indeed, the authors of the article clearly suggest that were it not for Gutiérrez's horrible life in Guatemala, he might not otherwise have been driven to lie about his age to the California social worker who first encountered him or engaged in any other misguided behaviors in his quest to secure a better life for himself (and his sister). In other words, if Gutiérrez cannot be held personally responsible for his individual choices as an immigrant, then he also cannot be considered "bad."

Given the nature of such claims, it is not surprising, then, that the authors of the article go to great lengths to also cultivate a particularly stark image of Gutiérrez's life in Guatemala, including his orphaned reality. As one subheading, "Tragedy upon Tragedy," implies, the description of this facet of Gutiérrez's story reads like a litany of misfortunes. First, there is the family's migration from the highlands to Guatemala City; then, the diagnosis and death of Gutiérrez's mother from tuberculosis in a poorly run state sanitorium, followed by the death of his two-year old sister due to their drunkard father's negligence and the separation from his older sister, with whom he wouldn't reunite until years later; and finally the demise of his father, who "dropped dead in a cheap hotel room" in front of him when he was eight (Arax et al.). Adding to these traumas is the extreme poverty and negligence Gutiérrez suffered in a country that seemingly could offer him only a life of petty crime on the streets and a brief stint in a city jail teeming with prison gangs. Tellingly, the only positive experiences Gutiérrez had growing up in Guatemala were his brief stays at an orphanage run by a US lay missionary as part of a New York–based Catholic program. Described as an "oasis," this US-linked institution is portrayed in a way that is consistent with the generally superior view of the United States espoused in the article, as a country that offered Gutiérrez the possibility of a better life and the care and kindness denied him as a child.

The notable elision of critical histories of colonization and US imperialism in Central America allow for the unfettered consumption by readers of this unflattering portrayal of Guatemala while also adding to the story's bleak and "compelling" nature. The backdrop to Gutiérrez's difficult childhood is the country's thirty-six-year civil war, which reached a peak during the 1980s and did not come to an end until 1996. Yet there are only two passing allusions to this reality in the article, one acknowledging the war and the other a reference to the military-sanctioned murder of the parents of one of Gutiérrez's adolescent friends (Arax et al.). Characteristic of the ways in which human-interest framing emphasizes the personal at the expense of the "larger picture," no direct correlations are drawn between these occurrences and the oppressive Guatemalan conditions otherwise depicted. There is likewise no acknowledgment of the Maya genocide that transpired during this same period and that prompted Gutiérrez's family to relocate to the city. Early in Specogna's documentary, the voice-over informs viewers, "In the late 1970s, the family [that of Gutiérrez] fled from massacres committed by the army like thousands of other Indian families seeking safety in the capital." The results of these omissions are, on one hand, to render Guatemala as inherently backward and deficient and, on the other, to represent it, ironically, as a country devoid of "Indians." Calling to mind both Quijano's notion of coloniality of power and Arias and Milian's coloniality of diaspora, this negation of the Indigenous and, relatedly, Gutiérrez's indigeneity is also emblematic of the mainstream media's more generalized role in his Latinoization.

As narrowly crafted as it is, this depiction of Gutiérrez's abject childhood in Guatemala lays the groundwork for a particularly potent and useful image of him as an orphan that, like his portrayal as a US marine and American hero, is also vital to the vision of neoliberal immigrant subjectivity affirmed in the article. Recalling the diverging portrayals of Guatemala and the United States, it was not only Gutiérrez's family that failed him but also his nation of origin. Guatemala was unable to provide Gutiérrez with the necessary care and nurturing (in the form of proper state services, discipline, and security) for him to become a productive member of society and an upstanding citizen. Gutiérrez is thus portrayed as doubly orphaned, or as an "orphan of Central America," who is devoid of both a viable family and nation or region of origin. This interpretation resonates with Macarena García González's analysis of the portrayal of transnational adoptees and undocumented immigrant children (conceived of as orphans of the global south) in contemporary works of Spanish juvenile fiction. According to González, the Third World countries from which transnational adoptees and immigrant children hail are posited in said literature "as unsuitable for families and unable to provide 'real' homes in which children can thrive," whereas destination and First World countries such as Spain are depicted as fit and capable of providing such homes (323).

Figuratively speaking, such a depiction of Gutiérrez as an orphan of Central America constitutes a disavowal of Guatemala and of Gutiérrez's ties to it. Although Gutiérrez is shown to maintain a distant connection to his sister Engracia, this relationship does not constitute the same concrete and direct link to his nation of birth and cultural identity that a bond with his biological parents would have. The fact that they died while he was so young marks a severing of such ties, as does Guatemala's perceived "abandonment" of him. This lack of familial and national ties signals to readers that Gutiérrez's Central American orphanhood is the impetus behind his quest for not only a new home and family life but also a new sense of cultural identity and national belonging in the United States. In this way, Gutiérrez's portrayal as an orphan exemplifies precisely what Diana Loercher Pazicky notes is the appeal of the orphan figure in the literary imagination, the fact that it "signals identity formation, not only individual but cultural" (xii). Such a "quest for identity hinges upon an understanding of the Self not as an essence formed in the past but as a dynamic, interactive process that takes place in the present and projects into the future" (xii). Indeed, in "Death of a Dream" Gutiérrez's image as an orphan is as much about illuminating his disenfranchised past to readers as it is about heralding the better future that awaited him in the United States, including his Americanization. In fact, by disarticulating Gutiérrez from his Guatemalan origins and culture, the article also foregrounds for readers his "adoptability," or potential for assimilation. Without the baggage of the former and given his youthful potential, Gutiérrez can more easily be cast as a nondescript Latinx minority exception and/or deserving immigrant, the kind of immigrant *we* should want in the country and whose acceptance makes *us* feel more "American."

Because of the problematic view of being Guatemalan it endorses and of how it facilitates Gutiérrez's becoming as an American, this notion of Central American orphanhood can also be seen as marking the metaphorical death of Gutiérrez's Guatemalanness, another precondition of Gutiérrez's belonging in the United States. In addition to his willingness to serve and die for the country (the basis of his posthumous citizenship), he is also expected to lose aspects of his identity that are deemed inferior and undesirable. Although not an explicit endorsement, quotes taken from Gutiérrez's letters to his sister referring to his birth nation as "a place where the angels reside in misery" and his projected loyalty to the United States hint at his own possible embrace of this idea (Arax et al.). That such an idea should be among the dominant messages transmitted to readers is unsurprising considering the neoliberal and assimilationist slant of the article. Still, it is notable that such notions are also clearly refuted in Specogna's documentary. Concerning Gutiérrez's relationship to his Guatemalan identity, his foster brother, David González, insists that Gutiérrez was proud of being Guatemalan and was reluctant to learn English so as to not lose his Spanish, a linguistic tie to his native country.

Coupled with his actual physical demise, this expectation of Gutiérrez's metaphorical death as a Guatemalan ultimately calls attention to the necropolitical nature of the inclusion afforded to youth like him within the neoliberal paradigm of immigration. In his well-known essay "Necropolitics," Achille Mbembe provides a working definition of sovereignty as "the capacity to define who matters and who does not, who is *disposable* and who is not" (27). This means of ruling or exerting power, which is rooted in death (not life), is what Mbembe refers to as "necropower," a "formation of terror" characteristic of the colony and late-modern colonial occupations (e.g., that of Palestine by Israel) that operate as states of exception or siege.[11] "Necropolitics" concerns itself with the wielding of this necropower, or "subjugation of life to the *power of death*" (39). Similarly implied by Cacho in *Social Death*, the US-led invasion of Iraq in 2003 and the ongoing war on terror of which it was a part, are likewise exercises in necropower (99–100). Under the mandate of fighting the global spread and threat of terrorism in the wake of 9/11, the George W. Bush administration targeted entire populations in the Middle East as "disposable" and as enemies. It did the same to Arab Americans, Muslims, and others living in the United States deemed potential threats through policies such as the United and Strengthening America by Providing Appropriate Tools Required to Intercept and Obstruct Terrorism Act, more commonly known as the USA Patriot Act, and the implementation of the National Security Entry-Exit Registration System. Both of these allowed federal and state institutions to operate in extrajudicial ways in their efforts to combat terrorism on the home front and, as a result, led to the erosion of civil liberties for the stated groups.[12]

One can likewise make the case, however, that it was not only "terrorists" and their allies who were deemed disposable and subject to the necropolitical imperatives of the United States but also immigrant youth like Gutiérrez who were offered citizenship in exchange for their military service. In stating this, I am not necessarily arguing against Cacho's claim that Gutiérrez's military service and patriotic death provided him a way of becoming eligible for personhood or of being recuperated as deserving (109). Rather, this means of transcending social death for Gutiérrez remained fundamentally premised on his willingness to die for the United States and on the expectation that this should be the price to be paid in order to become American. It is this notion that lies just beneath the surface of Gutiérrez's representation as a "good immigrant" and "American hero" and that is effectively being communicated to readers in "Death of a Dream." In a (perverse) manner of speaking, a "good Latino" or immigrant subject is thus understood to be a "dead Latino" or, at the very least, one who embraces his expendability and gladly subjects himself to death in order to belong. Hence, in the case of Gutiérrez, the unfortunate fact that he was a casualty of friendly fire and literally killed by the United States matters very little by comparison to his actual death or "ultimate sacrifice." What the related depiction of Gutiérrez as an orphan of Central America adds here is that such an expectation of dying encompasses other key aspects of his immigrant subjectivity, including a Guatemalan ethnic and cultural identity considered to be inherently problematic. This last point is of significant consequence in the more immediate context of undocumented youth migration from Central America in the Trump era.

TROUBLING "GOOD" AND "BAD" IMMIGRANTS

Much in the same way that undocumented youth migration from the Central American region has continued unabated since Gutiérrez's passing and, in more recent years, significantly increased, so, too, have the hostilities toward these immigrants and ways of preventing their legal and social integration into the United States. The reality confronting these youth, especially during the Trump presidency, is reminiscent of the 1980s. Racialized anxieties about demographic changes and a conservative backlash to the ongoing liberalization of society have been accompanied by a heightened sense of xenophobia, nativism, and increased political polarization. All of these were openly embraced and peddled by Trump and his allies in their efforts to "Make America Great Again." Also characteristic of this period have been efforts to restrict both legal and illegal immigration and to effectively erode any notion of "good" immigrants in favor of rendering all immigrants from undesirable countries as "bad." Take, for instance, Trump's rationale for rescinding DACA, which was partly based on the idea that DACA was attracting "young people who would become members of violent gangs throughout [the] country, such as MS-13" (Bump). Meant to substantiate the Trump administration's hard-line stance on illegal immigration and its "law and order" mandate, this deliberate conflation of DACA recipients, or Dreamers, as they are popularly known, and MS-13 gang members was also a thinly veiled attempt to refute the oft-perceived exceptionality of the former.[13] By effectively closing the gap between "good" undocumented youth immigrants such as DACA beneficiaries and all other undocumented youth from Latin America, who are seemingly prone to criminality, the Trump administration purposely blurred the distinction between the two.

Underscored in this same example is the increased level of visibility and notoriety that Central Americans once again achieved during the Trump presidency, which significantly contributed to the adversity that these immigrants faced. Akin to refugees from the region tainted by communism in decades prior, unaccompanied Central American youth, particularly males, were construed by the Trump administration and the right-wing media as would-be or actual MS-13 gang members who posed a grave security threat to the United States. Along with the termination of DACA, this means of criminalizing and signifying these adolescents in political discourse and across a wide range of mediums and public forums provided fodder for discriminatory policies directly targeting and disproportionately affecting Central American (im)migrants. One extreme result was the curtailing of the asylum process, which was the very avenue through which Gutiérrez procured his legal residency. Another effect was to indelibly brand these same undocumented immigrants with their Central Americanness. For male youth this means being linked to MS-13 as well as long-standing hegemonic representations of the region as racially, culturally, and politically inferior and of Central American men as violent, depraved, and a threat to the social order and security of the United States. Both elements—an especially hostile context of reception and the inability for these same immigrants to be seen outside of the parameters of their national or regional origins—has made their recuperation as "good" or model immigrants who merit belonging in the United States all but impossible.

Even with these mitigating factors, these undocumented youth are still, however, expected to prove their immigrant worthiness in similar fashion as that of model immigrants like Gutiérrez. In other words, they must perform acts that underscore their disposability and willingness to die. We see this in the case of Henry, an adolescent from El Salvador whose story is recounted in "A Betrayal," the first in a series of human-interest stories about Henry that appeared in *ProPublica* from 2018 to 2019.[14] The article also helped its author, journalist Hannah Dreier, win a Pulitzer Prize for Feature Writing in 2019.[15] "A Betrayal" chronicles Henry's evolution from a teenage member of MS-13 (a.k.a. "Triste") to an informant working with the Long Island FBI Gang Task Force, a role he took hoping to escape the gang life he had been unable to avoid by migrating to the United States from El Salvador. Despite his work with the task force while a sophomore and junior in high school,

Henry was detained by ICE shortly after turning eighteen. The deportation case initiated against him was, as the author states, based on information he offered the FBI to help arrest fellow gang members (Dreier). The failure by the FBI and immigration authorities to protect him from being outed as a "snitch" and from deportation back to El Salvador, both of which made him a target of MS-13 and jeopardized his life, is the "betrayal" at the crux of this article. As the caption of an image of Henry reads, "Henry thought that talking to the police would help him get out of MS-13. Instead, his cooperation put him on a path to deportation and his likely death" (Dreier).

Precisely because this article is an advocacy piece meant to raise awareness about and garner public support for Henry's legal fight to secure asylum,[16] the primary representation it affords of Henry is that of an asylum seeker with a legitimate claim. Drawing on her research concerning the depictions of asylum seekers and refugees in American human-interest stories, Sarah J. Steimel finds that these individuals mostly appear in the following ways: "(a) as prior victims; (b) as in search of the American Dream; and (c) as unable to achieve the American Dream" (219). Of these three representations, the first is most prevalent and is primarily achieved through "harrowing stories of victimization" (227). Henry's portrayal in "A Betrayal" largely corroborates these findings, as he is mainly envisioned as a youth victimized by MS-13, both in El Salvador and in the United States. What is more, he is also shown to be a victim of US state and federal agencies and, ultimately, the Trump administration. As Dreier forewarns readers in the opening paragraphs, "[u]nder normal circumstances, Henry's choice [to work with police] would have been his salvation. [. . .] But not in the dawning of the Trump era, when every immigrant has become a target and local police towns like Brentwood have become willing agents in a nationwide campaign of detention and deportation."

Notably, in seeking to make this case for Henry's legitimacy as an asylum seeker, the author also fundamentally makes a case for Henry as a deserving, or "good," immigrant in the neoliberal sense. Henry's representation in the article speaks not only to the logistical reasons why he cannot be sent back to El Salvador and needs to be given refuge and witness protection in the United States, but also to the reasons he merits the opportunity to become and be embraced as an American. One of the first and only details readers learn about Henry's early upbringing in El Salvador is that his parents migrated to the United States when he was very young, leaving him in the care of his elderly grandparents. The familial and financial void left by his parents made Henry especially susceptible to the gang and its coercive means of recruitment, as did the seeming powerlessness of the Salvadoran state to reign in MS-13 (Dreier). The fact that the only reference to Salvadoran federal and local agencies in the article pertains to the execution of a dirty cop by MS-13, which Henry witnessed, coupled with no mention of actions by these same agencies to effectively combat gangs such as MS-13, speaks to this very idea. The depiction of Henry in "A Betrayal" recalls that of Gutiérrez as an "orphan of Central America" in "Death of a Dream." Although Henry is not an orphan in the biological sense, he is still portrayed as a forsaken and vulnerable child driven into gang life by the abandonment of his parents as well as the inability of an impotent Salvadoran state to protect him. For example, while explaining the meaning behind Henry's gang moniker, the author states that "Triste," the Spanish word for "sad," is "[w]hat you become when your parents abandon you as a toddler and go to America and leave you behind in a slum." In rendering him as this doubly victimized child who cannot be held fully accountable for his past crimes and gang life, the article thus also foregrounds his moral nature and immigrant worthiness.

This sense of Henry's inherent decency is likewise fanned by allusions in the article to his different attempts to better himself and get out of the gang, such as when "[h]e approached US military recruiters in school, eager to join the Army" but was informed that he needed his parents' permission to do so because of his young age. It is Henry's willingness to put his life on the line as an FBI informant, however, that provides the most important proof of his "goodness" and deservingness. Speaking to this point is the central critique at the heart of the article regarding Henry's betrayal by the FBI and immigration services, as well as the noted "outrage" at Henry's situation expressed by the school administrators, law enforcement officers, and community activists quoted. Robert Feliciano, the head of the Suffolk County School Board, remarks that Henry was taken advantage of by the FBI and then dropped, which is something, Feliciano stresses, "[y]ou can't just do" (Dreier). In related fashion, Bob DeSena, the founder of a large gang-intervention program in New York, takes aim at Henry's FBI contact, who refused to testify on Henry's behalf at his asylum hearing. As DeSena states, "Rivera [Henry's contact], if he wasn't full of shit, should pick up the phone and say, 'Look, this guy helped us'" (Dreier). Underlying these sentiments is the notion that Henry's actions and service to the FBI merited him a second chance at a better life, including witness protection, and that the United States owed Henry as much but failed to live up to its end of the bargain. Like "Death of a Dream," "A Betrayal" thus also suggests and affirms for readers that what ultimately makes undocumented immigrant youth like Henry truly worthy of legal, if not social, belonging is their ability and willingness to subject themselves to death.

As this representation of Henry likewise conveys, his actions aiding the FBI are not, however, enough to make him worthy of inclusion. Henry may have paid the high cost of immigrant belonging exacted by the United States, but he is still incapable of being fully recuperated as a "good immigrant" because he cannot shed his Central Americanness in the same way. As a member of MS-13 (albeit one trying to leave the gang) Henry epitomizes the notion of the "bad" immigrant under neoliberalism as well as the very national security threat about which Trump and those in his political and media orbit continually warned the American public. Under these circumstances, Henry cannot be disarticulated from his Central American origins and gang past. Consequently, he is neither desirable nor assimilable like Gutiérrez, whose rendering as an orphan and, more important, status as a US marine and fallen hero did allow for his posthumous interpolation as an American. Dreier's very depictions of MS-13 prove this point. These narrative and visual portrayals of the gang, which are ironically meant to create a cognitive distance between Henry and the gang and to show him as somehow different from other MS-13 members, only make the imprint of his Central Americanness all the more pronounced.

In providing readers with a broader context regarding the gang, Dreier states that whereas other "criminal enterprises attract members who want to get rich and who sell drugs or women or stolen goods to achieve that aim," MS-13 "traffic[s] in a single product: violence." The gang's characterization as such is supported throughout the article with graphic illustrations of said violence, including Henry's traumatic "education" while a young member of the gang in El Salvador. As the author surmises, Henry's exposure to multiple murders taught him "how soft skin feels when you slice into it and how bodies, when they are sprayed with bullets, look like they are dancing." Photographs of desolate sites in Suffolk County, Long Island, where gang members are believed to hang out and where murder victims of MS-13 have been found, add to this sensationalistic and borderline fetishistic portrayal of the gang. One image, for example, shows readers a section of woods that is, as the accompanying caption states, "a favorite gang hangout." The otherwise serene and almost idyllic image is notably unsettled by the black graffiti that mars one of the trees, consisting of the numbers "503," the international calling code for El Salvador, and a childlike happy face with what appear to be devil horns.

Such an image capitalizes on the prominent role of forests and woods within the horror genre as ethereal and unpredictable sites where darkness and evil lurk. The absence of actual bodies, be it those of MS-13 members or their victims, adds to this fear by inviting readers to imagine the violence and depravity enacted in those places by the gang. Inasmuch as this depiction of MS-13 may help to underscore Henry's victimization and the real danger the gang poses to him, it is a depiction that nevertheless engages in the same fear-baiting tactics and reductionist perspectives regarding MS-13 that are widespread in news media and contemporary political discourse. As such, the danger that is MS-13 and all things Central American is amplified to the detriment of Henry's personal plight.

The only photograph of Henry included in the article falters along the same lines, failing to fully disarticulate him from his Central Americanness. The photograph, which appears at the very end of the article and is the last image readers see, shows Henry in the shadows. With his hands clasped near his mouth and his elbows resting atop a table, he stares to his left, away from the camera. The brightly lit, white background stands in sharp contrast to his dark silhouette, obscuring him all the more. The only hint of color in the photograph is provided by Henry's orange jumpsuit, the stock clothing of immigrant detainees. Intended to protect Henry, this cloaked image of him helps to draw readers into the mystery of who he is and of his story. There is nothing overtly threatening about Henry in this image. Indeed, the fact that he cannot be seen and is not facing readers directly makes Henry appear contrite and demure.

Yet, as Susan Sontag reminds us in "The Image-World," when something is photographed it "becomes part of a system of information, fitted into schemes of classification and storage" (351). In other words, despite how this single portrait of Henry may seek to favorably portray and shield him, it nevertheless remains part of the larger repertoire of photographs and other images used to tell his story. Among others, this repertoire includes the noted problematic images meant to convey the indiscriminate violence and ruthlessness of MS-13. Existing as part of this same repertoire, Henry's photograph has the potential to likewise portray him as a menacing figure, as another MS-13 gang member waiting in the shadows rather than the asylee in need of refuge that Dreier proclaims him to be. Consequently, this means of visually depicting Henry and adding to his story does little to humanize him, and actually runs the risk of reifying for readers his racialized otherness and criminality.

CHALLENGING NARRATIVES

According to the Pulitzer Prize awarding committee, Dreier garnered her award "[f]or a series of powerful, intimate narratives that followed Salvadoran immigrants on New York's Long Island whose lives were shattered by a botched federal crackdown on the international criminal gang MS-13" ("Hannah Dreier"). As the previous analysis of "A Betrayal" shows, these "intimate narratives" are not, however, without their inherent contradictions or ideological influences. They are also capable of doing much more than their intended purpose. The advocacy work undertaken in this article on behalf of Henry is undermined not only by the visual framing of his personal story but also by a neoliberal logic of immigrant worth that requires his subjection to death (in both a literal and a symbolic way). No matter how sympathetic, in this award-winning account, Henry can be understood and judged only as either a "good immigrant" who was forced to commit crimes through no real fault of his own and who must pay a high price in order to be admitted into the United States or as a "bad" immigrant who does not deserve a chance at redemption.

But stories such as that of Henry and the means of relating them in the mainstream media are not new. Echoes of contemporaneous accounts about undocumented youth from Central America are found in seemingly unlikely places, such as those of exceptional Latinos like Lance Corporal José Gutiérrez. Mythologized as an American war hero in the US popular imaginary, José Gutiérrez was the consummate "good immigrant." Yet, as the detailed account in "Death of a Dream" reveals, the price he had to pay for nominal inclusion as an "American" was just as high as that of Henry. It was only in death and on account of his "Central American orphanhood" that Gutiérrez became a desirable immigrant, one who *could* belong.

"Death of a Dream" was thus also an account that affirmed for its readership exclusionary ideals of what belonging in America means under neoliberalism. Indeed, this retelling of Gutiérrez's life and death underscored the institutionalization of such ideals and the necropolitics that undergird them but are often obscured. In this sense, then, Gutiérrez's case constitutes a foundation without which it is difficult to fully grasp the related plights of youth like Henry nearly two decades later. It is a case that also fundamentally underscores the need to actively challenge and seek alternatives to the neoliberal narrative of immigrant goodness and merit that has informed and continues to inform how undocumented Central American male youth and their stories are being represented. Without such an undertaking, the impossible expectations placed on these youth to belong will continue to be reified and, worse yet, celebrated as part of the "American way."

CHAPTER FOUR

Central American Crossings, Rightlessness, and Survival in Mexico's Border Passage

INDEPENDENT CINEMA IS ONE OF THE CULTURAL ARENAS in which the topic of Central American migration to the United States has gained the most traction in recent decades. Along with feature films based on fictional accounts, such as Cary Fukunaga's *Sin nombre* (2009), Luis Mandoki's *La vida precoz y breve de Sabina Rivas* (2012), and Diego Quemada-Diez's *La jaula de oro* (2013), a growing corpus of documentaries have been produced on this topic since the early 2000s, including *Asalto al sueño / Assaulted Dream* (2006), *De nadie (Border Crossing) / No One* (2007), *Wetback: The Undocumented Documentary* (2007), *La vida en la vía / Life on the Line* (2007), *Which Way Home* (2009), *María en tierra de nadie / Mary in No-Man's-Land* (2010), *La Bestia / The Beast* (2011), and *Who Is Dayani Cristal?* (2013).[1] Unlike their notable predecessor, Nava's epic *El Norte*, most of these cinematic productions do not emphasize the experiences of Central American political refugees and their arrival and adaptation to the United States. Instead, they register the economic disenfranchisement of Central American migrants in the current neoliberal economic paradigm and focus, almost exclusively, on the transmigration of these migrants through Mexico. The latter is arguably the most treacherous leg of the Central American migratory journey, and it's a reality that continues to be largely ignored within mainstream media and US debates about undocumented immigration from Latin America.

As these films chronicle, while en route in Mexico, Central Americans are susceptible to any number of physical dangers as well as emotional and psychological traumas. These are due to not only the undocumented status of these migrants but also their perceived lower cultural standing according to many Mexican nationals. Not surprisingly, populations that are among the most vulnerable in their home countries (e.g., women, children, ethnic and racial minorities, and members of the LGBTQ community) are similarly the most at-risk during these journeys. Even when migrants are fortunate enough to survive their illicit travels aboard La Bestia, or a "train of death" that is routinely patrolled by criminal youth gangs, they are still in danger of being harassed and exploited by corrupt government officials and drug cartels that prey on them with impunity, not to mention detained by Mexican immigration officials and incarcerated in substandard holding facilities before eventually being deported. Notably, in portraying these migrant hardships and bleak circumstances, these films also give way to an equally disconcerting image of Mexico as a veritable no-man's-land or site of unencumbered lawlessness where the Mexican state lacks the power (or refuses) to intervene to safeguard the basic human rights and lives of the undocumented. Indeed, it is during their journey through Mexico that the (American) dreams of these migrants are "assaulted" and dissipate, as the title of Uli Stelzner's documentary *Asalto al sueño* suggests. Migrants are likewise made to feel, as one man tearfully laments in *María en tierra de nadie*, as if they are "nothing."

In this chapter I examine the politics of emotion as well as the narrative and rhetorical strategies employed in the aforementioned films to represent the crossings of Central American migrants through Mexico, crossings that entail traversing not only national and legal boundaries but also those of gender, sexuality, race, ethnicity, and class. As I argue in the first part of the chapter, such films constitute a subgenre of human rights media on the basis not only that they have a specialized thematic focus on undocumented Central American transmigration and are activist films for migrant and human rights, but that they are also characterized by shared affective and representational politics. These documentaries are explored as part of a cohesive body—one, however, that is not necessarily monolithic, as my analytical emphasis on the three films *De nadie*, *María en tierra de nadie*, and *La Bestia* shows. Although all three films share the broader defining characteristics noted, including the use of an observational filming mode and the narrative thread of the epic migrant journey, they differ in other respects. Both Tin Dirdamal's *De nadie* and Pedro Ultreras's *La Bestia* employ the many dangers migrants face in their journeys as organizing principles of their narrative structures and as key themes, while Marcela Zamora Chamorro's *María en tierra de nadie*, the only film of those mentioned that is directed by a woman, explores the difficulties mothers contend with when they migrate and the particular dangers women face on the migrant trail.

My interest in these films lies in looking not so much at how they seek to humanize undocumented Central American migrants through highly emotive portrayals of their trials and suffering (though this is addressed) but more at how they strategically posit Mexico as both a border zone and, relatedly, a dehumanizing passageway for these same individuals. While key to the human rights agenda of these films, this two-prong construct of Mexico as a "border passage" also speaks more broadly to the guiding conceptual thread that runs throughout this book: the politics of US Central American non-belonging. This construct illuminates Mexico's active role as part of a broader US-Mexico interstate regime focused on immigration regulation and (US) national security that renders the lives of undocumented Central Americans expendable while also deeming these migrants as undesirable citizen-subjects of the United States prior to their arrival. Mexico's role as gatekeeper for the United States is not necessarily new. However, it is a role that Mexico has assumed more prominently and consistently since the 1990s. The Mexican state's cooperation with the Trump administration in policing Central American immigrants at the US-Mexico border and its acquiescing to the "Remain in Mexico" program that went into effect in 2019 is a case in point.[2]

By underscoring the Mexican government's efforts on behalf of US national security and foreign policy interests, this "border passage" construct also calls attention to the fact that the struggle of many undocumented Central Americans for civic and social belonging in the United States is not necessarily initiated at the hyper-visible US-Mexico border, a privileged geopolitical space of migrant crossing and civic negotiations in US media and immigration debates. Nor is it a struggle solely waged within the confines of the US nation. The criminalization and state of racialized rightlessness that undocumented Central American immigrants come to experience in the United States, where they are also deemed threats to the US body politic and undeserving of basic human and civil rights, is systematically ascribed to them in their passage through Mexico.

HUMAN RIGHTS ADVOCACY AND AFFECTIVE POLITICS
IN *MIGRA*-DOCUMENTARIES

In his book *Realer Than Reel: Global Directions in Documentary*, David Holgarth makes the claim that documentary film has undergone a process of globalization in recent decades whereby both its conditions of possibility and its diffusion are the result of a combination of local and global factors, particularly the transnational marketplace (32). The films in question, *Asalto al sueño*, *De nadie*, *Wetback: The Undocumented Documentary*, *La vida en la vía*, *Which Way Home*, *María en tierra de nadie*, *La Bestia*, and *Who Is Dayani Cristal?*, speak to this very notion of documentary globalization. All of them are, to varying degrees, products of transnational efforts by small production companies in Central America, Europe, Mexico, and the United States, having been financed by a combination of gifts from private foundations, public service media organizations, public education funds, international human rights organizations, and related nonprofit entities. And, despite not being part of the mainstream media, most of these films have enjoyed wide circulation in international and independent film festivals in Europe, Latin America, and the United States; via special film screenings at university campuses, community venues, and on local public television channels; on sites such as YouTube; and through DVD sales. Moreover, many have not only won and been nominated for prestigious awards at film festivals but also garnered significant attention from Hollywood. Such is the case of *Which Way Home*, which was nominated for an Academy Award for Best Documentary Feature in 2010.

Aside from their global dimensions, these documentaries are joined by their human rights–based agendas. As such, and although these films share a kinship with both the consciousness-raising documentaries that characterized the New Latin America Cinema movement of the 1960s and pro-immigrant documentaries produced since the 1990s in the United States,[3] they fall within the purview of what scholars have defined as human rights media. Such media aims to "generate unwanted attention and publicity" so as to "shame perpetrators of abuses (generally governments or large corporations) into changing policies or decreasing levels of violence" and to promote some degree of social mobilization and change in the form of transnational activist networks that are capable of exerting pressure domestically (Hinegardner 172–173). In keeping with this definition, the noted documentaries draw attention to and seek to shame the Mexican and US governments for contributing to the humanitarian crisis of unauthorized Central American migrants in Mexico and allowing it to continue unabated.[4] Mexican director Pedro Ultreras has stated, for example, that he made his documentary *La Bestia* "to try to awaken feelings" and "to start a debate that ends in actions and solutions" on behalf of undocumented Central Americans (in "Documentary"). Relatedly, interactive websites such as the one developed for the documentary *Who Is Dayani Cristal?*, a collaboration between director Marc Silver and famed Mexican actor Gael García Bernal, provide a platform for the type of social mobilization and cross-national activism that human rights media also hopes to generate. Visitors to the website whoisdayanicristal.com are provided with several options for getting involved, which range from donating money to nonprofit organizations and migrant shelters to petitioning Congress to change the government's current detention and deportation policies.

The fact that all of these documentaries center on the same topic and do so by using analogous narrative strategies and filming techniques makes them, however, a somewhat more specialized group of human rights media, what I term *migra*-documentaries. As a qualifying adjective, *migra* evokes the slang term that is widely used in the United States and parts of Latin America for the US border patrol and/or related immigration and state enforcement agencies. In her seminal work on the history of the US border patrol, Kelly Lytle Hernández notes the instrumentality of *la migra* in transforming immigration law enforcement into "a site of racialization and inequity in the United States" (3). Her research likewise reveals the extent to which modern migration control and border enforcement at the southern boundary has been a shared enterprise between the United States and Mexico, at least dating back to the 1940s. These films register similar nuances in terms of *la migra* and (im)migrant regulation and oppression in Mexico, revealing the latter to be a byproduct of an expansive US-Mexico interstate regime rather than just Mexican policies. The transnational border enforcement and securitization measures of this regime similarly exacerbate inequities and contribute to the racialization and gendering of migrant bodies in disenfranchising ways.

The "*migra-*" that serves to identify these films, however, also acknowledges their mobile nature as material and cultural objects as well as the subject matter they address. Resulting from transnational enterprises, the intended reach and activism of these documentaries depends on their physical and virtual circulation around the globe. Relatedly, the focal point of these documentaries are *migrantes* (migrants) and *migración* (migration). By virtue of their status as migrants, the Central American people depicted in these films are ones in transit, moving from and through one geographic space to another without a sense of national belonging. Akin to the notion of "passage," these migrants similarly transit from one state of existence to another. In their journeys through Mexico, migrants are stripped of their humanity through a conflation of binational immigration enforcement, the depraved indifference or corruption of Mexican authorities, and their subjection to extreme forms of violence at the hands of criminal entities seeking to make a profit. As these films reveal, migrants are transformed into nonbeings and commodities without a claim to even basic human rights. This process of dehumanization is among the key aspects of the bleak reality these films are invested in showcasing, as it forces viewers to inversely have to contend with the humanity of migrants and to recognize that migrant rights are human rights.

Deborah Shaw's classification "Central American/Mexican/US migration films" provides a necessary starting point for discerning the representational, ideological, and affective politics at play in *migra*-documentaries.[5] According to Shaw, this brand of migration film strives to render migrants and their struggles in more humane ways while hinting at, but not explicitly addressing, the broader geopolitical context that has engendered the very migratory flows and struggles depicted on screen. As Shaw specifically states, these films are more interested in showcasing the emotional weight shouldered by migrants and in laying the blame on immoral individuals such as "unscrupulous Mexicans" (e.g., coyotes and corrupt police officers) and "racist US citizens" than they are in revealing the "effect of national and transnational policies on migrants" (233). *Migra*-documentaries can be seen as existing along the same continuum as these Central American/Mexican/ US migration films in that the former also show the human face of migration. They do so, however, without allowing viewers to ignore the imperative links between the migratory subjects (and their predicament) being represented on screen and the enactment of "national and transnational policies" by nation-states. In effect, and as the political activism of many directors might suggest, *migra*-documentaries are films in which overt critiques of the structural inequities, government policies, and global systems of oppression that have given way to the human rights violations and violence against undocumented Central Americans in Mexico are commonplace.

Insisting on such connections and critiques, and thus giving way to a more nuanced view of the Central American transmigrant reality, not only is crucial to the emotional and political pull these films aim to have on viewers as global citizens but also influences and helps to explain the type of shared filming strategies and narrative structuring the filmmakers of these documentaries employ. Many of these *migra*-documentaries concentrate on a small group of undocumented migrants, often those who are preselected by the director and interviewed prior to embarking on their journeys. Notably, the migrants who are chosen and highlighted are overwhelmingly *mestizo/ ladino* or read as such. They also seemingly read as cisgender and heterosexual. Hence notwithstanding the fact that, as I suggest below, these films contest the trope of the forever illegal, they do so in a more generalized way and still manage to affirm other dominant views of Central American immigrants.

The migrants who are generally focalized in these films tend to be asked about their reasons for leaving their home countries as well as the expectations and hopes they have for the journey and their life in the United States. The film crew, then, trails and films the migrants throughout their travels, riding alongside them on top of the cargo trains for periods of time, and/ or meet up with them at designated *albergues*, or migrant shelters, along the way. Due to the uncertain nature of these journeys (mainly the fact that

4.1. *Honduran migrant children Kevin and Fito in* Which Way Home.

migrants can, at any moment, be detained or, worse yet, disappear without a trace) these key encounters at the shelters allow filmmakers to check in with migratory subjects and document their emotional trajectories and off-camera experiences via additional interviews. The interviews are often informal and, like the rest of the filming that takes place en route, make use of an observational mode of filmmaking, one meant to render the viewing audience intimate observers of the human drama unfolding in front of the camera and before their eyes. Visual aids such as maps of Mexico detailing the trajectory of the migrants and the routes of the trains they ride also tend to be standard in these films.

Though pivotal to the narrative thread of the epic journeys related in these documentaries, these primarily linear story lines centered on an identifiable group of migrants in transit are not the only ones of note in these films. Also included are the testimonies of migrants met along the way, mainly aboard the train and in shelters, as well as that of others who have had similar experiences and currently reside in the United States "without papers" or are back in their home countries. Interweaving these stories with those of the featured migrants adds significantly to the collective experience of migrant disenfranchisement depicted in these films and lends credence to the notion that the abuses perpetrated against undocumented Central Americans are a standard practice in Mexico with lasting repercussions for those who experience them. These secondary interviews often are also among the most unsettling and emotive. Such is the case of the account rendered in *La Bestia* by José Guardado, a Honduran migrant whose first failed attempt to cross through Mexico resulted in the loss of his hand while being robbed aboard a train. Guardado tells of his six children, whom he supports by begging on the streets in his native Honduras and for whose sake he is undertaking this dangerous journey a second time. As Guardado speaks, the camera's focus on him changes from a medium shot of his upper body to a close-up of his bandaged limb and then his face, which registers a host of emotions ranging from frustration to desperation to shame to sadness and, finally, to utter disillusionment. The segment concludes with Guardado's dim assertions that "el sueño americano lo lleva [a uno] a punto de perder la vida" (the American Dream takes you to the point of losing your life) and that in Mexico "hay caminos que no tienen regreso" (there are journeys with no return).[6] Soon thereafter, viewers learn that Guardado was forced to abandon his travels yet again after being the victim of another robbery.

This unapologetic means of capturing and rendering the various physical and psychological traumas that undocumented Central Americans experience is, on a basic level, an attempt to grant these migrants the humanity often denied them in public debates and discriminatory discourses in the United States about illegal immigration. The fact that these films humanize Central American (im)migrants in particular likewise underscores the active role of these films in making these same (im)migrants and their border crossings more legible to a US public that is largely accustomed to viewing and understanding issues related to immigration at the southern border primarily within the context of Mexican undocumented immigration. Indeed, I have made a similar case elsewhere with regard to the representation of Salvadoran migrant mothers in the film *María en tierra de nadie* by the Salvadoran director Marcela Zamora Chamorro.[7] In light of these efforts, one can further argue that these films enact or constitute counternarratives to the prevalent means of imagining US Central Americans as forever illegals even though the representations of Central American (im)migrants these films offer fail to fully account for the racial, ethnic, gender, and sexuality-based diversity of this population.

Nevertheless, as other film and cultural critics have argued, this intended goal of humanizing the Other (and its related possibilities), a process that in this case relies on the forging of an empathetic link between the viewer and the migratory subject(s) in pain, is not always achieved. In her discussion of emotion in documentary filmmaking, Belinda Smaill contends, for example, that empathy can be one-sided and does not always lead to an intersubjective link between the viewer and the subject portrayed on screen. Instead of prompting the viewer to feel or perceive as the subject does, such empathy-seeking portrayals can result in the viewer consuming "the representation of pain" of the Other without actively acknowledging them or the circumstances that have given way to their dire predicament (64). Similarly, in her introduction to *Compassion: The Culture and Politics of an Emotion*, Lauren Berlant makes the case that films that invite sympathetic responses from viewers, especially across international lines, can have the effect of reinscribing key distances and power differentials. In other words, the suffering and tragedies that befall individuals in other parts of the world, namely in the global south, are perceived as occurrences that happen over *there* to *them*, not *here* to *us*.

Admittedly, all the *migra*-documentaries in question run such a risk. Yet it is one that is also mitigated, to a certain extent, by another equally imperative element of these films: the expert accounts provided by representatives from human rights organizations, directors of migrant shelters, government officials, and local and state authorities. Filmed using more conventional methods such as standard headshots and scripted questions, such accounts help to underscore the vital nexus *migra*-documentaries stress between the disenfranchised state of undocumented migrants and geopolitical and socioeconomic structures. For example, most of the critiques, observations, and commentaries espoused by the stated experts reference the broader context of US-Mexico relations, governmental inefficiency, and widespread corruption that have contributed to the plight of Central Americans in Mexico. Many of these same individuals, especially the directors of shelters who interact most consistently and closely with migrants, likewise draw a direct link between these macro and micro realities of migration for audiences.

Viewed through the lens of the affective politics outlined here, these expert accounts emphasize "the relationship between pain and systems of power" (Smaill 70). Seeing them this way, as Smaill additionally posits, helps to circumvent the possibility of the viewer objectifying and consuming the Other's pain by prompting the viewer to recognize the Other not only as a victim but also as a political subject. Thus, and in keeping with Laura Podalsky's discussion of affect and emotion in contemporary Latin American cinema, one can argue that a key result of such mitigation is to invite viewers to "feel through" the depictions of migrant suffering on screen as opposed to merely "feeling" for migrants (129). In essence, this dual focus on migrant testimonies and expert accounts has the intended effect of, on one hand, emotionally *moving* viewers (inciting feelings of empathy, compassion, or even outrage at the injustices witnessed) and, on the other, *moving* them to take political action (prompting viewers to see the pain and predicament of these migrants as a consequence of larger systems of power and nation-states that they as global citizens have the power to push back against and hold accountable). The comments of Zamora Chamorro concerning the reception of her film *María en tierra de nadie* in Mexico are suggestive of this very idea. As she notes in a television interview from 2011, among the more widespread reactions to her film by Mexican audiences was a sense of indignation after learning about the dire predicament of Central American migrants in their country, followed by the need to take some form of action. The question "What can we do?" was, according to Zamora Chamorro, one of the most common responses ("CCEN Presentación").

What follows is a closer look at this interplay between, on one hand, human rights advocacy and discourse and, on the other, representational and affective politics. The discussion centers on the critiques, observations, and rhetoric of migrant directors and activists that render Mexico an extended border zone in which the lives and human rights of undocumented Central Americans are of little consequence. Also examined, however, are images, scenes, and emotionally laden testimonies of migrants, particularly those of women, that attest to the dehumanizing nature and consequences of such a process of borderization. A prime example is the transformation of migrants into human commodities and, hence, the unmaking of their humanity. These migrant-centered aspects give rise to yet another representation of Mexico: that of a harrowing and dehumanizing passageway for undocumented Central Americans. Taken together, these representations posit Mexico as a "border passage," a construct that helps to further the human rights–based agenda of these films and our understanding of US Central American non-belonging across borders.

FROM BORDER ZONE TO "BORDER PASSAGE"

One of the most well-known and outspoken advocates for migrant and human rights in Mexico is Father Alejandro Solalinde, director of the Hermanos en el Camino (Brothers on the Path) migrant shelter in Ixtepec, Oaxaca. Known as the "Romero" of Central American migrants, a reference to famed Salvadoran martyr Oscar Arnulfo Romero,[8] Solalinde's activism has made him the target of state and criminal organizations alike as well as led to attempts by the conservative echelons of the Catholic Church to curtail his growing influence. It is not surprising, then, that interviews with Solalinde are standard in these *migra*-documentaries nor that his statements often include scathing condemnations of the Mexican government's treatment of Central American migrants. In *La Bestia*, for example, Solalinde is critical of Mexico's strategy of systemic interior enforcement regarding immigration, stating that "México es el único país del mundo dónde se busca, persigue . . . encarcela los migrantes en todos los espacios, todo su territorio" (Mexico is the only country in the world where migrants are sought, pursued, found, and imprisoned throughout its territory). Unlike the United States, Mexico has not erected any physical barriers at its southern boundary with Belize and Guatemala so as to continue to facilitate cross-border markets. Instead, Mexico has implemented a network of immigration checkpoints throughout its entire territory along major highways and locations where undocumented migrants are known to transit. As Solalinde goes on to suggest, Mexico's singularity in this respect is not a source of pride but rather a source of embarrassment.

Solalinde's critique, one meant to shame the Mexican state by calling out its inhumane persecution of undocumented Central Americans, nurtures an image of Mexico as an extended border zone, a space of illicit and dangerous crossings, ongoing low-intensity conflict, and rampant violence. Fellow activist and director of the Casa del Migrante (House of the Migrant) shelter in Tapachulas, Chiapas, Father Flor María Rigoní, hints at the reason for this borderization later in the film, when he alleges that "México, bajo agua, se ha convertido en el guardian de Estados Unidos" (Mexico has become the unofficial gatekeeper of the United States). As "unofficial gatekeeper," the Mexican state functions as an extended arm of US immigration and national security policies. Lending credence to this claim is the notable expansion of Mexico's detainment infrastructure and significant increase in deportations within the span of the last two decades,[9] as well as the signing and implementation of regional agreements between the United States and Mexico such as the 2005 Security and Prosperity Partnership of North America (SPP) and the Mérida Initiative launched in 2007, both of which include significant provisions for border enforcement and security.[10] Agreements such as these, as Cecilia Menjívar notes, are part of the strategy of exteriorization or outsourcing of border controls adopted by powerful migration-receiving countries such as the United States ("Immigration Law"). They are also, however, agreements that signal the amalgamation of power between the US and Mexican states, or, more to the point, the rise of a US-Mexico interstate regime focused on curtailing the flow of undocumented migrants heading north (the vast majority of which are Central American) and protecting (US) national security.[11]

As part of this interstate regime, Mexico is not only facilitating the United States' expansion of its immigration and national security policies beyond the US-Mexico border but also helping to carry out the biopolitical imperatives inherent to such policies. These imperatives mark undocumented immigrants like Central Americans as undesirable citizen-subjects of the United States and deem their lives expendable. Speaking to this point are the observations made by Jonathan Xavier Inda, who posits in "The Value of Immigrant Life" that when the (US) state constructs undocumented immigrants as undesirable (as well as threats) and bars them from the United States, the state "also implicitly judges them to be expendable, suggesting that their lives are not quite worthy of being lived" (149). Essentially, the state makes a value judgment regarding which lives "deserve to be lived," those of US citizens, and which "can be disallowed to the point of death," those of immigrants who attempt to cross the border unauthorized (149). This value judgment is premised on the presumed criminality of "illegal aliens" and their undesirability based on their race, ethnicity, gender, sexuality, class, and the like. Thus, for Inda, the US state's banning of undocumented immigrants from the country and the unabated policing of the same by the US border patrol amounts to an exercise in what Foucault calls biopower, of which a key rationale is the "do[ing] away with life in the name of life itself" (150). Within the confines of the United States, such biopolitical imperatives are carried out via legal propositions and statutes similarly aimed at protecting the body politic by disenfranchising and endangering the lives of the undocumented (Inda, "Biopower" 104–109).

The expendability of undocumented Central American lives sanctioned by the United States and Mexico in the name of (US) national security also helps to partly explain the notable inaction of both countries regarding the exploitation and abuse of said migrants en route. Despite passing a series of comprehensive laws ensuring migrants' rights while in its territory, the Mexican state, for example, has failed to enforce any of them.[12] Mexico's immigration enforcement apparatus and state authorities have likewise been the subject of continuous scrutiny for violations of human rights and corruption.[13] For advocates working on behalf of migrants, such as Mauricio Farah of the National Commission of Human Rights in Mexico, this failure on the part of the Mexican state to guarantee basic protections for Central Americans independent of their legal status sends a powerful message to criminals that they can do as they will with migrants and suffer little or no repercussions. As Farah blatantly states in *María en tierra de nadie*, the Mexican government is literally "feeding migrants to criminals." Thus, beyond designating Central Americans as expendable Others in both Mexico and the United States and thereby reifying their lack of belonging in either nation, the US-Mexico interstate regime is also further fueling the targeting of undocumented migrants by criminal organizations and other would-be assailants, including corrupt government employees.

One of the most effective means used in these *migra*-documentaries to convey this notion of Central American disposability and rightlessness—in essence, social death—is the use of images of migrant disenfranchisement and testimonies that underscore, whether directly or symbolically, the transformation of migrants into human commodities and/or that suggest that these same flows of undocumented Central Americans are a potential source of cheap and exploitable labor for Mexico and the United States. Apart from tangential or minor story lines about the trafficking of women and children, this aspect of the Central American migratory experience is rarely engaged in mainstream media reporting, which tends to favor headlines concerning migrant apprehensions and detention. Yet it is one of the more pervasive and insidious forms of abuse and exploitation migrants encounter in their journeys. The degree to which all of the noted *migra*-documentaries routinely engage with this stark reality of migrant commodification is indicative of the latter and provides the basis for the image of Mexico as a dehumanizing passage for undocumented Central Americans that these films likewise project.[14]

Notably, whereas in these *migra*-documentaries the representation of Mexico as an extended border zone is conveyed through the expert opinions and critiques of shelter directors and migrant/human rights activists, this related portrayal of Mexico is mainly conjured through migrant testimonials and representations of human suffering. Moored more concretely to the affective politics of these films, these accounts and portrayals are one of the most effective means of communicating to viewing audiences the gravity of the Central American migrant crisis in Mexico, thereby also shaming the Mexican state and, by extension, the United States for their actions (or inaction) concerning this matter. Bringing this brutal reality to light in this way, however, also allows these films to effectively frame the "problem" of Central American undocumented transmigration in Mexico as a matter of human rights and broader systemic failures rather than immigration enforcement and binational securitization policies.

"*CUERPOMATICS*," NECROLOGICAL TRANSPORT, AND COMMODIFIED LABORERS

The unauthorized land-bound journeys to the United States undertaken by Central Americans are characterized by violent and traumatic experiences of human commodification within the scope of what can be conceived of as a web of migrant commodification.[15] In Mexico, profiting from undocumented Central Americans is an easy and lucrative business that originates in migrants' home countries and spans throughout Mexico and into the United States. Human smugglers demand high premiums from migrants or their families to transport migrants across Mexico and to the northern border. At the same time, these coyotes, or *polleros*, also have to pay their own bribes to transnational criminal organizations such as the Mara Salvatrucha and the Zetas to ensure a "safe" passage for all involved.

Corrupt immigration officials and police officers similarly profit from migrants through the direct solicitation of bribes or theft, as do criminal gangs and syndicates such as MS-13 and the Zetas, whose additional crimes include trafficking migrants in the sex trade or as indentured servants as well as abducting and holding them for ransom. Consequently, and as shelter director Pedro Pantoja bluntly informs a room full of migrants in a key scene of *María en tierra de nadie*, migrants are nothing more than "merchandise" for everyone. This sad truth is reflected by the neologism coined by Central American migrant women to refer to their own bodies as "*cuerpomatics*" (body-matics) or "cash machines" (Ó. Martínez xiv).

Vital to the subsistence of this web are the freight trains, which provide the noted criminal entities a seemingly endless supply of migrants to exploit for profit. Among the most compelling testimonies included in *María en tierra de nadie*, for example, are those of "Janeth" and "Irma," two migrant women who were abducted from the trains by the Zetas as part of a larger operation to kidnap and ransom migrants. Unlike their fellow captives, however, "Janeth" and "Irma" were forced to work as domestic servants and, in the case of Irma, also as a sex slave as a means of "paying" for their freedom. Such incidents, including routine muggings of migrants, are often facilitated by train conductors who purposefully delay, slow, or stop trains in remote locations so that would-be exploiters can have unencumbered access to the clandestine passengers onboard. These transactions take place under the threat of violence or death and involve the strategic use of terror against migrants, often in the form of rape and torture. To a certain extent, then, these trains and their surrounding areas constitute sites where the expendability and rightlessness of Central American migrants converges with the added traumas of violence and death.

A film that brings to bear this stark reality in searing ways is Tin Dirdamal's *De nadie*. Rather than prioritizing the experiences of migrants on the move, Dirdamal's film centers on individuals whose northbound journeys have been temporarily disrupted. One such migrant and, arguably, the film's protagonist, is a Honduran woman named María. Like countless other Central American women, María was driven to migrate to help financially support her family, which consisted of her four children and physically incapacitated husband. María was forced to abandon her travels after the migrant group she was traveling with on the trains was assaulted and robbed by members of the Mara. As viewers eventually learn, during this same encounter María was also raped. Her personal story, including her account of this ordeal and that of others, is rendered via a series of interviews filmed while María was temporarily housed at a shelter in Orizaba, Veracruz, Mexico. Portions of these interviews are interwoven throughout the film in keeping

4.2. *María in* De nadie.

with a set of themed segments and alongside those of fellow migrants. It is thus María's story of interrupted migration that serves as the film's consistent narrative thread and, just as important, one of the principal ways in which the film makes discernible how migrants are commodified and unmade as human beings.

Much of what María relates in the film, outside of her home life and reasons for leaving, is directly tied to what she has witnessed, heard, and personally experienced near or onboard the trains. In a segment of the film dedicated to the topic of the trains, "El tren: La bestia de hierro" (The Train: The Steel Beast), María references a graphic incident involving two young Salvadoran women who were raped, mutilated, and murdered by members of MS-13 (referred to throughout the film as simply "the Mara"). As María details, in addition to being sexually violated, both women were also shot multiple times and had their breasts cut off. María's inquiries to the filmmaker, "¿Te diste cuenta de eso? ¿Tu no sabes de eso?" (You weren't aware of that? You didn't know about that?), underscore how quickly this account has spread among the migrants at the shelter where María is staying. Coupled with María's eye-witness account at the beginning of this segment concerning a sixteen-year-old boy who fell from the train and lost an arm, this similarly horrific story helps to contextualize for viewing audiences the many dangers and deadly consequences of riding the "steel beast." It is not only the devouring trains that migrants need to be wary of, but also the human predators and opportunists that regularly board them and lurk in the surrounding areas.

María's recounting of this incident also helps to foreground the central role of the trains in the enterprise and process of migrant commodification. Instances of rape and other forms of violent sexual assault—mostly, but not exclusively, against women and girls—are highly prevalent on the migrant trail. Many female migrants who undertake this journey anticipate this very possibility by taking oral contraceptives (*United Nations* 44). Indeed, the experience of the two Salvadoran women referenced by María is one of four such instances of rape and murder by MS-13 on or near the trains that are discussed by migrants in the film. Not only do these public acts of sexualized terror signal the dominance of groups such as MS-13 over their victims, but they also are a strategic means of spreading fear throughout the broader migrant population. The circulation of the noted account of the Salvadoran women, along with María's added speculation that her children may fear for her safety because they, too, have likely heard about this attack, underscores just how effective such spectacles of horror are in generating a climate of fear in this Mexican border zone. Beyond this, however, such acts serve to erode the basic humanity of migrants and to undermine any sense of community and belonging they bring with them from home or forge along the migrant trail.

María's own personal and traumatic experience with MS-13, as related in the film, makes this notion painfully clear. Details of this encounter first emerge at the end of the segment "El Tren" during a sequence of alternating shots of María and two male companions speaking about the incident. All three detail the violent manner in which the men of the group were beaten and threatened with death by the gang. However, it is not until the film's end, when Dirdamal revisits this sequence of alternating testimonies, that a more complete account of the group's experience emerges, including the previously undisclosed fact that María was also gang raped. Tellingly, it is not María but her male companions who are the first to address and reveal on screen that she was sexually assaulted. Both men refer to the brutal way in which María's assailants treated her. One of the men states, "A ella la agarraron pues como animal" (They grabbed her like an animal). The other adds, "como quien agarra una bestia" (as if they were handling a beast). In speaking about the incident, both men avoid referring to María by name, choosing instead to use impersonal terms such as "ella" (her) or "la mucha-cha" (girl). This is a notable rhetorical move that, along with the nighttime setting of the interview and the dimly illuminated faces of the men sitting curbside, registers their unease in discussing the topic as well as a sense of emotional and psychosocial distance between themselves and María.

Speaking about the weaponization of rape during the Guatemalan and Peruvian civil conflicts of the 1980s and 1990s, Jean Franco notes that rape and execution "*perform* expulsion from the human, reducing its object to a state of abjection" (28). Citing Bülent Diken and Carsten Bagge Laustsen's "Becoming Abject: Rape as a Weapon of War," Franco explains this idea by stating that "[a]bjection places the victim outside the bonds of the human, for the abject is 'inscribed in a primordial chaos, marked by a primary indistinctness or formlessness. Which is to say that, before differentiation, ordering is a relation to lack of distinction. The abject is, in other words, not a pole in a binary distinction but indistinction itself'" (28). Franco goes on to add that such abjection is "maximized" by the treatment of raped women like animals, including the very positions they are forced to assume during their violations, as was the case in the Guatemalan and Peruvian examples that she references (28). The account of María's rape by her male companions aligns with Franco's observations and underscores María's state as abject. The fact that the men are unable to name María signals her expulsion from humanity and from the social (Franco 29). María has become something "other," resulting in her separation from her male companions and the straining of the communal bonds they share as fellow Hondurans and migrants. María's status as Other is visually manifested on screen. As the men conclude their testimonies, the camera pans out to reveal María standing just above them to the left. While her companions related her traumatic and personal experience, María remained silent and literally occupied the peripheral space off-screen.

Although the mass rapes committed during the Guatemalan and Peruvian conflicts were part of genocidal efforts by state governments against Indigenous communities, the same cannot be said of the prevalence of this type of sexualized violence on the migrant trail. The eradication of all migrants, or those of a particular ethnic background, is not the final endgame of criminal networks like MS-13. Rather, for these groups, the violation, torture, and indiscriminate killing of undocumented Central Americans is a key aspect of the migrant commodification enterprise. It is no coincidence that such violent acts and public displays tend to be carried out while migrants are robbed or used for other financial means. These cruel attacks are meant to reify the status of migrants as inhumane objects and ultimately as merchandise. In the case of women, whose bodies are already inherently viewed as items of consumption within patriarchal society, this is doubly so. The film stresses this point by way of María's experience with a potential employer who lures her to a job interview under the false pretext that she would be working at a circus. As María later reveals on camera, the employer took her instead to a strip club and offered her a job waiting tables almost nude. The unstated expectation was that she would prostitute herself to the primarily Mexican male clientele.

When María does finally address her own rape, we see the extent to which what she has witnessed and endured has served to make her state of rightlessness and extreme alienation as a Central American migrant and woman in Mexico all the more acute. In her account, which she has purposefully avoided relating in front of her male peers, María speaks of how her violation and humiliation have fundamentally changed her—killed her happiness—and consequently made it impossible for her to go back home. As she states, "Ya no voy a poder ser esposa a mi esposo. . . . Ya no siento que soy digna de que me abrace" (I won't be able to be a wife to my husband anymore. . . . I feel like I am not worthy of him anymore). Although María acknowledges that her rape was not her fault, her shame is too great, so much so that it also keeps her from speaking to her children, which she refuses to do throughout the entire film. Now, in addition to being abject to her fellow migrants and an outcast in the hostile national space through which she is traversing, María also perceives this to be the case in relation to her family and community back home.

This representation and understanding of migrant social death, which encompasses the rightlessness and commodification of migrants' bodies, is further reiterated in the film's title and music. The literal translation of *de nadie* is "belonging to no one," calling attention to the fact that Central American migrants like María do not belong in any given national space or community, even their own. As such, they are "nobodies" who do not matter to anyone. The film's feature song, "Los nadies" ("The Nobodies"), a musical adaptation by composer Alfonso M. Ruibal of Eduardo Galeano's famous poem by the same title, stresses the same idea. The "nobodies," as the song lyrics state, "no son seres humanos, sino recursos humanos" (are not human beings, rather human resources). "[N]o tienen nombres, sino números" (They do not have names, rather numbers). In other words, the "nobodies" are nothing more than a product to be consumed for money. They are nothing more than a number, a statistic.

Though highly effective, the engagement with and representation of stories like María's are not the only means by which *migra*-documentaries draw attention to the process of migrant commodification that undocumented Central Americans are subjected to throughout their journeys. Nor do such individualized stories encompass all aspects of this commodification process, which also entails the exploitation and consumption of migrant labor. Although unauthorized migratory flows from Central America to the United States have since the late 1970s been driven by a series of political, environmental, and social issues, economic factors have always been paramount. In the region, neoliberal policies and free-trade initiatives such as CAFTA-DR have had dire consequences for agriculture and subsistence farming, wages, and the environment, resulting in the displacement of countless workers and a loss of viable employment.[16] At the same time, these policies and initiatives have led to a related need by US companies for cheap (immigrant) labor in order to remain competitive in the global economy. These economic push-and-pull factors have been exacerbated or, in some cases, supplanted by other pressing concerns such as food insecurity, gender-based violence, and the escalating threat of gangs in the region.

Such circumstances have laid the groundwork for the expropriation and exploitation of Central American immigrant labor in Mexico and in the United States. As has been duly noted, Central American immigrant workers have become an increasing part of the racialized and disposable labor force on which the service sector and many industries in the United States rely (Brick et al. 11–12). The undocumented status of a large percentage of these workers is a key reason for this concentration, as it keeps many of these immigrants from moving up the social and economic ladder. Being undocumented likewise makes these immigrant laborers more susceptible to pervasive forms of discrimination and workplace harassment due to their race, ethnicity, gender, and/or sexuality. Fear of deportation or related threats add to these oppressive working conditions by ensuring the silence of these laborers and their continued subjugation. As with the general contexts and conditions under which many undocumented Central American migrants are forced out of their countries of origin, the ones in which these same migrants find themselves as disenfranchised laborers in the United States are similarly oppressive.

In *migra*-documentaries, this dimension of the migrant commodification process is conveyed via one of the most recognizable features of these films: stock images and/or extended scenes of Central American migrants illicitly riding freight trains. Mostly set during daylight hours and generally consisting of long shots of a moving train with migrants crowded on the tops of its wagons, these images and scenes serve as establishing shots that underscore the mass scale of the migratory phenomenon in question as well as the vulnerability of migrants and the deadly risks associated with riding the trains. In this sense, these images and scenes operate in a more nuanced and oppositional way within *migra*-documentaries than in US mainstream media, where they contribute to the notion of US Central Americans as forever illegals. The facts, however, that these migrants travel on trains tasked with transporting goods and that as migrants they also constitute a valuable resource and means of income for their countries of origin in the form of an exportable labor force suggest another interpretative possibility concerning these images and scenes. In effect, they can also be read as a symbolic rendering of these migrants as commodified laborers in their temporary (Mexico) and intended final (the United States) destinations. Consequently, despite the fact that *migra*-documentaries do not specifically address the social reality of undocumented Central Americans in the United States, they do foreshadow this added form of exploitation. And in so doing, these films further cement the image of Mexico as a dehumanizing passageway.

Far from providing any clear resolutions, *migra*-documentaries end in uncertainty and with the same sense of foreboding as that generated by the story lines and migratory journeys they depict. The ending to María's "story" in *De nadie* offers yet again a prime example of this characteristic filmic element. The last on-screen image of María is a black-and-white still, following a muted scene of María walking leisurely in a city park, eating ice cream. The caption accompanying the still informs viewers that María made it to Monterrey, Mexico, where she worked for several months and from which she sent money to her family, though they never received it. The film then fades and cuts back to the earlier shot of María in the city park, this time showing her walking away from the camera. The image freezes into another black-and-white still, with a new caption that stresses María's resolve to get to the United States and the fact that, following her abrupt departure from the city, the film crew never heard from her again. For viewers who have been witness to María's migrant journey thus far, such an ending is less than satisfactory, denying any possibility of narrative and emotional closure. Much like María's unknown fate, viewers are left in limbo.

As with the other representational and affective elements of *migra*-documentaries discussed in this chapter, this thwarted or open ending serves the human rights–based agenda of these films. The inconclusive nature of the migrant journeys depicted, even in the case of migrants who successfully cross into the United States but whose undocumented status leaves them similarly disenfranchised, is yet another means of underscoring the precarious and dehumanizing nature of Central American passages through Mexico. The fact that María can so easily disappear into the unknown both on-screen and in life—a point accentuated in the film through the use of the fade-ins and muted sound—marks the vulnerability and relative lack of value of "nobodies" like her. Indeed, the Associated Press reported that close to four thousand migrants went missing or died while transiting Mexico in the span of 2014 to 2018, estimates that are likely an undercount (Da Silva). By calling attention to this very reality, these films ultimately compel viewers to see migrants as human beings and to reckon on an emotional and political level with the injustices committed against them by local actors and national powers such as the governments of Mexico and the United States. In so doing, these films also offer alternatives to mainstream news media images of Central American "illegals" who, though visible, remain illegible.

In related fashion, and just as importantly, these films widen the purview for understanding Central American non-belonging. The multiple forms of marginalization and loss of humanity that undocumented Central Americans experience in Mexico are instrumental to establishing their perceived inferiority and undesirability once in the United States. The factors that make these populations easy targets for predators in Mexico—their Central American national origins, their general lack of education, the fact that many are young families or women with small children fleeing violence and poverty—are also grounds for criminalizing them as potential "threats" to the US body politic and rendering them incapable of successfully integrating and contributing to American society. Echoing Rosa's painful realization in *El Norte*, *migra*-documentaries underscore the geopolitical terrains and sociocultural axes within which and through Central Americans in and outside of the United States come to experience not belonging. However, as I have also been arguing and shown, this condition of otherness does not preclude these same individuals from forging alternate notions and means of belonging, be it en route or once in the United States. In the following chapter, centered on US Central American struggles for space, visibility, and voice in Los Angeles, I offer the most extensive example yet of the latter.

CHAPTER FIVE

The Cachet of Illegal Chickens in Central American Los Angeles

R ESIDENTS AND VISITORS OF ECHO PARK AND SILVER Lake are no doubt familiar with the vibrant murals of cartoon chickens painted on several walls throughout these two Los Angeles neighborhoods. These murals are the work of a local graffiti writer turned street muralist from Guatemala who goes by the name Cache (pronounced *caché* in keeping with the Spanish translation of the French *cachet*).[1] A unique balance between the whimsical and the political, Cache's wall art and colorful characters are a strategic means of social commentary. Inspired by Carlos Castañeda's theory of *humaneros*, or "human coops," Cache's chickens are visual metaphors for humans who are trapped in the "coop" of a socially and economically stratified society that is largely driven by consumerism and that emphasizes uniformity (Lurie 21). His chicken murals speak to both the oppressive reality of this entrapment and the possibility of fighting against it, whether the chickens depicted are white, rotund, and cute or more humanized and multihued or brown (the latter recalling chicken breeds used in the poultry industry). Thus it is not uncommon to see Cache's chickens partaking in anti-gubernatorial forms of resistance such as antiwar rallies and Occupy LA marches alongside a black-clad cartoon Zapatista, a symbol of popular struggle in the Americas and the signature character of fellow street artist Eye One.[2] Nor is it unusual to see these same birds standing defiantly—in some cases even thrusting a clenched fist in the air—while rising above the bubbly murkiness and the far-reaching mechanical tentacles (of society) that threaten to encase them.

Like other forms of what has broadly been termed street art,[3] Cache's murals evince the production of an "oppositional political-aesthetic stance" that "registers dissatisfaction" with oppressive economic, social, and political structures (Boykoff and Sand 17). This critical intervention is enacted on the visual playing field of the public spaces and walls of the city and achieved precisely through Cache's unique use of branding, one that draws on contemporary street art practices as well as the identity and communal politics of graffiti. In keeping with the anti-corporatist bent of street art production since the 1990s, Cache's trademark chickens are, as he notes, a tool for combatting the "censored and diluted media assault on the human psyche" by corporations and the government; it's an "assault" that not only engenders uniformity but also speaks to the visual power wielded by the marketing world and government institutions ("Cache").

Branding, however, also speaks to Cache's identity and communal responsibility as a graffiti artist. As was the case with the tag artists of the New York graffiti movement of the 1970s and '80s for whom tagging, or writing "graff" (not only stylized letters but also cartoon characters), was a form of self-promotion and representation, Cache's chickens are a type of personal signature.[4] Along with distinguishing him from the crowd and solidifying his street credentials, this signature provides Cache an avenue for communal engagement and empowerment. As Cache states, he is "one of the few people in the community with a voice," and he wants to use it to affect change in and for that community, one largely composed of working class or impoverished people of color, including undocumented immigrants, who are often relegated to the city's margins and barred from being "true" Angelenos (Lurie 21).

The fact that most of Cache's murals have been painted illegally plays just as pivotal a role in the "oppositional politico-aesthetic stance" taken up through his art as branding (Alegría). In producing unsanctioned art on city walls and private property, Cache reframes the aesthetic and official politics within and against which he works. In other words, he forces a reconfiguration of what is conceived of as "art" and "the law." Regardless of the fact that street artists and their work often straddle the line between the mainstream and the periphery, street art remains an art "from below," to borrow from Rebecca E. Biron's discussion of the city and art in Latin America (19). It is an urban art form meant to be accessible to everyday people in the communal spaces they inhabit and, as such, pushes back against the ideal of "high art." It likewise challenges legal discourses "from above" that tend to construe street art, particularly graffiti, as vandalism and those who produce it as criminals. The eleven-year mural moratorium (2002–2013) in Los Angeles, a city that has a long and vibrant tradition of public murals, speaks precisely to this last point. In banning uncommissioned murals on private property as unsanctioned forms of advertising, even in cases where the owner of said property had provided consent, the city, in effect, used official channels to wage a war on public art, vilifying and rendering unlawful street murals and street artists alike.

Although contextualizing Cache's murals within this broader framework of street art and graffiti oppositional politics is essential for understanding his work, in this chapter I also endeavor to highlight the impact that Cache's immigrant background and ethnic identity as a Guatemalan and, more broadly, as a US Central American has on his street art. Thus, I also read Cache's art as an example of what Paul DiMaggio and Patricia Fernández Kelly denote as immigrant art. Such art functions through a dialectical exchange in which art constitutes a window into the immigrant experience in all of its complexities and, similarly, immigration constitutes a lens for comprehending the diverse employment and transformation of artistic genres by immigrants (DiMaggio and Fernández Kelly 1–22). Situating Cache's work at this provocative intersection between "street" and "immigrant" art imbues his cultural production with another layer of meaning as a visual expression of the Central American immigrant experience in the United States. Although admittedly not all of Cache's art lends itself to this type of interpretation, as the following analysis of three examples of his art suggests, being Central American is a key dimension of his work. This discussion of Cache's art not only presupposes an understanding of Cache's identification as a Guatemalan in Los Angeles and his subjectivity as a graffiti artist as mutually constitutive elements but also allows for a critical possibility with regard to his art that has gone unexplored due to the premium placed on anonymity within street art.[5]

As Martin Irvine argues, street art is invested in toppling "regimes of visibility" that distribute and regulate power through the partitioning of visibility. These are the regimes of government (politics, law, property) and the aesthetic (a legitimizing art world that decrees what is and is not art). Working within their own set of rules and codes, such regimes determine "what can be made visible or perceptible, who has the legitimacy to be seen or heard where, and who can be rendered invisible" (Irvine 250). Indeed, as Cache's use of branding and the illegality of his murals reveal, his street art works against such regimes. His art contests not only the appropriation and distribution of visibility in what concerns public space by corporations and the government but also the marginalization and silencing of disenfranchised communities that are relegated to the background of the broader urban landscape even while paradoxically being one of its most visible elements. Similarly, by painting unsanctioned murals on city walls to engage community, Cache disrupts the regime of art and its means of policing what is "high" versus "low" art and who has access to either one.

However, when viewed through the lens of Cache's Central Americanness and its manifestation in his street art, his work evinces a challenge to these and other regimes of visibility concerning how, when, where, and under what circumstances Central Americans are seen or not seen in Los Angeles and, to a certain extent, the greater United States. Los Angeles is home to the largest community of Central American immigrants and US-born generations in the United States. The minor presence of Central Americans in the city during the 1940s and 1950s was drastically transformed by the massive influx of immigrants, primarily from El Salvador and Guatemala, in the late 1970s and 1980s (Segura 9). Relative newcomers, Central Americans have marked their presence in Los Angeles through the establishment of businesses, cultural associations, and yearly celebrations, as well as political organizations and community outreach centers. Similar to other immigrant groups and ethnic communities, they have also claimed a sector of the city as their own: the Westlake and Pico-Union neighborhoods, popularly known as "Little Central America." Ongoing endeavors to have portions of this area officially sanctioned as commemorative sites of Central American culture and history reveal the stake Central Americans have in acquiring a legitimizing form of visibility and the struggles they face in doing so.

Such communal efforts have been and continue to be complicated by the core issue of undocumented (im)migration. As discussed in chapter one, significant portions of the US Central American population are unauthorized. In what specifically concerns Los Angeles County, Salvadorans and Guatemalans alone account for nearly 20 percent of the overall undocumented population ("Profile"). This reality is amplified by prominent representations of forever illegals, making visibility an even more contested battleground for US Central Americans. Because undocumented Central Americans are seen first and foremost as a criminal and demographic threat to American lives and society, their exploitability, particularly as a labor force, remains relatively hidden from view. In other words, and drawing on Nicholas De Genova's concepts of "the scene of exclusion" and the "obscene of inclusion," the "illegality" of undocumented US Central Americans, which punctuates their exclusion in visible ways, works to obscure the obscenity of the subordinated and racialized ways in which they are otherwise included into the nation for profit ("Spectacles" 1182–1186). Consequently, for US Central Americans in Los Angeles and beyond, being seen is not just a matter of competing for visibility and struggling against the regimes of a city government that grants it, but also a question of negotiating the regimes of industry and law that keep many of them in the shadows.

The three works by Cache examined here expose and work against the bearing that such regimes of visibility have on US Central American sociocultural and legal struggles for voice and validity. In so doing, these art pieces offer counternarratives to generalized views of US Central Americans as undesirable Others while also evincing an example of the alternate ways in which US Central Americans like Cache simultaneously define and enact their own sense of belonging. The first piece analyzed consists of a street mural in Echo Park that Cache completed in 2013.[6] An expression of Cache's self-identification as a Guatemalan Angeleno, this piece is a testament to the roots that the Central American immigrant population has put down in Los Angeles and its transformative presence in the city. In this sense, and akin to other community-sponsored projects, Cache's mural is invested in legitimating US Central Americans and their contributions to the city. His street art, however, is effective in this regard precisely because of its ability to challenge official structures, in part due to its unsanctioned nature, and because it offers an inclusive and broad understanding of US Central American visibility that moves beyond the city's delineated limits.

The other two pieces by Cache differ significantly from this street mural in that they are sculpture-based installations on exhibition in gallery and museum settings. Sharing many of the same props and materials, both of these untitled and interrelated works constitute critical responses to immigration policies and calls for immigration reform. These pieces counteract derogatory notions of (im)migrant "illegality" (Central American or otherwise) that obscure the realities of labor exploitation and the inhumanity of targeted immigration laws, which are neither comprehensive nor fully inclusive. The installation piece featured in the *By the Time I Get to Arizona* show held at Mid-City Arts gallery in June 2010, for example, contests the exclusionary and racial underpinnings of Arizona's controversial Senate Bill 1070 (the Support Our Law Enforcement and Safe Neighborhoods Act). The law makes it a state crime to be in the country illegally and requires police officials to check the immigration status of any individual they suspect of being undocumented. In addition to its overt political statement, Cache's work can also be understood as a commentary on the paradoxical construction of Central American undocumented laborers, in particular women, as simultaneously visible and invisible subjects in the United States.

Cache's linked artistic contribution to the *Dreams Deferred: Artists Respond to Immigration Reform* exhibition, which ran from December 2010 to May 2011 at the Chinese American Museum in Los Angeles, renders a similarly poignant critique of the country's failing immigration system and the inclusionary limits of the 2010 Development, Relief, and Education for Alien Minors Act. The DREAM Act was a bipartisan bill first introduced in Congress in 2001 and then for several years thereafter, never garnering the necessary votes in the Senate to be adopted as law. Indeed, the bill also failed to pass in

2010 when the Senate was controlled by Democrats, prompting then President Obama to take executive action to implement DACA. Unlike DACA, however, the DREAM Act offered undocumented youth a pathway to US citizenship.[7] Cache's work for this exhibit responds to the DREAM Act's failure to also address the predicament of undocumented parents whose children stood to benefit from the bill, leading consequently to potential family separations. This issue strikes close to home for Cache and, more generally, the US Central American immigrant population.

US CENTRAL AMERICANS IN THE CITY

To a certain extent, Cache's mural located on Sunset Boulevard, just east of Coronado Street, is an ode to Los Angeles. A collaborative effort with fellow street artists ZES (from Los Angeles) and Askew (from New Zealand), the mural features as its central focal point the city's name painted in neon lime and written in graffiti. The futuristic style of the lettering channels the work of LA graff writers of the 1980s, whose influences included East LA cholo tags of the 1970s and whose own unique style set them apart from New York artists (Deitch 166). The graffiti of the city's name appears against a space-like backdrop with red and orange hues, evoking the lights and nonstop movement of the city at night. Some of the chickens that populate the piece, also in red, orange, and purple hues, are angular and edgy, giving the mural an ultramodern feel. Other chickens, located farther away from the words "Los Angeles," are bubbly and playful in nature, much like their bright neon colors.[8] As is also characteristic of Cache's artwork, the chickens and graffiti are immersed in a light blue cloud-like matter. Emerging from the depths of this matter are tentacles, painted in candy-striped light blue and white, that seemingly threaten to overtake the city and those who inhabit it.

The graffiti of the city's name, surrounded by tentacles, is the only remnant of a previous mural by Cache painted on the same wall. In its initial form, the mural featured an idyllic day scene in the city inhabited by a host of anthropomorphic and animated characters, including cats, dogs, turtles, chickens, aliens, and walking boom boxes. As Stefano Bloch's work reveals, this older work was part of a series, *Los Angeles: Untitled*, of "graffiti-murals" painted on retaining walls along Sunset Boulevard by Cache and Eye One (111). The murals marked a significant break with the tradition of officially sanctioned works in the city by Chicano muralists/activists, while making a statement against hipster gentrification in the Echo Park and Silver Lake communities (Bloch 121).

5.1. *Pedestrian walking by Cache's mural on Sunset Boulevard. Photograph by the author.*

5.2. *Cache's chickens, Sunset Boulevard mural. Photograph by the author.*

The visual priority of "Los Angeles" and its constancy from one mural to the next speaks to the fact that street art is an engagement with the city, one that gives way to a "city re-imaged and re-imagined" (Irvine 237). Notably, in this instance, Cache's process of re-imaging and re-imagining the city is one mediated through his sense of being Guatemalan in Los Angeles. When asked via email whether or not he considers himself to be Guatemalan American or US Central American, or if he even cares for such labels, Cache responded, "I am a guatemalteco with a US citizenship, but consider myself an earth-ling that bleeds Los Angeles." (Cache, "Two more questions"). This answer registers a wide range of subject positions that hinge upon national affinities, notions of legal and global citizenship, and locality. Yet the emphasis placed on being Guatemalan and Angeleno are undeniable. In stating that he is a "guatemalteco with a US citizenship," Cache draws a distinction between his national and cultural identification with Guatemala and his legal status as a citizen of the United States. The latter does not necessarily connote a similar sense of American national and cultural belonging. A similar distinction is made in Cache's articulation of self as an "earthling that bleeds Los Angeles." Although Cache considers himself to be a global citizen, or "earthling," he remains at his very core an Angeleno. He carries the city in his blood.

This notion of being Guatemalan Angeleno is manifested via the tentacles featured in the mural, which, like the city's name, have been carried over from one mural to the next. The light blue and white colors used by Cache in the tentacles are reminiscent of the Guatemalan flag. These colors, however, also appear on the flags of El Salvador, Honduras, and Nicaragua, and constitute national markers of identity for immigrants from these countries. The blue-and-white sign of the Cuscatleca Bakery, a Salvadoran-owned business located across the street from Cache's mural, exemplifies the symbolic currency of these colors. In using such hues, Cache thus showcases not only his national background but also his belonging to a broader Central American immigrant community in Los Angeles, and attests to the transformative presence of this growing population in the city. Unlike his other murals, in which tentacles are connected to alien ships and painted grey, these Central American signifiers are unattached and devoid of their meaning as the extending arms of a stratified society that entraps humans. They remain, nevertheless, alien and somewhat threatening as they register the existence of a community that, like other ethnic groups before it, is changing the spatial and cultural logics of the city.

Cache's visual representation of US Central Americans in Los Angeles parallels ongoing efforts by US Central American groups and organizations to have their historical contributions and cultural heritage officially recognized by the city. Since 2007, groups have petitioned the Los Angeles City Council to declare the Westlake and Pico-Union neighborhoods the Central American Historic District, or a similar derivative, the Central American Cultural District, following designations such as Little Armenia, Koreatown, and Historic Filipino Town (Bermudez 2012). Even though this measure has yet to be approved, the US Central American community has succeeded in having the city declare a section of Vermont Avenue populated with Salvadoran businesses the El Salvador Community Corridor. They have likewise procured two commemorative sites honoring Monseigneur Oscar A. Romero, the archbishop of El Salvador who was an advocate of human rights and a martyr of the Salvadoran civil war (1980–1992).[9] Such initiatives reflect a conscious understanding that visibility and, relatedly, the ability to control how one is seen equals power. The latter is of essence to a community whose quest for voice as one of the seemingly newer arrivals is further compounded by the fact that they inhabit one of the most impoverished and densely populated areas of the city.

Like these efforts, Cache's painting of the mural in question is invested in making US Central Americans visible through the acquisition of public space and its redefinition as a marker of Central Americanness. Yet whereas these same community-led initiatives remain beholden to the city council's power to partition visibility and, therefore, publicly validate US Central Americans as Angelenos, Cache's mural does not. As a work of street art that illegally co-opts city space, Cache's artwork circumvents such official routes, calling them and the regime of governance and visibility they sustain into question. Furthermore, it is a work that espouses a broader and more inclusive notion of US Central American visibility. The majority of the aforementioned endeavors to legitimize the place of US Central Americans in the city have been spearheaded primarily by Salvadorans, whose status as the largest group within the LA-based Central American community as well as history of social activism in the United States dating back to the solidarity movements of the 1970s and '80s tends to eclipse the presence of other US Central American groups. They are also initiatives that have centered almost exclusively on claiming space within the noted Westlake and Pico-Union neighborhoods. Though a logical and relevant objective given this area's historical and present significance to Central American immigrants and newer generations, it nevertheless runs the risk of limiting the US Central American experience to that of living in an enclave.

Inasmuch as Cache's strategic use of light blue and white conveys his individual identity as a Guatemalan Angeleno, it also connotes a sense of a Central American collectivity or regional identity. Employing these colors without any specific identifiers for any one Central American country allows them to function as signifiers of a unified presence and of belonging for a number of US Central American groups in the city. Notably, this is an artistic and symbolic move that corresponds with what Maritza E. Cárdenas notes is the strategic adoption of a Central American regional identity by US Central Americans in large metropolitan and Latino-dominant areas such as Los Angeles as a means of ensuring greater visibility, community, and exerting agency.[10] Similarly, by painting his mural in Echo Park, just a few miles north of the Westlake and Pico Union neighborhoods but still outside of them, Cache decenters the notion of where and under what circumstances US Central Americans are and can be seen. "Little Central America" may be a key settlement site, but it also functions as a port of entry. Many US Central Americans reside in other parts of Los Angeles, such as Hollywood, Van Nuys, North Hollywood, and South Central, not to mention farther removed cities and suburban areas throughout Los Angeles County. Allowing US Central Americans to be seen outside of the epicenter of their cultural, financial, and political activity shows that their transformative potential is not confined to a specific location. As the tentacles in Cache's mural suggest, US Central Americans are rising from the depths and are spreading, slowly but surely Central Americanizing Los Angeles.

COUNTERPUBLICS, ALTERNATIVE NARRATIVES,
AND POLITICAL CHICKENS

Having one's artwork displayed in a gallery and museum setting constitutes a notably different spatial interface than that of painting unsanctioned murals on the public streets of the city. Accordingly, a case could be made that because the installation pieces Cache contributed to the *By the Time I Get to Arizona* and *Dreams Deferred* exhibits appeared in legitimizing institutions such as a gallery and a museum, they do not hold the same agency as the works he produces and displays in the streets. To make this case, however, would be to ignore the fact that both spaces in question— Mid-City Arts and the Chinese American Museum—are instrumental in the construction of what Nancy Fraser terms subaltern counterpublics that enrich, rather than detract from, the critical interventions made by Cache's artwork (67).

As local art blogger Mark Vallen noted in his post about the *By the Time I Get to Arizona* exhibit opening, the Mid-City Arts building has its own colorful past, having been a popular gathering space for some of the first hip-hop DJs in Los Angeles during the 1980s and later becoming a hip-hop record store in the early 2000s. While still in business and under the ownership of street artist Viejas del Mercado, who, like Cache, is also of Guatemalan descent, Mid-City Arts continued to play a key part in the cultivation and promotion of aesthetic countercultures, such as graffiti and street art, that significantly share an intimate history with hip-hop.[11] Existing as a composite of three different spaces—an exhibition hall, an aerosol paint shop, and an open-air performance space—the gallery served as a meeting ground for street artists from all over the globe as well as a shared space that put these same artists and their work in dialogue with the diverse community in which they were located.[12] Notably, almost half of Mid-City is composed of US-born Latinx populations and Latin American immigrants from Mexico and El Salvador ("Mid-City Profile"). It is also in close proximity to Little Central America, just five miles west on Pico Boulevard.

Precisely because of its emphasis on street art, its location, and the demographic of its patrons, Mid-City Arts was a space that challenged elite notions of art and the power of visibility wielded by hegemonic artworld institutions. In essence, it functioned as a zone of opposition from which alternate discourses could be launched that contested the status quo of the public sphere. Moreover, given that the *By the Time I Get to Arizona* exhibit was an act of creative resistance against Arizona's exclusionary immigration measure S.B. 1070, the alternate discourses articulated within this subaltern counterpublic also opposed discriminatory and dominant views of undocumented immigration and immigrants. What became most paramount within this gallery setting and context, then, was not necessarily debates related to the dichotomy between high and low art and how the exhibition of street art in a gallery robbed or imbued it with different aesthetic and market signification (though these issues remained present), but rather what the art on display called into question and, ultimately, revealed.

The Chinese American Museum functions in a similar capacity. Working at the intersections of history, local art, and immigration politics, the museum also allows for the engendering of subaltern counterpublics through which communal empowerment and counternarratives of resistance can be enacted. Not only is the building that houses the museum the last vestige of what was the city's original Chinatown, but it is also part of the El Pueblo de Los Angeles Historical Monument, hailed as the birthplace of the city and a testament to its diverse roots, including its Spanish and Mexican origins. Inaugurated in 2003, after nearly twenty years of dedicated community activism, the museum, as its website proclaims, is a testament to the more than 150-year history of Chinese immigration and settlement in the city ("Mission"). Along with its mission to foster engagement with and educate the public concerning this history and its legacy, the museum aims to highlight the evolving experiences of Chinese Americans and their ongoing contributions to the broader United States ("Mission").

Coupled with the museum's symbolic location, the sustained efforts of the Chinese American community and related organizations to make the museum a reality provide yet another example (in addition to that of previously discussed US Central American initiatives in the Pico-Union District) of claims to belonging by immigrant and/or historically marginalized groups that challenge the city's regimes of visibility. The greater history of immigrant labor and disenfranchisement of Chinese Americans that the museum focalizes in exhibitions and in its research/educational initiatives, beginning with the Chinese Exclusion Act of 1882, is, relatedly, a means of refuting and/or fruitfully complicating what is often a purely celebratory and forgetful discourse of "immigrant America." The aim of the *Dreams Deferred* exhibit, which ran concurrently with another one focused on Angel Island,[13] underscores this very notion. Among other things, *Dreams Deferred* was meant to illuminate the shared histories and struggles of Los Angeles's diverse immigrant communities, including having to contend with the

5.3. *Cache's untitled installation for the* By the Time I Get to Arizona *exhibit. Photograph by the author.*

effects of racially biased immigration laws and the need for policy reforms ("Dreams Deferred"). Much like the Mid-City Arts gallery, the museum's engagement with art (and history) does not seek to uphold power structures and inequities, rather to expose them and offer alternate visions.

By the Time I Get to Arizona

The untitled, three-dimensional installation that Cache fashioned out of papier-mâché sculptures and other household materials for the *By the Time I Get to Arizona* gallery show features one of his trademark chickens staring intently at a hamburger that is surrounded by a white picket fence. The hamburger has an American flag planted in its center and rests atop a mousetrap, depicting it as bait for the chicken that desires it from the other side of the fence. Like the hamburger, the chicken, which is suggestively brown, is encased by a thin wall of poultry mesh, the type used in the construction of chicken coops. The floor underneath the entire installation is covered with a thin layer of sand spotted with mini potted cacti and small black pebbles. Coupled with the walls of fence and mesh, this flooring evokes the treacherous desert terrain of the US-Mexico border that undocumented migrants risk their lives to cross in their quest for the American Dream, symbolized here by a cornerstone of American popular cuisine, the hamburger.

Like many of the other works on display at the Mid-City Arts show, Cache's critical reflection regarding Arizona's S.B. 1070 manifests many of the concerns held by critics of the law, who maintain that it green-lights racial profiling and amounts to a targeted attack against Mexicans and other Latinx populations. Such concerns are linked to larger socio-political issues such as racism, the violation of human and civil rights, racial inequality, and the anxiety that fuels the "Latino Threat Narrative," which posits Mexicans and, by extension, other Latin American immigrants as "an invading force from south of the border that is bent on reconquering land that was formerly theirs (the US Southwest) and destroying the American way of life" (Chavez, *Latino Threat* 2). These issues are often sublimated by the hypernationalist, criminalizing, and racializing discourses surrounding undocumented immigration from parts of the so-called Third World, and their emphasis on sovereignty, that have historically been and continue to be a part of immigration debates and policy making in the United States. S.B. 1070 is no exception.

Key elements of Cache's installation—the white picket fence and the "hamburger trap" it encloses—speak to the exclusionary politics and racism at the center of Arizona's bill. Although codified as a law to help secure Arizona's border and the state's legal inhabitants against the threat of illegal aliens, the law allows for the policing of undesirable migrants and ethnic Others construed in the popular imaginary not only as criminals but also as foreigners who refuse to assimilate. Such individuals must be barred from the nation lest they corrupt the "American way of life." Cache's provocative inclusion of a white picket fence, which conjures an image of the predominantly Anglo suburban neighborhoods of 1950s America, underscores this seeming need for protection and attempt to preserve what is "ours." The wooden barrier protects what it fences in—the cornerstone of America's way of life, the American Dream—while also establishing a territorial, cultural, and racial boundary for would-be trespassers and unwanted guests. Moreover, in using the metaphor of a hamburger, a highly commercialized form of fast food and one that in this installation is a bait for a mouse trap, Cache also forces viewers to consider the nature of the American way of life and ideal of success that US citizens protect so vehemently and that undocumented migrants risk their lives to attain.

In effect, Cache's installation posits the American Dream as a commodity for sale that has been successfully marketed to US citizens and foreigners alike. It remains valuable as long as everyone wants to buy it and buy into it. It is also clear that the undocumented migratory subject, represented by the chicken gazing at the hamburger, is willing to do so, but at what cost? Keeping in mind Cache's metaphorical use of chickens in his street art, the price to be paid by undocumented migrants is that of becoming individuals trapped in a consumer-driven society plagued by economic, racial, and gender inequality. This predicament is made even more dire for migrants by their criminalization as "illegals" and their existence as "impossible subjects," individuals "whose inclusion within the nation [is] simultaneously a social reality and a legal impossibility," being "barred from citizenship without rights" (Ngai 4). The poultry mesh that encases the chicken foregrounds this reality, symbolizing the migratory subject's entrapment in the "coop" of society and, by the same token, the subject's potential imprisonment in a deportation facility.

The exposure of these discriminatory politics and the discourses that work to both obscure and fuel them is the basis of the overall critical commentary that drives Cache's piece. However, it is not the only form of unveiling that Cache's art performs. In *Double Exposures: The Subject of Cultural Analysis*, Mieke Bal argues that exposition or the gesture of exposure, such as that of artists who put their work on display in museums, can be conceived of as a performative speech act that produces meaning (2). The artist (first person) communicates with the viewer (second person) about the object (third person), which, despite its silence, remains physically present. Within this exchange, it is the object (third person) that is of most consequence, given its function as a sign and producer of meaning. Despite its actual visibility, the object on display comes to stand for something else, the statement being made about it to the viewer by the artist or exposer. Equally imperative to this discursive exchange is the narrative that links the object's "present" to the "past" of its "making, functioning, and meaning" and that of the master narrative of the exposition as a whole that viewers experience as they tour the museum (Bal 4). These narratives act as filler between the object and the statement being made about it, creating the possibility for ambiguity and discrepancies. Conceptualizing exposition in this manner allows Bal to destabilize the subject-object dichotomy created by this act, which presupposes that the object is present only to substantiate the statement being made about it to the knowledgeable viewer by the artist. In essence, Bal suggests that, among other things, the object can exist or *mean* in ways other than those intended by the artist.

Bal's discussion is useful, as it foregrounds the possibility of Cache's installation piece as capable of also producing meaning or making a statement about Central American undocumented migration and labor exploitation. Cache's portrayal of the undocumented migratory subject as a brown chicken insinuates a link between this subject and the meatpacking and poultry industry. It likewise hints at the important gendered dimensions of such a relationship. As noted previously, this type of brown chicken calls to mind breeds, such as ISA browns, that are genetically engineered hybrids for the purpose of egg laying and others that are grown specifically for their meat. A high premium is placed on females, given their capabilities as reproducers of marketable goods (eggs). In this case, the chicken represented by Cache does not necessarily evoke the product itself, but rather the cheap and highly productive workforce needed to guarantee its production. This is a workforce that in recent decades has become not only increasingly Mexican and Central American but also more female.

This seeming reference to the growing female presence within the poultry industry adds further nuance to the broader critique made via this installation piece regarding the exploitation of undocumented Central American workers. Women employed in poultry plants are generally responsible for some of the most physically taxing and hazardous forms of assembly line work, including having to hang, slice open, and empty chicken carcasses of their entrails at high speeds and in substandard working conditions. The intense and debilitating nature of this work is made more acute by abuses of supervisorial power aimed especially at women, such as sexual harassment and lower wages. Like the ISA brown breeds that Cache's chicken in this installation piece recalls, women employed in these plants are expected to be high producers, valued only for how quickly and efficiently they can move products through the processing line. Within what is already a disenfranchised population of undocumented workers who lack citizenship-based rights, immigrant women find themselves even more stigmatized and subordinated on account of their gender.

The successful functioning of the agricultural industry depends on the purposeful obscuring and docility of the broader undocumented immigrant workforce it employs. Were this necessary invisibility to be compromised, however, undocumented Central Americans would indeed be seen but only as criminal illegal aliens. Highly publicized events such as the 2008 immigration raid at the kosher meatpacking plant Agriprocessors Inc. in Postville, Iowa, is a case in point. Following the raid, approximately 290 undocumented Maya Guatemalans were convicted of document fraud. The majority served five months in prison and were eventually deported, while the owners of the plant were not charged with any criminal charges for violating immigration and labor laws.[14] Embedded in an alternate narrative of immigrant labor and exploitation, Cache's installation piece, like his street mural, becomes an expression of another key facet of the Central American immigrant experience in the United States. In effect, it reveals the contradictory positioning of Central Americans as, on one hand, visible illegal aliens and, on the other, invisible laborers maintained as such by the regimes of government, law, and the agricultural industry.

Dreams Deferred: Artists Respond to Immigration Reform

Cache's installation piece for the *Dreams Deferred* exhibition at the Chinese American Museum in Los Angeles incorporated many of the same props and materials that were the basis of his sculpture for the Mid-City Arts gallery show, with one key exception. Rather than a hamburger trap, the brown chicken on the other side of the white picket fence has her gaze fixated on two white eggs, which rest on a patch of artificial grass. By making this substitution, Cache transforms his piece from one that excoriates the American Dream as a consumerist fallacy that ensnares immigrants and depends on their exploitable labor to one that similarly calls out the short-sightedness of immigration policies like the DREAM Act. As Cache's piece suggests, legislative measures such as the DREAM Act, which also remain wedded to the problematic ideal of the American Dream, sanction the inclusion of a privileged few deemed as "exceptional" (the undocumented youth who stand to benefit from the passage of the bill), to the detriment of those who fail to live up to and meet certain standards of merit and immigrant "worthiness" (e.g., the parents of Dreamers, among others). The adoption and implementation of such policies, as Cache's work ultimately emphasizes, would lead to the further oppression of immigrant communities by effectively instituting a form of de facto family separation.

Notably, it is not just the possibility of acquiring legal status that would give way to a division between Dreamers and their similarly undocumented parents or other family members. As Claudia A. Anguiano and Karma R. Chávez explain in their analysis of Dreamers discourse, "DREAMers are exceptional in that they are unlike other immigrants, both because of their education and ability to adopt many of the characteristics desired in US citizens, and also because, unlike adult immigrants such as their parents, DREAMers did not *choose* to migrate to the United States" (90, emphasis in original). In other words, Dreamers are also set apart from their parents because of their perceived "Americanness" and potential for belonging as well as their absolution from criminal border crossings. Indeed, these are notions that President Obama underscored when announcing his decision to implement DACA in 2012, following the failure of Congress to pass the latest version of the DREAM Act. As he stated to the nation, the undocumented youth in question are "Americans in their heart, in their minds, in every single way but one: on paper. They were brought to this country by their parents—sometimes even as infants—and often have no idea that they're undocumented." ("Remarks").

Such divisions effectively designate Dreamers "good immigrants" who affirm the reality of the American Dream through their ethos of hard work and unblemished moral behavior, whereas their parents, who presumably did make a choice to break the law and bring their children to the United States without authorization, are deemed "bad immigrants." The juxtaposition in Cache's piece between the two chicken eggs and their surroundings and the presumed mother hen and her surroundings speaks precisely to this distinction between "good" and "bad" immigrants. Nesting atop a patch of green grass behind a white picket fence, which demarcates the confines of the ideology of the American Dream, the unhatched chicken eggs are signifiers of the potential of Dreamers to successfully assimilate into American society, from both a financial and cultural standpoint. This success is understood in individualistic terms, as a result of Dreamers' self-motivation and drive, and independent of any nurturing from their parents. It is the same notion of success, rooted in neoliberal ideals of responsibility and immigrant merit, that was repeatedly affirmed in mainstream retellings of José Gutiérrez's "heroic" life and death explored in chapter three. By contrast, the mother hen who is barred from her eggs and the American Dream is encased in a circle of chicken wire mesh that, as in the previous installation, hints at the possible imprisonment or deportation and perceived criminality of undocumented parents. This wall of wire mesh likewise symbolizes the inability of these same parents to be a part of and share in the everyday lives and American dreams of their "exceptional" children.

This critique regarding the potential of the DREAM Act to separate immigrant families on legal and sociocultural grounds echoes that of immigrant rights activists, including many Dreamers themselves.[15] Cache's particular take on this legislation is, however, also born out of personal experience. Cache's migration to the United States in the late 1980s, along with that of his brother, was predated by that of his mother, who had migrated to the country on her own a few years prior. Although Guatemala was at the height of its civil war, her main motivations for migrating to the United States were related to her spouse's alcoholism and the emotional and economic strain it placed on the family and marriage (Cache, Interview). As Cache recalls, his family also resided in Guatemala City and were somewhat removed from the fighting and violence being carried out primarily in rural and highland areas. The temporary separation from his mother, and later the long-term separation from his father, that Cache and his brother endured as young children may have resulted from different circumstances than those that would typically affect Dreamer families if legislation like the DREAM Act were passed. Nevertheless, they remain experiences that impacted Cache and, like him, many other US Central Americans.

Indeed, one can make a case that family separation is yet another staple of the Central American (im)migrant experience in the United States. As I have noted elsewhere, Central American women have had, at times, a pioneering and steadily increasing role in international flows from the isthmus since, at least, the 1960s (Padilla, "Central American Transnational Imaginary" 155). Many of these women, as suggested by Cache's own immigrant story as well as the cultural works referenced and explored in the previous chapter,[16] have been mothers forced to migrate to ensure the survival and well-being of their children. Such migrations have come at a high cost for both migrating mothers and the children they leave behind, namely having to endure being separated from one another for indeterminate periods of time. Whereas civil conflicts in Central America, along with enduring violence and economic uncertainty in the postwar years, have further propelled these familial separations, the passage and implementation of more restrictive immigration policies in the United States have made reunifications nearly impossible.

In this sense, Cache's contribution to the *Dreams Deferred* exhibit enacts more than just a broad criticism of the exclusionary pitfalls of the DREAM Act. Like his installation for the *By the Time I Get to Arizona* gallery show, this piece opens itself up to alternate interpretations linked specifically to the realities and struggles of US Central Americans. In this case, we are talking about a history of family separations occasioned not only by a host of factors in Central American sending countries but also by domestic and immigration policies geared toward reducing or preventing at all costs the continued presence of undesirable immigrants in the United States. Such an interpretation is even more poignant when we likewise consider the inhumane policy of separating children from their parents at the US-Mexico border enacted by the Trump administration in 2018 to "dissuade" undocumented Central American migrants from seeking asylum in the country. Cache could not have necessarily foreseen these unfortunate developments, yet his piece seems to eerily foreshadow them just the same. Much like the "story" of José Antonio Gutiérrez, which offers insight into the plight of undocumented (male) youth in the Trump era, Cache's work offers a wider vantage point from which to understand contemporaneous threats and assaults on the Central American (immigrant) family structure.

CENTRAL AMERICANIZING THE UNITED STATES

This final chapter is, at its core, an inquiry into the critical possibilities that exist when street art, immigration politics, and being Central American in Los Angeles converge. Seeing the art of graffiti writer Cache from this intersectional vantage point reveals his work to be a unique visual engagement with the Central American immigrant reality, including notions of what it means to belong and not belong in the United States. As street art that also functions as a form of immigrant art, the examples of Cache's work analyzed here both expose and challenge the regimes of visibility (those of government, the law, and industry) that determine to what extent, where, and how US Central Americans are made visually legible and, consequently, deemed welcomed additions to LA's diverse community. In Cache's Echo Park mural, candy-striped light blue and white tentacles and neon hues provide an apt metaphor for Cache's representation of his own Guatemalan Angeleno identity as well as the transformative and growing presence of Central Americans in the city. In his sculpture-based installations for the *By the Time I Get to Arizona* gallery show and the *Dreams Deferred* exhibition, it is his well-known signature as a street muralist—his politicized chickens—that serves as the signifier of Central Americanness. In the first instance, he calls attention to the plight of undocumented Central American workers who are kept by the regimes of government, the law, and industry in the impossible predicament of needing to remain invisible as laborers and, when visible, are seen only as "illegals" who are unauthorized to be within the confines of the nation. In the second, he shines a light on the history and centrality of family separations that are an inherent aspect of the Central American immigrant reality.

Although different in many respects, these three works are part of the same conversation. Whereas in his mural Cache remarks on the Central Americanization of Los Angeles that he sees around him and of which he is a part, his installation pieces show this process to also extend beyond the city. The narrative of Central American immigrants as an exploitable labor force within the agricultural industry has taken shape in the last decades not necessarily in Los Angeles, but rather in other parts of the country. It is the narrative of thousands of Central American immigrants that left the city in the early 1990s, or never settled there, and that now call other destinations in the Midwest and the US South home. It is likewise a narrative with increasing relevance to how we think about the Central American experience in the United States and whose importance is certainly not lost on someone like myself, a transplanted Angelena who currently resides in Northwest Arkansas. Aside from being the corporate home of Tyson Foods, one of the leading companies in the global poultry industry and an active recruiter of immigrant labor, this geographic region is the site of a growing Central American community, as evidenced by the *mercados, pupuserías,* and *panaderías* with their telltale light-blue and white signs.

In similar fashion, Cache's installation piece critiquing the 2010 DREAM Act allows for a broader contemplation of the ongoing reality of family separations in Central American immigration to the United States. This, too, is a form of revelation that allows US Central Americans to be seen in new ways and beyond the demarcated limits and spaces of Los Angeles. Such an act of exposure, like that enacted by and through all the works in question, is at its core a refutation of the ways in which US Central Americans have been denied a sense of belonging and deemed to not belong. At the same time, however, this added revelation is also a claim to visibility and belonging, one ultimately rendered on Cache's terms.

Conclusion

SEEING BEYOND THE DOMINANT

*T*HROUGHOUT THIS PROJECT I HAVE SHOWN THE DEGREE to which the visibility afforded to US Central Americans in the national popular imaginary has largely marked their exclusion. Grounding my discussion in an analysis of hegemonic representations of US Central Americans as threatening guerrillas, political refugees, *domésticas*, MS-13 gang members, and forever illegals, I have argued that these populations have been generally construed as Others who do not and cannot belong. The representations in question, emerging in the span of nearly four decades from 1980 to 2020, have played a key role in this process of ostracization through the means by which they signify US Central Americans and work intertextually as part of an expanding regime of representation.

Yet, as signifiers whose meanings are not fixed, these prominent depictions can likewise constitute potential sites for contesting this same material and symbolic marginalization of US Central Americans. In many instances, this resistance consists of illuminating nuanced histories and experiences of Central American (im)migration to the United States that underscore just how decontextualized and ideologically invested portrayals of US Central Americans in the mainstream media are. Other types of challenges take the shape of articulations of belonging from within the margins that do not conform to the traditional narrative of immigrant assimilation and its corollary, the ideal of the American Dream. Despite being a secondary focus of this project, this added dimension of the work of signification that these hegemonic representations do remains significant nevertheless, helping to further disclose the ways in which not belonging, and belonging, are imbricated for US Central Americans. It is in this sense, then, that these prevalent means of envisioning these populations have helped to fashion as well as disclose the contours of a Latinx/US Central American experience largely defined by non-belonging.

129

Working with these representations, however, provides a key (though not the only) avenue for engaging with the cultural politics of US Central American non-belonging. And this approach, as fruitful as it is, is also not without its limits. As noted in the introduction, these imaginings are hegemonic products of their First World contexts and the special interests of power brokers such as the US government, the media, and corporate industries. These depictions make discernible the paradoxical visibility of US Central Americans but also contribute to it, allowing these populations to be "seen" but not necessarily in a way that makes the nuances of their histories and their lives legible. Moreover, because these portrayals also affirm racialized hierarchies rooted in colonialism as well as class divisions and gender/sex norms, they contribute to the further marginalization and, to a certain extent, erasure of Indigenous, Afro-descendant, and LGBTQ Central Americans in the United States and the added dimensions of their realities as immigrants and subsequent generations.

Thus, and as a means of concluding what I have envisioned as a fundamental but also first conceptual incursion, I would like to gesture toward some of the other critical possibilities of this "working" paradigm. The provocative works of US Central American cultural producers Roy G. Guzmán and Breena Nuñez as well as a brief contemplation of how local and regional politics are likewise implicated in notions of US Central American non-belonging provide the basis for such a discussion. Like many other children of the Central American diaspora who either came to the United States at a young age or are the children of immigrants, Guzmán's poetry and Nuñez's comics shed light on experiences that resonate with those explored throughout this book. They infuse these experiences, however, with intergenerational perspectives that bring to the fore LGBTQ and Black identities, adding further layers of nuance to what it means to be Central American in the United States. Indeed, in their works we see reflected many of the same discourses and concerns raised in the Twitter communities of #CentAmStudies and #CentralAmericanTwitter. However, despite the fact that the works of Guzmán and Nuñez likewise offer the possibility of pushing back against dominant views of US Central Americans, especially that of the forever illegal, they are not necessarily invested in working with or through these same tropes.

Part of his collection *Catrachos* (2020), Guzmán's poem "Payday Loan Phenomenology" is, as the title implies, a meditation on the significance and experience of having to get predatory "payday loans" for Latinx/Central American immigrants. The poem's opening verses conjure the sense of defeat and angst felt by the speaker's family on their drive to get the loan, feelings that are made more acute by the car's broken air conditioner. Written in a prose-like form, the speaker's memories and thoughts are separated throughout by spaces as if marking the absences and silences that also condition this experience. Rising to the surface are the speaker's recollections of his and his mother's past in Honduras, including their economic hardship, and the realization that in the context of their new lives in the United States they are still struggling to survive, caught up in a cycle of never having enough.

Pulling up to the payday loan office and waiting in line for their turn to apply for and receive their loans triggers another set of memories and observations regarding traumas shared collectively with others, traumas stemming from not only living such a precarious financial existence but also being (formerly) undocumented. As the poet writes, "we carry blue passports everywhere we go / to remind us of how others have been snatched from their dreams / our skin callused from too much persecution" (87). Amid the patrons, the speaker also recognizes "people who look like us who sound / like us when they say gracias [. . .] grieve like us because our bones cry the same way" (88). And when they return home "to an apartment [they] can't accept [they] can't afford" (89), the speaker and his family will do so in shame, "crawl[ing] away from each other's gaze" (90).

In writing from the vantage point of his and his family's economic disenfranchisement and "social expendability" (87), the poet makes discernible for readers an experience of US Central American not belonging that is pervasive, cyclical, and endured collectively. It is underpinned by multiple traumas and disillusionment and, for the poet, his added identity as a gay young man. Tellingly, the poet characterizes the cops that patrol near the payday loan office, who are "evidently Latinos," as ones who "will batter you when they catch you hustling / but dance with you during pride parades" (87), underscoring the threat these cops pose to immigrant and gay communities independent of their race and ethnicity, what may be their own queerness, and/or their willingness to partake in pride festivities. In the related verses "the Black cops enjoying Latin music *I know / you want me* with my hands up *you know I want cha* legs / spread apart," the poet drives this point home. Interspersing lyrics from Pitbull's well-known dance song "I Know You Want Me (Calle Ocho)" with an image of him being potentially arrested and body-searched creates an unsettling juxtaposition between what could be an erotic/sexually charged situation (that is not necessarily dangerous) and a threatening one. In this way, Guzmán complicates notions of non-belonging from the vantage point of being both US Central American/Honduran and queer.

Breena Nuñez's comics offer a similar intervention and means of broadening our understanding of US Central American non-belonging. An educator and cartoonist, Nuñez self-identifies as an Afro-Guatemalan Salvadoran.

Her zines and comic strips engage with topics such as anti-blackness, colorism, internalized racism, being multiethnic, and, more broadly, US Central American identity. In addition to having her comics appear in *The New Yorker* and *The Nib*, Nuñez maintains an active social media presence on Twitter, Instagram, and via her own website, where she likewise shares her artwork. In one of Nuñez's comic strips in the series *From There to Here*, she explores the complexities and frustrations of figuring out her identity in light of the fact that she was raised in a predominantly Chicanx neighborhood in San Francisco and the anti-blackness inherent to Latinx/US Central American communities. The first tier of the comic consists of an initial panel in which a five-year-old Nuñez asks her mother if they are Mexican, followed by another of Nuñez in college being asked by a fellow student if she had African relatives because, according to him, she looks "hella Ethiopian." The second tier then shows a visibly confused, frustrated, and angry Nuñez literally "blowing her top" in the first panel and completely spent in the second while the student who inquired about her racial identity tells her, "OK, relax! It was just a question." In the caption accompanying this last panel, Nuñez writes, "My young brain refused to believe that blackness existed in the Americas. And to this day I wondered why I did."

Nuñez's interrogation of her own inability to acknowledge and accept her blackness points to the larger issue of anti-blackness in the Americas as well as the erasure of these populations within the more specific regional context of Central America. Notably, in another comic strip series titled *I Exist*, Nuñez specifically examines the denial of both blackness and the existence of Black populations in El Salvador. This query and broader critique, which is likewise tied to the legacy of colonialism in the Americas, is at the heart of Nuñez's related questioning of her ethnic identity, which is how the comic begins. Hence, Nuñez is engaged in and, by the same token, alludes to the process of decolonization that is needed for her to be able to recognize and own both her (US) Central American ethnic and cultural identity and her blackness. Both of these can give her a sense of community that has eluded her, a notion explored in another comic from the same series. Just as importantly, Nuñez offers her readers a counternarrative to exclusionary and racist notions of regional or national belonging for Central Americans premised on hegemonic discourses of *mestizaje* and the prevalence of representations of US Central Americans as *mestizos* or *ladinos*.

Along with these works by Guzmán and Nuñez, which evince underrepresented experiences of queer and Black US Central Americans, a better understanding of how the local and the regional affects the cultural politics of US Central American non-belonging is also a needed and crucial enterprise. As Ana Patricia Rodríguez stresses in her call to look beyond the trope of "invisibility," the presence of US Central Americans must be understood in and across different sites ("Toward" 106). Within the local and regional geographic spaces they reside in, many US Central Americans also negotiate their non-belonging in relation to other (dominant) Latinx groups and their claims to inclusion. For US Central American populations residing in the Southwest, a regional space in which Mexican Americans and Mexican immigrants are the Latinx majority and that Chicanxs claim as their rightful patrimony, this means having to navigate non-belonging within the scope of intra-ethnic relationships.[1]

The essay "Gallina Ciega: Turning the Game on Itself" by US Salvadoran performance artist and poet Leticia Hernández-Linares offers a compelling and intimate portrait of this reality. In this essay, Hernández-Linares reflects upon the difficulties of being a "Salvadoran who grew up Chicana," an experience that defies the boxes people try to put her in as well as the identity labels with and through which she works (112–113). Hernández-Linares's contemplations of these matters reveal her struggles to have a sense of true belonging as a Salvadoran in a state like California, where Mexican and Chicanx histories and cultural paradigms of identity predominate. She recognizes the need to own her Salvadoranness and the importance of excavating the specific histories of US Central Americans. By the same token, she also acknowledges the ways in which US Central Americans like herself have "entered into" Chicanx identity and "begun to expand it" (113). These last observations are vital, as they constitute a declaration of belonging on Hernández-Linares's own terms and based on her own experiences, while still rejecting the nationalism of the "Mexican/Chicana/o and Salvadoran sides of the room" (113).

Another related example that shows the vitality and critical potential of looking at the local and regional dynamics of non-belonging can be found in the *migra*-documentaries explored in chapter four. The main focus of my analysis in this chapter was how *migra*-documentaries represented Mexico as a "border passage" for undocumented Central American migrants. I argued that, among other things, this construct underscored the ways in which Central Americans were deemed undesirable and unbelonging citizen-subjects while transiting through Mexico, long before arriving in the United States. In chronicling the perilous journeys of Central Americans through this border passage, these *migra*-documentaries, however, also offer a depiction of these migrants as literal and metaphorical "border crossers." As Nestor Rodríguez observes, in their journeys Central American transmigrants transverse not only geographic boundaries but also "social planes of race, class, and gender relations" (83). To the latter we could also add social planes of sexuality, language, age, and culture.

Conceiving of Central American transmigrants as border crossers creates new possibilities for contemplating borderlands subjectivities that are rooted in Central American–specific experiences and histories of "crossing." In her seminal work *Borderlands/La Frontera: The New Mestiza*, Gloria Anzaldúa articulates a vision of the US-Mexico border as "*una herida abierta*," or open wound, "where the Third World grates against the first and bleeds" (3). This understanding of the border as not only a territorial but also a colonial divide between an imperialist North and an oppressed global South is central to the grand narrative of the US-Mexico borderlands institutionalized by the Chicanx and border studies scholarship of the 1980s and '90s.[2] Notably, in Anzaldúa's verses, Mexico is a metonymical stand-in for the Latin American continent and its peoples as well as the colonized world and its others, including disenfranchised minorities in the United States.

This view of the US-Mexico dyad provides the basis for the notion of borderlands subjectivity that Anzaldúa likewise posits. Like the unnatural boundary created by the violent imposition of the US-Mexico border on Mexican land and its people, she too must contend with the cultural and psychic traumas of being torn.[3] One of the ways in which Anzaldúa contends with this "splitting" as a Chicana in the borderlands is by asserting her ties to a pre-Colombian Indigenous past and culture in Mexico. As scholars have noted, this return to the "homeland" and idealization of Indigenous roots by Chicanxs is a response to the Anglo-American culture that surrounds and excludes them. In essence, it is an attempt to create a "narrative of belonging" in the face of alienation even though Chicanxs also have an ambivalent relationship to Mexico (Contreras 6).[4] However, as other scholars have also observed, this vision of Mexico and means of engendering a sense of belonging occludes the material realities of the US-Mexico borderlands, in particular what transpires on the Mexican side.[5]

The portrayals of Central American border crossings afforded by *migra*-documentaries unsettle this dominant narrative of the US-Mexico borderlands and, relatedly, the Chicanx paradigm of borderlands subjectivity. As we see in these films, when it comes to undocumented Central American transmigrants, the Mexican state does not stand in opposition to the United States, nor is it a source of potential resistance to the alienation and oppression of these border crossers. As an integral part of a US-Mexico interstate regime of immigration enforcement and securitization, Mexico takes part in the imperialistic endeavors of the United States against Central Americans. With their focus on what happens south of the US-Mexico divide, *migra*-documentaries also make it difficult to ignore the material reality on the ground for undocumented Central Americans. These films thus provide insight into the formation of borderlands subjectivities that are also taking shape within the US-Mexico (extended) borderlands, but in ways that force a rethinking of the US-Mexico dyad and the Chicanx concept of border subjectivity wedded to it. Contemplating US Central American borderlands subjectivities thus requires working in relation to but also moving beyond dominant paradigms of the US-Mexico borderlands. Recalling Hernández-Linares's own maneuvering between her Salvadoran and Chicanx identities, this type of critical enterprise is a claim to belonging that also marks the presence of US Central Americans in the border spaces they inhabit.

Independent of these new potential directions for further exploring and expanding the concept of non-belonging, I also know that the focus on national belonging maintained in this project will remain paramount. Non-belonging raises questions about national affiliation premised on racist discourses of legal and cultural citizenry, social and economic integration, and the biopolitics of keeping the country safe. These questions remain pivotal to the US Central American communities that continue to grow and thrive across the country and as Central American migration to the United States continues to be a lynchpin in national debates on immigration. As I write this, thousands of Central American immigrants are being held indefinitely in detention centers, awaiting deportation; many will be deported back to dangerous situations. Others are still languishing in Mexico with, as of yet, no real possibility of claiming asylum in the United States, and nearly six hundred children still remain separated from their parents as a consequence of the Trump administration's immigration policies.

Although Joseph R. Biden defeated Trump in the November 2020 presidential election and has vowed to overturn many of the cruel and inhumane policies of the previous administration, progress is slow on this front, and, in fact, many of these same policies are still in place under his new presidency.[6] Furthermore, the mainstream news media has once again turned its attention to the new "crisis" unfolding at the US-Mexico border and the latest "surges" of unaccompanied youth from Central America's Northern Triangle. Right-wing politicians and media pundits have decried both as consequences of Biden's election and lenient views on immigration. Indeed, some of these same politicians are advocating a return to Trump-era policies because they "work." Thus, it is still unclear what the legacy of the Trump administration's approach to immigration and border enforcement and securitization practices will be and, relatedly, the extent of their ongoing damage to the US Central American immigrant community and others. Like Reagan's machinations in the Central American region and his domestic policy agenda in the 1980s, have the actions of the Trump administration provided the foundation for even more restrictive and dehumanizing means of dealing with the "immigration problem" and future "border crises"? Or will these effectively be repudiated, as the Biden administration has claimed? What we do know is that these actions have impacted and will continue to impact the legal, social, and cultural struggles of US Central Americans for greater representation and inclusion. And as these actions do this, US Central Americans and others will also continue to resist, further expanding the cultural politics of non-belonging.

Notes

1. Trump officially announced his candidacy for president of the United States on June 16, 2015. In his now-infamous speech, Trump stated the following about Mexico and Mexican immigrants: "When Mexico sends its people, they're not sending their best. They're not sending you. They're sending people that have lots of problems, and they're bringing those problems with us. They're bringing drugs. They're bringing crime. They're rapists. And some, I assume, are good people." Trump added that this type of immigration was not just coming from Mexico but from "all over South and Latin America" ("Here's Donald Trump's"). Although Trump began by maligning Mexicans specifically, "Mexican" ultimately meant all those coming from Latin America. As his presidency progressed and migration from Central America became a key issue, he increasingly also targeted Central American (im)migrants.

2. In this study, I employ the term "US Central American" as a means of collectively referring to both Central American immigrants and subsequent US-born populations. Theoretically speaking, my use and preference for this term aligns with the conceptualization of US Central American provided by Karina O. Alvarado, Alicia Ivonne Estrada, and Ester E. Hernández in the introduction to the edited volume *U.S. Central Americans* (2017). This preference is worth noting given alternative terms such as "Central American-American," "American Central American," and "*centralamericanos*" that have likewise been conceptualized and advanced by other US Central American scholars, including Arturo Arias, Claudia A. Milian, and Maritza E. Cárdenas. As Alvarado et al. posit, the "US" in "US Central American" marks, among other things, the "social and national location" from which members of the Central American diaspora construct "identities, histories, communities, and cultures," while "Central American" emphasizes a regional identification that unsettles nationalistic paradigms and US-based ethnic identities that delineate Americanization (23). In this sense, "US Central American" also emphasizes "the multiple

137

ways in which Central American diasporas experience belonging and nonbelonging in both the United States and Central America" (29). This particular emphasis on "belonging and nonbelonging," along with the term's more general means of accentuating the diasporic and transnational dimensions of US Central American communities, makes it particularly apropos to this project.

3. The Sandinista National Liberation Front (FSLN) was founded in 1961. The "Sandinistas" took their namesake from the famed revolutionary leader Augusto César Sandino, who led an armed insurrection against the US Marine's occupation of Nicaragua (1927–1932). In 1934 Sandino was assassinated by Anastasio Somoza García, a military leader trained and fully supported by the US government. Although Somoza García took control of Nicaragua as a "liberal," he, along with his two sons, Luis and Anastasio (Somoza Debayle), ruled the country as dictators. The "conservative" Somoza dynasty lasted from 1932 to 1979, when the Sandinistas succeeded in overthrowing Anastasio. The United States sought to undermine the socialist-based Sandinista government by funding the military efforts of the "Contras," a group of right-wing Somoza loyalists and ex-National Guardsmen. The latter engaged in a US-backed counterrevolutionary war against the Sandinistas throughout the 1980s.

4. Nicaragua's "Contra War" lasted approximately from 1981 to 1989. In 1990, the Sandinistas lost the democratically held presidential elections. The Salvadoran civil war began in 1980 and ended with the signing of peace accords in 1992. Guatemala's civil conflict was the longest of the three, beginning in 1960 and ending with the signing of peace accords in 1996.

5. The Immigration and Nationality Act of 1965 was signed into law by Lyndon B. Johnson. It constituted a reform of the immigration system and policies established under the Johnson-Reed Act of 1924 that relied on a national origins quota system, which privileged European immigrants of Northwestern and Germanic origins. Although the 1965 law abolished the quota system and ended the practice of admitting immigrants based on racial hierarchies, thus paving the way for significant immigration from Asia, Africa, and Latin America, it continued to allow for the use of numerical limits on immigration from countries and established a system of preferences for immigrants.

6. The United States is home to populations from all seven of the isthmian nations: Belize, Costa Rica, El Salvador, Guatemala, Honduras, Nicaragua, and Panama. All of these racially, ethnically, and linguistically diverse communities, including Indigenous and Afro-descendant populations, have unique histories of migration and settlement in the United States, some dating as far back as the mid- to late nineteenth century.

7. Honduran migration to the United States dates back to the late nineteenth century and had a notable uptick in the 1980s. The late 1990s and early 2000s, however, witnessed the largest increases in Honduran immigration, which were fueled by a combination of natural disasters (Hurricane Mitch in 1998), economic factors, and politically motivated and gang-based violence. Estimates suggest that the Honduran

immigrant population in the United States grew from 109,000 in 1990 to close to 523,000 in 2010 (Reichman).

8. "Ladino" is a term akin to "mestizo" that is used in Central America. When speaking specifically of US Central Americans, I evoke both terms in this book.

9. Most of the studies on Indigenous and Afro–Central Americans in the United States have focused on Mayan and Garifuna communities. Included among these studies are Anderson's *Black and Indigenous: Garifuna Activism and Consumer Culture in Honduras*; Batz's "Maya Cultural Resistance in Los Angeles"; Boj Lopez's "Mobile Archives of Indigeneity" and "Weavings That Rupture"; Estrada's "Ka Tzij" and "(Re)Claiming Public Space and Place"; England's *Afro Central Americans in New York City* and "Afro-Hondurans in the Chocolate City"; Fink's *The Maya of Morganton*; and the edited volumes *The Maya Diaspora* by Loucky and Moor and *The Mayans among Us* by Sittig and González. It is also important to note that although I am drawing a distinction here between Afro-descendant and Indigenous US Central Americans, populations such as the Garifuna identify as both Black *and* Indigenous.

10. This notable increase in migration from the region, especially that of undocumented youth and family units, is addressed in chapter one.

11. See the volumes edited by Mitchell and Hansen as well as Kellner and Durham, and Hall's primer *Representation: Cultural Representations and Signifying Practices* along with his related articles, "Race, Culture, and Communications" and "Cultural Studies and Its Theoretical Legacies."

12. In addition to the mainstream news media coverage of undocumented migration from Central America during Trump's presidency, alternative media venues such as *Vice News Tonight* on HBO have featured several exposés on Central American asylum seekers and immigration. HBO also aired *Torn Apart: Separated at the Border* (2019), a documentary about the Trump administration's policy of separating Central American children from their parents at the US-Mexico border implemented in 2018, and *Icebox* (2018), a drama about a twelve-year-old Honduran boy who seeks asylum as an unaccompanied minor in the United States. The Showtime series *Shameless* also incorporated a secondary storyline revolving around unaccompanied minors and immigrant youth detention during its ninth season in 2019. Popular dramas on national television networks such as NBC's *Law and Order: SVU (Special Victims Unit)* and ABC's *Grey's Anatomy* followed suit with episodes based on the family separations at the US-Mexico border. *Law and Order: SVU* aired the episode "Zero Tolerance" in 2018, and *Grey's Anatomy* aired "What I Did for Love" in 2019.

13. DACA was a response to the failed efforts by Congress to pass the DREAM Act (Development, Relief, and Education for Alien Minors Act) in 2011, which I discuss at more length in chapter five. As instituted by the Obama administration, DACA provided recipients with a two-year deferment from deportation and the ability to obtain a work permit. To be eligible for DACA, undocumented youth needed to have arrived in the United States prior to turning 16; have resided in the country continuously since June 15, 2007; have been enrolled in school or graduated from a high school, and/or served in the Coast Guard or Armed Forces of the United

States; have not been convicted of a felony or significant misdemeanor; and not otherwise be a national security or public safety threat.

14. @realDonaldTrump. "Many Gang Members and some very bad people are mixed into the Caravan heading to our Southern Border. Please go back, you will not be admitted into the United States unless you go through the legal process. This is an invasion of our Country and our Military is waiting for you." *Twitter*, 29 Oct. 2018, 9:41 a.m., twitter.com/realdonaldtrump/status/1056919064906469376?lang=en.

15. See, for example, DeCesare, and Zilberg's "Fools Banished from the Kingdom" and *Spaces of Detention*.

16. Some inroads are being made in this area. Cárdenas's article "Is Carlos Mencia a White Wetback?" explores how the media contributes to the erasure of US Central Americans within the broader Latinx imaginary. Mata's *Domestic Disturbances* includes analyses of US Central Americans in contemporary films within the scope of her book's broader emphasis on Latina representations of immigration and labor. Finally, in *Salvadoran Imaginaries*, Rivas provides, among other things, a nuanced exploration of the "mediated" accounts of Salvadoran migration and diasporic belonging afforded in Salvadoran print and online news media.

17. See, for example, Arias's *Taking Their Word*, Cárdenas's *Constituting Central American-Americans*, Caso's *Practicing Memory in Central American Literature*, Rivas's *Salvadoran Imaginaries*, Rodríguez's *Dividing the Isthmus*, my own *Changing Women, Changing Nation*, and the edited volumes *U.S. Central Americans* by Alvarado et al. and *Indigenous Interfaces* by J. G. Menjívar and Chacón.

18. For further discussion of how this emergent field has been defined, see Baker and Hernández, Arias's "What Are Central American Studies?," and Rodríguez's "Toward a Transisthmian Central American Studies." In their discussion Baker and Hernández define "Central American Studies" as "an interdisciplinary field that bridges ethnic studies and area studies," recalling the broader notion of Latin American studies (86). In line with a transisthmian vision of Central American studies, Rodríguez adds that the notion of "US Central American studies [. . .] operates from an expanded notion of Central America in which the diaspora is essential to the construction of transnational cultural identities and imaginaries in the twenty-first century" (104). The monograph-length studies mentioned in the previous endnote, as well as numerous articles, book chapters, and special editions of journals, speak to the strength of cultural studies–based analyses within the field of (US) Central American studies.

CHAPTER ONE: SIGNIFYING US CENTRAL
AMERICAN NON-BELONGING

1. Prior to the late 1970s and 1980s, Central American migration to the United States consisted primarily of small waves of laborers and privileged elites, many of which worked, vacationed, and/or settled in urban centers such as New York City,

New Orleans, San Francisco, and Los Angeles. These smaller migratory waves date back to the late nineteenth century. For more information regarding this earlier immigration history, see Orlov and Ueda; Repak; Rodríguez, "Salvadoran Immigrant Acts"; Segura; and the chapter on Hondurans in Sluyter et al., *Hispanic and Latino New Orleans*.

2. The IRCA provided a pathway to permanent residency for a large number of unauthorized immigrants in the country (approximately 2.7 million) while also laying the groundwork for future restrictions on immigration and legalization (Chishti et al.). Implemented in an uneven manner, the law applied only to those who had been in the country since 1982, who had no criminal record, and who could also prove that they would not be a "public charge." Those who met these initial qualifications then had to demonstrate a certain level of English language competency and knowledge of American civics. In essence, applicants had to prove that they were morally worthy and of economic value to the country to even be considered viable candidates. At the same time, and as a means of counterbalancing the limited "amnesty" it was providing to some, the IRCA also included provisions for increased border security, employer sanctions (with no real designs for holding them accountable), and accommodations for the farming industry, showing that, fundamentally, this was a law motivated by economics—the country's need for cheap foreign labor, particularly in the agricultural sector—rather than concerns over social injustice, inequity, and greater inclusion.

3. According to recent census data, Salvadorans alone constitute the third-largest population of Hispanic origin living in the United States (Noe-Bustamante et al.)

4. As is also noted in chapter four, the adoption of neoliberal policies in the Central American region and free trade agreements such as the Dominican Republic-Central American Free Trade Agreement (CAFTA-DR) have likewise contributed to these migratory flows. Ratified in the mid-2000s, CAFTA-DR has had dire consequences for agriculture and subsistence farming, wages, and the environment in Central America, leading to decreased employment opportunities and population displacement.

5. Individual estimates from the Pew Research Center regarding the number of unauthorized immigrants pertaining to each of the noted countries are as follows: Salvadorans (51 percent), Guatemalans (56 percent), and Hondurans (60 percent) (Cohn et al., *Rise in U.S. Immigrants* 14).

6. In 2014, the Obama administration also sought to deter migration and asylum seekers from Central America by keeping entire families in detention, so as to quickly process and deport them back to their home countries. To this end, the administration opened two family holding facilities in Texas, adding to an existing facility in Pennsylvania. The policy of family detention under Obama, however, was challenged in court by immigrant rights activists under the Flores Agreement. This settlement agreement stemmed from a 1985 court case, *Flores vs. Reno*, involving the mistreatment of an unaccompanied minor from El Salvador, Jenny Lissette Flores, who fled the war and was held in custody with adult migrants. The settlement

resulting from this case set the government standard for the length of time and the conditions under which unaccompanied minors can be held in detention: twenty days. In the case against the Obama administration, the Ninth Circuit sided with immigration activists, ruling that the Flores Agreement also included accompanied children but did not address the issue of their parents. Consequently, the Obama administration made it a practice, for the most part, of releasing families after the allotted twenty-day detention period rather than separating them.

7. This program was also established by the Obama administration in an effort to curtail the unauthorized migration of unaccompanied minors from the isthmus.

8. See Associated Press, "More than 5,400 Children Split at the Border, According to New Count." According to this news story, the Trump administration reported separating 2,814 children from their parents between June and July 2018, when a federal court in San Diego ordered the administration to halt the practice. An additional 1,090 children were separated from their parents following the court order. Reports by the ACLU note, however, that the Trump administration also admitted to separating 1,556 children from July 2017 to June 2018, before its "zero tolerance" policy became official and went into effect.

9. In November 2019, the Trump administration issued yet another rule stating that it would seek out and implement "Asylum Cooperative Agreements" with El Salvador, Guatemala, and Honduras. Under said agreements, the United States would have the authority to deport potential asylum seekers back to one of the cooperating countries to have their asylum claims processed there instead. The premise was that these countries are "safe third countries." However, as critics have noted, this policy, like the related measures instituted, jeopardized the lives and well-being of asylum seekers because the "safe third countries" in question are the same nations from which the majority of these asylum seekers hail. Rather than an effective policy, these "agreements," as critics of the measure have suggested, provided yet another means of driving down the number of asylum seekers at US ports of entry.

10. President Joseph R. Biden, who defeated Trump in the November 2020 presidential election, campaigned on the promise that he would overturn many of the policies affecting Central American asylees at the US-Mexico border. Following his inauguration in early January 2021, Biden rescinded the zero-tolerance policy and signed executive orders directing the Department of Homeland Security to establish a task force to reunite nearly six hundred children with their parents and to consider reinstating the CAM program. Under Biden the MPP program has also been halted, and efforts have been made to begin processing the asylum claims of those individuals currently in the program. As of March 2021, closures of the US borders with Mexico and Canada remain in effect, as does the added measure of allowing CBP officials to automatically turn away unauthorized immigrants apprehended at either border, except for unaccompanied minors who are seventeen or younger.

11. This rescission was challenged in US district courts in California, New York, Maryland, and the District of Columbia, a litigation fight that eventually made its way to the US Supreme Court. In June 2020, the court ruled in a 5–4 decision

that the Trump administration's termination of the DACA program was unlawful because the administration had failed to sufficiently explain its reasons for doing so and had not considered alternatives to a complete rescission in keeping with the Administrative Procedure Act (APA). Thus, the court left open the possibility that the Trump administration could terminate the program if it followed proper procedures. Following the ruling, the Trump administration reinstated the program but sought to implement significant changes that would make renewals for active DACA recipients more expensive and difficult as well as curb new applications. Although the Biden administration fully reinstated the program, in July 2021 a federal judge ruled in a separate lawsuit, initiated by the State of Texas in December 2020, that DACA was illegal. The Biden administration is appealing the decision.

12. Pending legal challenges to the Trump administration's efforts to end TPS for individuals from the Central American countries of El Salvador, Honduras, and Nicaragua, as well as from Haiti, Nepal, and Sudan, have prevented these terminations from going into effect. Biden has pledged to undo Trump-era policies related to the TPS program and has proposed a pathway to citizenship for TPS holders as part of his immigration plan ("Fact Sheet: President Biden Sends Immigration Plan to Congress").

13. As England notes in *Afro Central Americans in New York City*, northbound migration by the Garifuna in Honduras has been primarily economically driven and predates the period of the 1980s and 1990s. However, the economic and political changes during these decades in the United States and Central America did impact the migration processes and patterns of the Garifuna. Similar to other Central American groups, rates of Garifuna migration to the United States have not decreased despite it being more difficult for the Garifuna to enter the country legally (64). The United States has likewise become a singular destination site for migrants, and Garifuna communities in Honduras have become more dependent on remittances for survival (64).

14. The genocide of the Maya population during Guatemala's thirty-six-year civil war has been well documented. According to the Truth Commission Report *Guatemala Memory of Silence*, produced by the Commission for Historical Clarification on Guatemala, 83 percent of the more than 200,000 civilians who were targeted and killed by government forces during this period were Maya (85).

15. The US Salvadoran humorist Wilfredo Santamaria is generally credited with launching the hashtag #CentralAmericanTwitter (Izaguirre).

16. Hall's basis for this notion is Foucault's concept of knowledge/power, which Hall explains in the following manner: "Knowledge when linked to power not only assumes the authority of 'the truth' but has the authority to *make itself true*. All knowledge, once applied in the real world, has real effects, and in that sense at least, 'becomes true'" ("Work" 49). Constituted through power (understood as decentralized), but also capable of inducing power, knowledge that takes on the appearance of truth can then be used to regulate/discipline the conduct of others and to oppress them, as Foucault effectively argues in *Discipline and Punish*.

17. As Stephen Benz elucidates, one of the enduring motifs that runs through US literature on Central America, dating back to the early nineteenth century, is

that of US travelers having to resist the dangers of the Central American tropics (52). It is not only the region's Edenic allure and the natives—portrayed as, among other things, simple and lazy, harbingers of disease, and depraved—against which North Americans must guard, but also a Central American culture that has spawned a violent and dysfunctional social order (56–57). Arguably, it is this US-centric view of the isthmian tropics, one that has historically been used to justify imperialist exploits in the region (60), that is channeled in the representations of war-torn Central America and its guerillas in the films in question.

18. Graden; Martin; and Zelazny provide further insight regarding the political prerogatives of the directors of these films.

19. See note 1 in this chapter.

20. See note 4 in this chapter.

21. Dalton employs this phrase in his well-known "Poema de amor" (Love Poem), which is an ode to the resiliency of the Salvadoran people in the face of numerous adversities. More than a description of the legal state of residing unauthorized in another country, Dalton's depiction of Salvadorans as "los eternos indocumentados" who labor in the United States and throughout parts of Latin America captures the sense of perpetual marginalization and rootlessness that is also part of the experience of being undocumented (36).

22. Consider another photograph that likewise achieved iconic status in 2018 at the height of the child-separation catastrophe at the US-Mexico border. The photograph shows a Honduran toddler crying hysterically while looking up at her mother, who is being arrested by a US border patrol agent. This image circulated widely in news media outlets and was featured on the cover of the July 2018 issue of *Time* magazine, titled "Welcome to America," with one notable difference: the crying child is alone and is looking up at Donald Trump. In this altered rendition of the photograph, the immigrant child epitomizes the complete infantilization of the Central American asylum seekers against whom the Trump administration waged a legislative and media war.

CHAPTER TWO: DOMESTICATED SUBJECT? THE SALVADORAN
MAID IN US TELEVISION AND FILM

1. Morrison appeared in a total of sixty-eight episodes during the show's first eight seasons.

2. Morrison announced her retirement from acting in 2017, just prior to the show's revival, and passed away in 2019.

3. See "Will and Grace Scene about Election Special."

4. Clara E. Rodríguez ("Introduction" 2); Valdivia (92); and Lichter and Amundson (65–67) all briefly note the typecasting of Latinas as the maid or as welfare mothers in films and television. These scholars view and contextualize this Latina image as consistent with a more general stereotype of women of color and do not engage or explore this image in further detail.

5. I am among the few Central Americanist scholars who have published work on this specific topic. Along with the original article "Domesticating Rosario," which serves as the basis for this chapter, see also "Migrant Marías" and "The Central American Transnational Imaginary."

6. *Maid in Manhattan* is a combination fairy-tale romance and rags-to-riches story. Lopez plays a Bronx-born maid and single mother who works in the hotel industry but dreams of being something more, and who falls in love with an Anglo Republican senatorial candidate. By the end of the film, she acquires both a successful career in hotel management and a "lasting relationship" with the newly elected senator. In *Spanglish*, Vega plays an immigrant maid from Mexico trying to provide for herself and her daughter by working for a wealthy and dysfunctional Anglo family in Los Angeles. The story is partially narrated by the maid's daughter, who is writing about her mother as the topic of her college entrance exam. In essence, the daughter is a living embodiment of the American Dream, which Vega's character earned via her hard work.

7. With regard to *West Side Story*, see the works by Jímenez; Pérez; and Sánchez.

8. Studies on the figure and image of the mammy are numerous. Notable works include Wallace-Sanders's *Mammy*; Morgan's "Mammy the Huckster"; Collins's chapter "Mammies, Matriarchs, and Other Controlling Images" in *Black Feminist Thought*; and Harris's earlier literary-based analysis *From Mammies to Militants*.

9. One of the last shows to feature an African American maid working for an all-Anglo middle-class family was the 1950s show *Beulah*, which ceased to exist, in large part, due to the protests and boycotts by African American civil rights groups (Lichter and Amundson 57–59).

10. The persistence of this image is not indicative of a lack of Chicanx-based activism against the limiting portrayals and images of Chicanx and Latinx peoples on screen. In his seminal work on Chicanx films and resistance, Chon Noriega notes that the 1960s and '70s Chicanx cinema that emerged as part of the Chicanx civil rights movement was very much an attempt by Chicanx filmmakers and video artists to create and represent alternatives to what were "abusive stereotypes" (xviii).

11. In his discussion concerning the difficulties of studying representation within the situational comedy, Brett Mills contends that sitcom analysis must take into account not only a particular program's jokes but also the genre's narrative aspects, for "[w]hile a specific joke may rest on stereotypes and may be told by a character who supports such stereotypes, the narrative within a specific episode, or that stretched across the series as a whole, may suggest a very different reading" (107). Mills also argues that looking at performance, especially performances in excess (physical or emotional), which is a conventional trait of sitcoms, can be equally revealing. Such observations are suggestive of the fact that the situational comedy is a rather complex form that has the potential to provide critical representations even while making use of stereotypes. As I detail in my analysis of Rosario, however, this character and the narrative of servitude constructed about and around her do little to challenge the stereotype of the Latina maid.

12. Mitchell makes the related argument that the show's "contained images" of

gayness and lack of diversity work to reaffirm "oppressive ideologies of class, race, sexuality, and patriarchy" (1052).

13. Gerken writes, "According to neoliberal political ideology in the mid-1990s, the emphasis on free trade, open markets, and personal merit [that were key to such ideology] was not only inherently race and gender neutral but was actually designed to further antiracist and antisexist policies" (76). The neoliberal mindset that permeated the Clinton administration's governance of the country in the 1990s was thus seen as "progressive." The opposite is, in fact, true, with many of the neoliberal policies and reforms instituted under Clinton proving detrimental to communities of color, in particular African Americans and (Latin American) immigrants. Here I am thinking of the 1994 North American Free Trade Agreement (NAFTA), the 1994 Crime Bill, the 1995 Illegal Immigration Reform and Immigrant Responsibility Act (IIRIRA), the 1996 Personal Responsibility and Work Opportunity Reconciliation Act (PRWORA), and the 1996 Antiterrorism and Effective Death Penalty Act (AEDPA).

14. Cooper offers a more in-depth discussion of gay humor and the use of camp on the show.

15. On this point, see Arias's discussion in *Taking Their Word* (206–213).

16. Gregory Hines had a brief guest appearance on the show as Will's boss and Grace's love interest during the second and third seasons. The series' revival has been similarly criticized for its lack of racial and ethnic diversity. See Barnes.

17. I discuss the 1996 IIRIRA in chapter one and chapter three.

18. Indeed, in the series' original finale, Grace has a dream in which Karen and Rosario are in a romantic relationship.

19. The *Will and Grace* official website has since been updated for the reboot and no longer features this information. It originally appeared under the cast description for Shelley Morrison.

20. These include *True Love* (1989), *Household Saints* (1993), and *The 24 Hour Woman* (1999), featuring Rosie Perez as a single mother struggling to successfully balance her career and family life. Savoca's other notable films include *Dogfight* (1991), *If These Walls Could Talk* (1996), and *Union Square* (2012).

21. Although it merits further exploration, it is important to note that the film's soundtrack, edited by Suzana Peric, is another important site of *Latinidad*. The soundtrack draws from a numerous selection of artists and musical styles from throughout Latin America, Spain, and the United States, including the Latin Playboys (David Hidalgo and Louie Pérez of Los Lobos), who composed the original score and two original songs for the film.

CHAPTER THREE: LANCE CORPORAL JOSÉ GUTIÉRREZ AND
THE PERILS OF BEING A "GOOD IMMIGRANT"

1. The other three green card soldiers whose deaths influenced the passage of this act were Marine Lance Corporal Jesús Suárez del Solar and Corporal José Angel Garibay from Mexico, and Army Private First Class Diego Rincón from Colombia.

2. Building on the tenets of an executive order signed by George W. Bush the year prior that granted automatic citizenship to noncitizens who enlisted in the armed forces, this law also shortened the qualifying time that noncitizen military personnel who were currently serving had to wait in order to apply for citizenship.

3. See, for example, Nomad; Godinez; and Ordoñez. Unlike the other two entries, Ordoñez's news article does not reference Gutiérrez's story within the written text; rather it includes a photograph of Gutiérrez's funeral services in Guatemala, in which his graduation portrait as a US marine factors prominently. This image is used to visually frame the article's news narrative.

4. A media frame consists of "the words, images, phrases, and presentation styles that a speaker (e.g., a politician, a media outlet) uses when relaying information about an issue or event to an audience" (Haynes et al. 18).

5. Regarding these two points, see Neuman et al.; Valkenburg et al.; and Haynes et al.

6. The issue of noncitizen veterans being subject to deportation precedes the Trump administration. However, the administration's anti-immigrant efforts, including a 2017 executive order signed by the president expanding the definition of who can be classified as a criminal and therefore prioritized for deportation, are seen as one of the reasons why there was an uptick in noncitizen veteran deportations after Trump took office. Some cases concerning the detention and deportation of noncitizen veterans have garnered national attention, such as that of José Segovia-Benitez, a Marine Corps veteran who was deported back to El Salvador in 2019. Like Gutiérrez, Segovia-Benitez served in the Iraq War, during which he sustained a traumatic brain injury, resulting in his honorable discharge from the military in 2004. Segovia-Benitez was deported on account of the felony convictions he incurred following his service years and while also battling PTSD.

7. On this topic, see Mariscal, "Homeland Security, Militarism, and the Future of Latinos and Latinas in the United States."

8. Gerken refers specifically to the Personal Responsibility and Work Opportunity Reconciliation Act (PRWORA) and the Antiterrorism and Effective Death Penalty Act (AEDPA), which were both passed by Congress and signed into law by Bill Clinton in 1996. Included in the many provisions of the PRWORA, which was meant to reform the federal welfare system, were several new funding restrictions and citizenship requirements for immigrants seeking public benefits. The AEDPA, passed in the aftermath of the 1995 Oklahoma City bombing, greatly expanded the grounds for detaining and deporting immigrants, including long-term residents. This law also laid the foundation for the prolonged detention of immigrants, the fast tracking of deportation procedures, and the curtailing of asylee rights that is widespread today.

9. One of Gutiérrez's adult foster sisters, for instance, is quoted as stating something similar in a *USA Today* article: "Gutiérrez 'wanted to give the United States what the United States gave to him. He came with nothing. This country gave him everything'" (Kasindorf).

10. The online version I am referencing here appears with the title "Green Card

Marines: A Guatemalan Orphan—Artistic, Poetic—Sought a Better Life in the U.S." on the *Los Angeles Times* website (www.latimes.com/local/california/la-me -green-card-marines-gutierrez-archives-snap-htmlstory.html).

11. In such states, "power (and not necessarily state power) continuously refers to and appeals to exception, emergency, and a fictionalized notion of the enemy. It also labors to produce the same exception, emergency, and fictionalized enemy" (Mbembe 16). Those in control, or wishing to control, therefore exercise their right to kill indiscriminately and to operate outside of the judicial order.

12. The USA Patriot Act was signed into law by President Bush six weeks after the attacks on 9/11. It effectively changed surveillance laws, allowing the FBI to conduct surveillance without a warrant, expanding the use of national security letters, and greenlighting searches of homes or businesses without the owners' consent or knowledge. It also allowed for the indefinite detention of immigrants, even if they were not charged with or suspected of terrorism. The National Security Entry-Exit Registration System, also known as NSEERS, was essentially a screening system that required certain noncitizens to register domestically and to be monitored when leaving and entering the United States. Individuals from Muslim countries composed the vast majority of the those targeted and forced to register. Several thousand were also consequently placed in deportation proceedings. However, the implementation of this system, which operated in some form or another from 2002 to 2016, never led to any terrorist-related convictions.

13. On this point, see my discussion of the 2010 DREAM Act and the rhetoric surrounding Dreamer exceptionality in chapter five.

14. The remaining articles in the series include "Former MS-13 Member Who Secretly Helped Police Is Deported"; "Teen Who Faced Deportation after He Informed on MS-13 Gets Temporary Reprieve"; "Teenage MS-13 Gang Informant Heads into Final Asylum Hearing"; and "Were Henry's Civil Rights Violated?" Most of these articles were also simultaneously published in *New York Magazine.*

15. The other two feature stories for which Dreier garnered the Pulitzer Prize were not about Henry. However, they still consisted of human-interest pieces that, like "A Betrayal," revealed the discriminatory nature and shortsightedness of Trump administration policies intended to crack down on MS-13. Both stories were likewise focused on Salvadoran immigrant youth residing in Long Island, New York.

16. These advocacy efforts also included a GoFundMe campaign, "Save Triste's Life," started by Henry's immigration lawyer, as well as an eight-minute video titled "Triste's Story," which makes use of Henry's own words and animation to tell his story. The video was featured as part of the article "A Betrayal" on the *ProPublica* website and can also be found on YouTube. As Dreier notes in the related piece "Former MS-13 Member Who Secretly Helped Police Is Deported," the substantial amount of money raised through this campaign from reader donations was used to relocate Triste to Europe after his deportation back to El Salvador.

1. Related print media and journalistic accounts, which notably have achieved far greater visibility and circulation than the documentaries listed, include Sonia Nazario's *Enrique's Journey: The Story of a Boy's Dangerous Journey to Reunite with His Mother* and Óscar Martínez's *The Beast: Riding the Rails and Dodging Narcos on the Migrant Trail*. Nazario's book, a national bestseller, first appeared as a series of Pulitzer Prize–winning articles published in the *Los Angeles Times* in 2002.

2. In 2019, after significant pressure from the Trump administration to help stop the flow of undocumented Central American migrants to the United States, the Mexican government sent nearly fifteen thousand members of the National Guard to the US-Mexico border. It also deployed another two thousand troops to Mexico's southern border with Guatemala and Belize (T. Arias).

3. Julianne Burton's edited volume *The Social Documentary in Latin America*, in particular her introductory chapter, "Toward a History of Social Documentary in Latin America," provides an essential foundation for understanding the history and development of the New Latin American Cinema movement as well as the centrality of documentary filmmaking within it. Regarding US-based documentaries about "illegal immigration" that are more immigrant-centered, see Anne Teresa Demo's "Decriminalizing Illegal Immigration: Immigrants' Rights through the Documentary Lens."

4. Critiques of Central American governments are also evident in these films, although they are conveyed in a less forceful manner. In their condemnations of Mexico and the United States, many directors of migrant shelters and human rights activists, for example, also address the failure of Central American governments to educate their citizens about the dangers of migrating through Mexico as well as the lack of power these same governments have to advocate on behalf of their citizens once abroad.

5. Shaw's analysis is concerned with a subgenre of mostly fiction-based migration films that first emerged in the early 2000s. She provides readers with a survey-like assessment of these films, emphasizing works such as Cary Fukunaga's commercially successful independent feature *Sin nombre*. Although Shaw does make note of documentaries such as *De nadie* and *Crossing Arizona* (2006), suggesting that they, too, fall within the category of "Central American/Mexican/U.S. migration films," she does not discuss these films or any such documentaries at length in her article.

6. Except for the translation of this passage, which is my own, the translations from Spanish to English of statements made by individuals featured in these documentaries and song lyrics correspond to the DVD subtitles or related materials. Translations of names of shelters and government agencies, official titles of individuals working in certain capacities, and the like that are not otherwise provided in these DVDs are also my own.

7. See my article "Migrant Marías."

8. Oscar Arnulfo Romero was the archbishop of San Salvador in the late 1970s.

His growing advocacy on behalf of the poor, social justice, and human rights led to his assassination in 1980 at the start of the Salvadoran civil war (1980–1992). Since then, Romero has become a hero for advocates of liberation theology and a key symbol of resistance and national pride both in and outside of El Salvador (see, for example, my discussion in chapter five regarding efforts led by the US Salvadoran community in Los Angeles to honor Romero's legacy). In 2015, Romero was also officially declared a martyr by Pope Francis and beatified as a saint.

9. Mexico more than doubled the number of detention centers in its territory in the eight-year span from 2000 to 2008, going from twenty-two to forty-eight (Alba). Recent reports likewise detail a significant rise in deportations from Mexico and confirm its ranking among the highest of immigration-detaining countries in the world, next to the United States. According to statistical data provided by the Global Detention Project, from 2015 to 2019 Mexico detained an average of 150,000 individuals per year. In 2019 alone, Mexico detained over 180,000, ranking among the highest detainee countries in the world. The number of voluntary returns and deportations for 2017 (the most recent year available) was 82,237. That same year, most of the individuals apprehended were from El Salvador, Guatemala, and Honduras ("Mexico Immigration Detention Profile"). Given the continued increase in migration from the region in the years since, it is likely that these same individuals continue to account for the majority of those detained.

10. Like its 1994 predecessor, the North American Free Trade Agreement (NAFTA), the SPP focuses on the expansion of commerce and trade between Canada, the United States, and Mexico. It also, however, includes significant provisions in terms of border enforcement and securitization that NAFTA did not. Pacts such as the SPP, which have become more paramount as immigration, terrorism, and national security have been increasingly linked in the post-9/11 era, are most beneficial to developed nations such as the United States that have the means to offer less powerful bordering nations such as Mexico "various concessions on trade and foreign assistance while exerting pressure on them to clamp down on transit migration" (Menjívar, "Immigration Law" 358). Similar dynamics characterize the Mérida Initiative, a binational agreement focused more specifically on crime and securitization that calls for the allocation of 2.5 billion dollars in US aid to Mexico for the purposes, among other things, of combating drug trafficking and internal corruption, and aiding in the establishment of a "21st century border" (Seelke and Finklea 14).

11. The United States-Mexico-Canada Agreement (USMCA), which went into effect in July 2020, did not significantly change the immigration and securitization measures stipulated in NAFTA, the trade agreement that the USMCA renegotiated and replaced.

12. Mexico participated in the Memorandum of Understanding for the Dignified, Orderly, Swift, and Safe Repatriation of Central American Migrants by Land in 2006, which outlined Mexico's responsibilities to provide safe transfer and care for Central American migrants who were arrested and repatriated back to their home countries (Cruz 1032). In 2011, the Mexican government updated its immigration

law to include key provisions that uphold Mexico's unwavering commitment to ensuring migrants' human rights independent of their legal status and that aim to ensure equality between Mexican nationals and immigrants. Included in the new law were also provisions for immigrant children and the detainment and processing of undocumented youth (Alba). The passage of this law was partly in response to the international pressure and public outcry against the Mexican government over the abduction and massacre of seventy-two undocumented migrants in the northern state of Tamaulipas (one hundred miles from Brownsville, Texas) in August 2010. As was widely reported, this kidnapping and mass killing was carried out with the aid of local police ("Mexico Becoming").

13. Human rights organizations, civil NGOs, and migrant advocacy groups have long been critical of how the Mexican state enforces its immigration and border security policies. Although officials from the National Immigration Institute (INM) are the only ones legally authorized to ask for proof of citizenship status from suspected migrants and to detain them, federal agencies such as the Department of Exterior Relations and the Department of Public Security, including the Federal Preventive Police, as well as local and state police units also routinely engage in these types of immigration enforcement. Corruption is rampant among these groups, as these officials often subject migrants to forms of abuse ranging from bribes to kidnapping for ransom and have no fear of legal repercussions. Further compounding this situation are the abuses perpetrated against undocumented migrants during their arrests and detainment in unsanitary holding facilities.

14. Edur Velasco Arregui and Richard Roman likewise conceive of Mexico as a "passage" for Central Americans in their article "Perilous Passage: Central American Migration through Mexico." As part of their social science–based framework, Arregui and Roman, however, analogize the migration of Central Americans through Mexico with that of African slaves across the Atlantic. While acknowledging that these processes cannot be unequivocally compared, they nevertheless highlight key parallels between the two, primarily on the basis of socioeconomic factors. For example, they state that Central American migrants also provide "cheap and 'flexible' labor for U.S. capital" and must contend with "a state-inflicted system of brutality and exploitation" in their journey (38–39). They also note that although "coercion is not the main direct mechanism in the 'recruitment' of Central American labor," as was the case for African captives, "it is present at a variety of levels, from the use of force to impose market relations that destroy traditional ways of earning a livelihood to the experience of coercion in the journey north" (39).

15. Wendy A. Vogt's ethnographic study *Lives in Transit* offers a similar understanding of what she terms the "*cachuco* industry," "*cachuco*" (dirty pig) being a derogatory term referring to Central American migrants in Mexico. Vogt contends that the "*cachuco* industry," which is buttressed by "the systematization of kidnapping, smuggling, and extortion" and is "where violence becomes the central mechanism through which vulnerabilities are produced and profits derived," represents a new phase in the commodification process of migrant labor under capitalism (86).

16. The importation of lower priced agricultural products from the United States

has made it impossible for local farmers to compete, while workers concentrated in export assembly plants (one of the few sectors of growth resulting from this free trade deal) continue to be paid low wages and subjected to multiple forms of abuse, including hazardous working conditions. The extraction of national resources by transnational corporations has also taken place with little or no environmental protections in place, leading to the pollution of water sources, as in the case of the toxic mining industry. Both the destabilization of agricultural industries and increased environmental hazards have led to the displacement of various communities in Central America and increased international migration.

CHAPTER FIVE: THE CACHET OF ILLEGAL CHICKENS IN
CENTRAL AMERICAN LOS ANGELES

1. Images of Cache's chicken murals are easily accessible on various Los Angeles–based blog sites. Also available via YouTube are the short documentary videos "Cache: Don't Be a Chicken" and "Cache's Chickens."

2. For more information on Eye One's art, see his website EyeOne/Seeking Heaven at www.eyelost.com/eyeoneblog/index.php?catid=11 and the YouTube clip "Art and Activism with Eyeone."

3. "Street art" is a broad term that refers to both a global movement that has steadily gained ground since the 1980s and the wide array of urban art expressions that characterize it. These include but are not limited to graffiti (simple "tags" of the artist's name made with a marker or aerosol paint, or more complex pieces with highly stylized or bubble-style letters and images), stenciling, murals, stickerbombing (placement of stickers, usually with a distinct image on various public surfaces), subvertising (alterations made to advertisements), wheatpasting (the adhesion of posters previously made by the artist on walls or other surfaces), and street sculpture (the placement of objects made by the artist in public spaces). The class backgrounds and skill level of those who practice this form of art are as varied as the works they produce; practitioners range from self-taught or intuitive artists who have honed their skills in graffiti crews to classically trained artists who attended world-class art institutes and universities. Not all individuals who have been associated with the term embrace it fully, as in the case of Cache, who prefers to be referenced as a graffiti writer rather than labeled a street artist despite the fact that he does produce street art.

4. Concerning the beginnings, evolution, and broader social and cultural significance of this movement, see Austin; Snyder.

5. Although the work of many street artists, in particular those who have acquired broad notoriety such as Banksy or Shepard Fairey, reflects a unique style or trademark that is easily recognizable, in general such works do not reveal individual or personal attributes of the artists themselves. As Allan Schwartzman suggests, unlike graffiti artists who use their art to stand apart from the crowd, street artists seek "to merge with the crowd" and "vehemently cour[t]" anonymity (62).

6. As of this writing, this mural is still in existence.

7. To be eligible for the benefits of the 2010 DREAM Act, undocumented youth needed to have arrived in the United States prior to the age of sixteen and have a clean criminal record; in other words, they had to prove their good moral standing and character. Having met these initial requirements, Dreamers would be granted conditional legal status that would protect them from deportation and allow them limited benefits such as the ability to apply for a driver's license and pursue employment and/or a higher education degree. During the ensuing six-year period, they would continue to be subject to criminal background checks and reviews. They would also be expected to complete two years of college education or service in the military and pay for all fees related to the processing of their immigration case, after which they would be able to apply for legal permanent status. Many of these requirements mirror those that were instituted as part of the DACA program.

8. These more whimsical figures are newer updates, added by Cache sometime after the mural's initial completion in 2013.

9. The first of these sites is a busy intersection at the corner of South Vermont Avenue and West Pico Boulevard that was declared Msgr. Oscar A. Romero Square in 2012. The second is a plaza in MacArthur Park, a hub of Central American social and political activity located in the Westlake neighborhood, which was inaugurated in 2013.

10. See Cárdenas, "Performing *Centralamericanismo*."

11. See, for example, Ferrell's discussion of "hip hop graffiti" in *Crimes of Style*. Austin and Snyder each also provide discussions of the historical and ongoing links between hip-hop and graffiti.

12. Although it is not clear when exactly Mid-City Arts went out of business, postings for shows and events at the gallery seem to indicate that it closed in the early 2010s.

13. *Remembering Angel Island* ran from June 2010 to December 2012 at the museum. It commemorated the one hundredth anniversary of the opening of Angel Island, the first immigration station on the West Coast. During its thirty years of operation, from 1910 to 1940, the station processed more than one million immigrants from over eighty countries, including 175,000 Chinese people.

14. In 2019, the largest workplace raid to date transpired in Morton County, Mississippi. According to media accounts, ICE raided six poultry processing plants and detained somewhere between 680 and 700 undocumented workers. The raid was carried out on the first day of school, sparking public outrage, as several children had one or both of their parents detained and were, in effect, terrorized by the prospect of not knowing whether they would see their parents again or who would care for them in the interim. A large portion of the immigrant workers taken into custody were also of Central American descent, particularly from Guatemala. As happened in Postville, Iowa, employers of the processing plants have not been subjected to the same level of legal scrutiny and actions. In fact, none of the employers of the plants have been brought up on criminal charges of any kind.

15. A similar critique has likewise been made of the DACA program and its recipients.

16. I am referring specifically to Nazario's *Enrique's Journey* as well as the documentary films *De nadie* and *Maria en tierra de nadie*.

CONCLUSION

1. For further discussion of US Central American and Chicanx/Mexican American intra-ethnic relationships, see Karina O. Alvarado; and Cárdenas's "Performing *Centralaméricanismo*" and chapter four of her book *Constituting Central American-Americans*.

2. For example, Anzaldúa; Calderón and Saldívar; Hicks; and Rosaldo.

3. In the opening verses of her book, Anzaldúa writes, "1,950 mile-long open wound / dividing a *pueblo*, a cultura, / running down the length of my body, / staking fence rods in my flesh, / splits me splits me / *me raja me raja*" (2).

4. In addition to Contreras's *Blood Lines*, on this topic concerning the relationship between Chicanxs and Mexico, see Bruce-Novoa's essay "Mexico in Chicano Literature" in *Retrospace*.

5. See, for example, Vila; and Johnson and Michaelsen.

6. See chapter 1, notes 10, 12, and 13.

Works Cited

Abbott, Paul, and John Wells, creators. *Shameless*. Bonanza Productions, 2011.

Abrego, Leisy J. "#CentAmStudies from a Social Science Perspective." *Latino Studies*, vol. 15, no. 1, 2017, pp. 95–98.

Agencia EFE. "Documentary Looks at Migrants' Plight in Mexico." *PV Angels*, 1 Mar. 2013, www.pvangels.com/news-mexico/5770/la-bestia-documentary -looks-at-migrants-plight-in-mexico.

Alba, Franciso. "Mexico: The New Migration Narrative." Migration Policy Institute, 24 Apr. 2013, www.migrationpolicy.org/article/mexico-new-migration-narrative.

Alegría, Andrea. "Political Chickens in Whimsical Worlds." *Eastside Living LA*, 21 Feb. 2009. *Internet Archive Wayback Machine*, https://web.archive.org/web /20090307202653/www.eastsidelivingla.com/?p=808. Accessed 4 Aug. 2021.

Alvarado, Karina O. "An Interdisciplinary Reading of Chicana/o and (U.S.) Central American Internarrations." *Latino Studies*, vol. 2, no. 3, 2013, pp. 366–387.

Alvarado, Karina O., et al., editors. *U.S. Central Americans: Reconstructing Memories, Struggles, and Communities of Resistance*. University of Arizona Press, 2017.

Amaya, Hector. "Dying American or the Violence of Citizenship: Latinos in Iraq." *Latino Studies*, vol. 5, no. 1, 2007, pp. 3–24.

———. "Latino Immigrants in the American Discourses of Citizenship and Nationalism during the Iraqi War." *Critical Discourse Studies*, vol. 4, no. 3, 2007, pp. 237–256.

Anderson, Mark. *Black and Indigenous: Garifuna Activism and Consumer Culture in Honduras*. University of Minnesota Press, 2009.

Anderson, Mark, and Sarah England. "¿Auténtica cultural africana en Honduras? Los afrocentroamericanos desafían el mestizaje indohispano en Honduras." *Memorias del Mestizaje: Cultura política en Centroamérica de 1920 al presente*, edited by Darío A. Euraque et al., Cirma, 2004, pp. 253–294.

Anguiano, Claudia A., and Karma R. Chávez. "DREAMers' Discourse: Young Latino/a Immigrants and the Naturalization of the American Dream." *Latina/o*

Discourse in Vernacular Spaces: Somos de Una Voz?, edited by Michelle A. Holling and Bernadette M. Calafell, Lexington Books, 2011, pp. 81–99.

Anzaldúa, Gloria. *Borderlands/La Frontera: The New Mestiza*. Aunt Lute, 1987.

Aparicio, Frances R. "Jennifer as Selena: Re-thinking Latinidad in Media and Popular Culture." *Latino Studies*, vol. 1, no. 1, 2003, pp. 90–105.

Aparicio, Frances R., and Susana Chávez-Silverman, editors. *Tropicalizations: Transcultural Representations of Latinidad*. Dartmouth College Press, 1997.

"Approximate Active DACA Recipients: Country of Birth. As of September 30, 2020." U.S. Citizenship and Immigration Services, 2020, www.uscis.gov/sites/default/files/document/reports/DACA_Population_Receipts_since_Injunction_Sep_30_2020.pdf. Accessed 10 Mar. 2021. PDF.

Arax, Mark, et al. "Death of a Dream: A Guatemalan Orphan—Artistic, Poetic—Sought a Better Life in the U.S." *Green Card Marines, Los Angeles Times*, 25 May 2003. *ProQuest*, www.proquest.com/newspapers/green-card-marines-death-dream-guatemalan-orphan/docview/421785565/se-2?accountid=8361.

Arias, Arturo. *Taking Their Word: Literature and the Signs of Central America*. University of Minnesota Press, 2007.

———. "What Are Central American Studies?" *Latino Studies*, vol. 15, no. 1, 2017, pp. 99–102.

Arias, Arturo, and Claudia Milian. "US Central Americans: Representations, Agency, and Communities." *Latino Studies*, vol. 11, no. 2, 2013, pp. 131–149.

Arias, Tatiana. "Mexico Sends Nearly 15,000 Troops to the US Border." CNN, 24 June 2019, www.cnn.com/2019/06/24/americas/mexico-sends-15000-troops-to-us-mexico-border-intl/index.html.

Arregui, Edur Velasco, and Richard Roman. "Perilous Passage: Central American Migration through Mexico." *Latino Los Angeles: Transformations, Communities, and Activism*, edited by Enrique C. Ochoa and Gilda L. Ochoa, University of Arizona Press, 2005, pp. 38–62.

"Art and Activism with Eyeone." *YouTube*, uploaded by LA Street Art Gallery, 14 Jan. 2013, www.youtube.com/watch?v=z65RAV5kwbA.

Asalto al sueño. Directed by Uli Stelzner, Gruppe ISKA, 2006.

As Good as It Gets. Directed by James L. Brooks, Tristar Pictures, 1997.

Associated Press. "More than 5,400 Children Split at Border, According to New Count." NBC News, 25 Oct. 2019, www.nbcnews.com/news/us-news/more-5-400-children-split-border-according-new-count-n1071791.

Austin, Joe. *Taking the Train: How Graffiti Became an Urban Crisis in New York City*. Columbia University Press, 2001.

Babel. Directed by Alejandro González Iñárritu, Paramount Pictures, 2006.

Baker, Beth F., and Ester E. Hernández. "Defining Central American Studies." *Latino Studies*, vol. 15, no. 1, 2017, pp. 86–90.

Bal, Mieke. *Double Exposures: The Subject of Cultural Analysis*. Routledge, 1996.

Barnes, Brooks. "'Will and Grace' Is Back. Will Its Portrait of Gay Life Hold Up?" *New York Times*, 14 Sept. 2017, www.nytimes.com/2017/09/14/arts/television/will-grace-debra-messing-eric-mccormack.html.

Battles, Kathleen, and Wendy Hilton-Morrow. "Gay Characters in Conventional Spaces: *Will and Grace* and the Situation Comedy Genre." *Critical Studies in Media Communication*, vol. 19, no. 1, 2002, pp. 87–105.

Batz, Giovanni. "Maya Cultural Resistance in Los Angeles: The Recovery of Identity and Culture among Maya Youth." *Latin American Perspectives*, vol. 41, no. 3, 2014, pp. 194–207. *JSTOR*, www.jstor.org/stable/24573923.

Bell, Vikki. "Performativity and Belonging: An Introduction." *Performativity and Belonging*, edited by Bell, Sage Publications, 1991, pp. 1–10.

Benz, Stephen. "Through the Tropical Looking Glass: The Motif of Resistance in U.S. Literature on Central America." *Tropicalizations: Transcultural Representations of Latinidad*, edited by Frances R. Aparicio and Susana Chávez-Silverman, Dartmouth College Press, 1997, pp. 51–66.

Berlant, Lauren. "Compassion (and Withholding)." Introduction. *Compassion: The Culture and Politics of an Emotion*, edited by Berlant, Routledge, 2004, pp. 1–14.

———. *The Queen of America Goes to Washington: Essays on Sex and Citizenship*. Duke University Press, 1997.

Bermudez, Esmeralda. "Pico-Union Intersection to Be Named for Salvadoran Archbishop." *L.A. Now* (blog), *Los Angeles Times*, 20 Jan. 2012, www.latimesblogs.latimes.com/lanow/2012/01/pico-union-intersection-to-be-named-for-salvadoran-clergy.html.

Biron, Rebecca E. "City/Art: Setting the Scene." Introduction. *City/Art: The Urban Scene in Latin America*, edited by Biron, Duke University Press, 2009, pp. 1–35.

Bloch, Stefano. "The Illegal Face of Wall Space: Graffiti-Murals on the Sunset Boulevard Retaining Walls." *Radical History Review*, no. 113, 2012, pp. 111–125.

Boj Lopez, Floridalma. "Mobile Archives of Indigeneity: Building La Comunidad Ixim through Organizing in the Maya Diaspora." *Latino Studies*, vol. 15, no. 2, 2017, pp. 201–218, doi.org/10.1057/s41276-017-0056-0.

———. "Weavings That Rupture: The Possibility of Contesting Settler Colonialism through Cultural Retention among the Maya Diaspora." *U.S. Central Americans: Reconstructing Memories, Struggles, and Communities of Resistance*, edited by Alvarado et al., University of Arizona Press, pp. 108–203.

Boykoff, Jules, and Kaia Sand. *Landscapes of Dissent: Guerrilla Poetry and Public Space*. Palm, 2008.

Brantner, Cornelia, et al. "Effects of Visual Framing on Emotional Responses and Evaluations of News Stories about the Gaza Conflict 2009." *Journalism and Mass Communication Quarterly*, vol. 88, no. 3, 2011, pp. 523–540.

Brick, Kate, et al. *Mexican and Central American Immigrants in the United States*. Report. Migration Policy Institute, June 2011, www.migrationpolicy.org/research/mexican-and-central-american-immigrants-united-states. Accessed 7 June 2013. PDF.

Bruce-Novoa, Juan. *Retrospace: Collected Essays on Chicano Literature, Theory, and History*. Arte Público, 1990.

Bump, Phillip. "The White House Statement on DACA, Annotated." *Washington Post*, 5 Sept. 2017, www.washingtonpost.com/news/politics/wp/2017/09/05/the-white-house-statement-on-daca-annotated/.

Burton, Julianne. *The Social Documentary in Latin America*. University of Pittsburgh Press, 1990.

"Cache." *Beautiful Decay Artist and Design*, 12 Apr. 2010, *Internet Archive Wayback Machine*, https://web.archive.org/web/20100415161811/beautifuldecay.com/2010/04/12/cache/. Accessed 4 Aug. 2021.

Cache. Interview. Conducted by Yajaira Padilla, 9 Sept. 2013.

———. "Re: Two more questions . . ." Received by Yajaira Padilla, 12 Sept. 2013.

"Cache's Chickens." *YouTube*, uploaded by Fairdale Bikes, 1 Nov. 2016, www.youtube.com/watch?v=V44IO-ik2BM.

Cacho, Lisa Marie. *Social Death: Racialized Rightlessness and the Criminalization of the Unprotected*. New York University Press, 2012.

Calderón, Héctor, and José David Saldívar, editors. *Criticism in the Borderlands: Studies in Chicano Literature, Culture, and Ideology*. Duke University Press, 1991.

Cárdenas, Maritza E. *Constituting Central American-Americans: Transnational Identities and the Politics of Dislocation*. Rutgers University Press, 2018.

———. "Is Carlos Mencia a White Wetback? Mediating the (E)Racing of U.S. Central Americans in the Latino Imaginary." *Race and Contention in Twenty-First Century U.S. Media*, edited by Jason A. Smith and Bhoomi K. Thakore, Routledge, 2006, pp. 70–84.

———. "Performing *Centralaméricanismo*: Isthmian Identities at the COFECA Independence Day Parade." *U.S. Central Americans: Reconstructing Memories, Struggles, and Communities of Resistance*, edited by Karina O. Alvarado et al., University of Arizona Press, 2017, pp. 127–143.

Caso, Nicole. *Practicing Memory in Central American Literature*. Palgrave Macmillan, 2010.

Castillo, Ana. *Sapogonia (An Anti-romance in 3/8 Meter)*. Anchor Books/Doubleday, 1994.

"CCEN Presentación Documental María en Tierra de Nadie, Buenos Días Nicaragua, Canal 12." *YouTube*, uploaded by Crea Comunicaciones, 13 Apr. 2011, www.youtube.com/watch?v=LaebOvFMY_M.

Chavez, Leo R. *Covering Immigration: Popular Images and the Politics of the Nation*. University of California Press, 2001.

———. *The Latino Threat: Constructing Immigrants, Citizens, and the Nation*. Stanford University Press, 2008.

Cherry, Marc, creator. *Devious Maids*, ABC Studios, 2013.

Chishti, Muzaffar, et al. "At Its 25th Anniversary, IRCA's Legacy Lives On." Migration Policy Institute, 16 Nov. 2011, www.migrationpolicy.org/article/its-25th-anniversary-ircas-legacy-lives.

Clueless. Directed by Amy Heckerling, Paramount Pictures, 1995.

Cohn, D'Vera, et al. "Many Immigrants with Temporary Protected Status Face Uncertain Future in U.S." Pew Research Center, 27 Nov. 2019, pewresearch.org/fact-tank/2019/11/27/immigrants-temporary-protected-status-in-us/.

———. *Rise in U.S. Immigrants from El Salvador, Guatemala, and Honduras Outpaces Growth from Elsewhere*. Report. Pew Research Center, 7 Dec. 2017, www

.pewresearch.org/hispanic/2017/12/07/rise-in-u-s-immigrants-from-el-salvador
-guatemala-and-honduras-outpaces-growth-from-elsewhere/.

Collins, Patricia Hill. *Black Feminist Thought: Knowledge, Consciousness, and the Politics of Empowerment*. Routledge, 1991.

Contreras, Sheila Marie. *Blood Lines: Myth, Indigenism, and Chicana/o Literature*. University of Texas Press, 2008.

Cooper, Evan. "Decoding *Will and Grace*: Mass Audience Reception of Popular Network Situation Comedy." *Sociological Perspectives*, vol. 46, no. 4, 2003, pp. 513–533.

Cortez-Davis, Evelyn. *December Sky: Beyond My Undocumented Life*. Cuicatl Productions, 2003.

Coutin, Susan Bibler. *Legalizing Moves: Salvadoran Immigrants' Struggles for U.S. Residency*. University of Michigan Press, 2003.

Crane, David, and Marta Kauffman, creators. *Veronica's Closet*. Bright/Kauffman/Crane Productions, 1997.

Crittle, Simon. "In Death, a Marine Gets His Life Wish." *Time*, 28 Mar. 2003, www.content.time.com/time/world/article/0,8599,438626,00.html.

Crossing Arizona. Directed by Dan DeVivo and Joseph Mathew, Rainlake Productions, 2006.

Cruz, Evelyn H. "Through Mexican Eyes: Mexican Perspectives on Transmigration." *Valparaiso University Law Review*, vol. 46, no. 4, 2012, pp. 1019–1052.

Dalton, Roque. "Poema de amor / Poem of Love." *Volcán: Poems from Central America, A Bi-lingual Anthology*, edited by Alejandro Murguía and Barbara Paschke, City Lights Books, 1983, pp. 36–37.

Da Silva, Chantal. "Nearly 4,000 Migrants Have Died or Gone Missing Trying to Get to the U.S." *Newsweek*, 4 Dec. 2018, www.newsweek.com/nearly-4000-migrants-have-died-or-gone-missing-trying-get-us-1243242.

DeCesare, Donna. "The Children of War: Street Gangs in El Salvador." *NACLA*, vol. 32, no. 1, 1998, pp. 21–31.

De Genova, Nicholas. "Spectacles of Migrant 'Illegality': The Scene of Exclusion, the Obscene of Inclusion." *Ethnic and Racial Studies*, vol. 36, no. 7, 2013, pp. 1180–1198.

Deitch, Jeffrey. *Art in the Streets*. Skira Rizzoli Publications, 2011.

De La Cruz, Rachael. "No Asylum for the Innocent: Gendered Representations of Salvadoran Refugees in the 1980s." *American Behavioral Scientist*, vol. 6, no. 10, 2017, pp. 1103–1118, doi.org/10.1177/0002764217732106.

Demo, Anne Teresa. "Decriminalizing Illegal Immigration: Immigrants' Rights through the Documentary Lens." *Border Rhetorics: Citizenship and Identity on the U.S.-Mexico Frontier*, edited by D. Robert DeChaine, University of Alabama Press, 2012, pp. 197–212.

De nadie. Directed by Tin Dirdamal, Producciones Tranvía, 2007.

Diken, Bülent, and Carsten Bagge Laustsen. "Becoming Abject: Rape as a Weapon of War." *Body and Society*, vol. 11, 2005, pp. 111–128, doi.org/10.1177/1357034X05049853.

DiMaggio, Paul, and Patricia Fernández-Kelly. "The Diversity and Mobility of Immigrant Arts." Introduction. *Art in the Lives of Immigrant Communities in the United States*, edited by DiMaggio and Fernández-Kelly, Rutgers University Press, 2010, pp. 1–22.

Dirt. Directed by Nancy Savoca, Canned Pictures Inc., Exile Films, 2004.

Dogfight. Directed by Nancy Savoca, Warner Bros, 1991.

Down and Out in Beverly Hills. Directed by Paul Mazurky, Touchstone Pictures, 1986.

"Dreams Deferred: Artists Respond to Immigration Reform Press Release." Chinese American Museum Los Angeles, 16 Nov. 2010, http://camla.org/wp-content /uploads/2013/06/Dreams%20Deferred%20Press%20Release.pdf. PDF.

Dreier, Hannah. "A Betrayal." *ProPublica*, 2 Apr. 2018, features.propublica.org/ms -13/a-betrayal-ms13-gang-police-fbi-ice-deportation/.

———. "Former MS-13 Member Who Secretly Helped Police Is Deported." *ProPublica*, 22 Jan. 2019, propublica.org/article/ms-13-member-who-secretly-helped -police-is-deported.

———. "Teenage MS-13 Gang Informant Heads into Final Asylum Hearing." *ProPublica*, 5 Apr. 2018, propublica.org/article/triste-henry-teenage-ms-13-gang -informant-heads-into-final-asylum-hearing.

———. "Teen Who Faced Deportation after He Informed on MS-13 Gets Temporary Reprieve." *ProPublica*, 6 Apr. 2018, propublica.org/article/ms-13-gang -informant-deportation-ice-asylum-hearing-temporary-reprieve.

———. "Were Henry's Civil Rights Violated?" *ProPublica*, 27 Apr. 2018, propublica .org/article/were-henry-civil-rights-violated.

Dunkerley, James. *The Long War: Dictatorship and Revolution in El Salvador*. Verso, 1982.

Dyer, Richard. *The Culture of Queers*. Routledge, 2005.

El Norte. Directed by Gregory Nava, Criterion, 2008.

The End of Violence. Directed by Wim Wenders, CiBy, 2000.

England, Sarah. *Afro Central Americans in New York City: Garifuna Tales of Transnational Movements in Racialized Space*. University Press of Florida, 2006.

———. "Afro-Hondurans in the Chocolate City: Garifuna, Katrina, and the Advantages of Racial Invisibility in the Nuevo New Orleans." *Journal of Latino/Latin American Studies*, vol. 3, no. 4, 2010, pp. 31–54, doi.org/10.18085/llas.3.4.g778 18x261q80158.

Estrada, Alicia Yvonne. "Decolonizing Maya Border Crossings in *El Norte* and *La Jaula de Oro*." *The Latin American Road Movie*, edited by Verónica Garibotto and Jorge Pérez, Palgrave Macmillan, 2016, pp. 175–193.

———. "Ka Tzij: The Maya Diasporic Voices from Contacto Ancestral." *Latino Studies*, vol. 11, no. 2, 2013, pp. 208–227, doi.org/10.1057/lst.2013.5.

———. "Latinidad and the Mayan Diaspora in the United States." *Latinos and Latinas at Risk: Issues in Education, Health, Community, and Justice*, edited by Gabriel Gutiérrez, Greenwood, 2015, pp. 145–150.

———. "(Re)Claiming Public Space and Place: Maya Community Formation in Westlake/MacArthur Park." *U.S. Central Americans: Reconstructing Memories, Struggles, and Communities of Resistance*, edited by Karina Oliva Alvarado et al., University of Arizona Press, pp. 166–187.

Eye One. *EyeOne/Seeking Heaven*. http://eyelost.com/eyeoneblog/index.php?catid=11&startpos=3. Accessed 13 May 2020.

"Fact Sheet: President Biden Sends Immigration Plan to Congress as Part of His Commitment to Modernize our Immigration System." Briefing Room, The White House, 20 Jan. 2021, www.whitehouse.gov/briefing-room/statements-releases /2021/01/20/fact-sheet-president-biden-sends-immigration-bill-to-congress-as -part-of-his-commitment-to-modernize-our-immigration-system/.

Ferrell, Jeff. *Crimes of Style: Urban Graffiti and the Politics of Criminality*. Northeastern University Press, 1996.

Fink, Leon. *The Maya of Morganton: Work and Community in the Nuevo New South*. University of North Carolina Press, 2003.

Foucault, Michel. *Discipline and Punish: The Birth of the Prison*. Translated by Alan Sheridan, Vintage Books, 1995.

Franco, Jean. "Rape: A Weapon of War." *Social Text*, vol. 25, no. 2, 2007, pp. 23–37.

Fraser, Nancy. "Rethinking the Public Sphere: A Contribution to the Critique of Actually Existing Democracy." *Social Text*, no. 25/26, 1990, pp. 56–80, doi.org /10.2307/466240.

Garcia, Gregory Thomas, creator. *My Name Is Earl*. 20th Century Fox Television, 2005.

Gay and Lesbian Alliance against Defamation. "GLAAD Calls '98 Season Lineup an Increasing Reflection of Gay Community." Press release. *Queer Resources Directory*, 19 Aug. 1998, qrd.org/qrd/media/television/1998/GLAAD.calls.season .lineup.an.increasing.reflection.of.gay.community-08.19.98. Accessed 8 June 2020.

Gerken, Christina. *Model Immigrants and Undesirable Aliens: The Cost of Immigration Reform in the 1990s*. University of Minnesota Press, 2013.

Godinez, Henry. "Too Much to Lose under Trump's Immigration Policies." *Chicago Tribune*, 14 Mar. 2017, www.chicagotribune.com/opinion/commentary /ct-immigration-deportation-trump-american-dream-perspec-0315-jm-20170314 -story.html.

González, Juan. *Harvest of Empire: A History of Latinos in America*. Penguin Books, 2011.

González, Macarena García. "Imagining Transnational Orphanhoods: Nation-as-Family in Recent Spanish Children's Books." *Children's Literature Association Quarterly*, vol. 4, no. 4, 2015, pp. 322–336.

Graden, Dale T., and James W. Martin. "Oliver Stone's "Salvador" (1986): Revolution for the Unacquainted." *Film and History*, vol. 28, no. 3, 1998, pp. 18–27.

Guatemala Memory of Silence: Report of the Commission for Historical Clarification: Conclusions and Recommendations. Commission for Historical Clarification, 1999.

Human Rights Data Analysis Group, hrdag.org/wp-content/uploads/2013/01
/CEHreport-english.pdf. Accessed 16 Mar. 2021. PDF.

Gutiérrez, Gabe, and Corky Siemaszko. "Photographer Reveals Story behind Iconic
Image of Fleeing Migrants at Mexico Border." *NBC News*, 26 Nov. 2018, www
.nbcnews.com/news/us-news/photographer-reveals-story-behind-iconic-photo
-fleeing-migrants-mexico-border-n940271.

Guzmán, Roy G. *Catrachos*. Graywolf, 2020.

Gzesh, Susan. "Central Americans and Asylum Policy in the Reagan Era." *Migration
Policy Institute*, 1 Apr. 2006, www.migrationpolicy.org/article/central-americans
-and-asylum-policy-reagan-era.

Hall, Stuart. "Cultural Studies and Its Theoretical Legacies." *Stuart Hall: Critical
Dialogues in Cultural Studies*, edited by David Morley and Kuan-Hsing Chen,
Routledge, 1996, pp. 261–274.

———. "Introduction." *Representation: Cultural Representations and Signifying Practices*, edited by Hall, Open University, Sage Publications, 1997, pp. 1–12.

———. "Race, Culture, and Communications: Looking Backward and Forward at
Cultural Studies." *Rethinking Marxism*, vol. 5, no. 1, 1992, pp. 10–18.

———. "The Spectacle of the 'Other.'" *Representation: Cultural Representations and
Signifying Practices*, edited by Hall, Open University, Sage Publications, 1997, pp.
223–290.

———. "The Work of Representation." *Representation: Cultural Representations and
Signifying Practices*, edited by Hall, Open University, Sage Publications, 1997,
pp. 13–74.

"Hannah Dreier of ProPublica." *The Pulitzer Prizes*, 2019, www.pulitzer.org/winners
/hannah-dreier-propublica. Accessed 19 May 2020.

Harris, Trudier. *From Mammies to Militants: Domestics in Black American Literature*.
Temple University Press, 1982.

Haynes, Chris, et al. *Framing Immigrants: News Coverage, Public Opinion, and Policy*. Russell Sage Foundation, 2016. *JSTOR*, www.jstor.org/stable/10.7758/97816
10448604. Accessed 20 May 2020.

"Here's Donald Trump's Presidential Announcement Speech." *Time*, 16 June 2015,
www.time.com/3923128/donald-trump-announcement-speech/.

Hernández, Kelly Lytle. *Migra!: A History of the US Border Patrol*. University of California Press, 2010.

Hernández-Linares, Leticia. "Gallina Ciega: Turning the Game on Itself." *This Bridge
We Call Home: Radical Visions for Transformation*, edited by Gloria E. Anzaldúa
and Analouise Keating, Routledge, 2002, pp. 110–116.

"He's Come Undone." *Will and Grace*, created by David Kohan and Max Mutchnick, season 2, episode 2, Three Sisters Entertainment and NBC Studios, 8 Feb.
2000. NBC, www.nbc.com/will-and-grace-original/video/hes-come-undone/35
57856. Accessed 16 Aug 2021.

Hicks, Emily D. *Border Writing: The Multidimensional Text*. University of Minnesota
Press, 1991.

Hinegardner, Livia. "Action, Organization, and Documentary Film: Beyond a Communications Model of Human Rights Videos." *Visual Anthropology Review*, vol. 25, no. 2, 2009, pp. 172–185.

Holgarth, David. *Realer Than Reel: Global Directions in Documentary*. University of Texas Press, 2006.

Holmlund, Chris. "Introduction: From the Margins to the Mainstream." *Contemporary American Independent Film*, edited by Chris Holmlund and Justin Wyatt, Routledge, 2006, pp. 1–19.

Hondagneu-Sotelo, Pierrette. *Doméstica: Immigrant Workers Cleaning and Caring in the Shadow of Affluence*. University of California Press, 2001.

Household Saints. Directed by Nancy Savoca, Jones Entertainment, 1993.

Huebner, Andrew J. *The Warrior Image: Soldiers in American Culture from the Second World War to the Vietnam Era*. University of North Carolina Press, 2008.

Hutcheon, Linda. *A Theory of Parody: The Teachings of Twentieth-Century Art Forms*. Methuen, 1985.

Icebox. Directed by Daniel Sawka, Gracie Films, 2018.

If These Walls Could Talk. Directed by Nancy Savoca, HBO, NYC Productions, 1996.

Inda, Jonathan Xavier. "Biopower, Reproduction, and the Migrant Woman's Body." *Decolonial Voices: Chicana and Chicano Cultural Studies in the 21st Century*, edited by Arturo J. Aldama and Naomi Hi. Quiñonez, Indiana University Press, 2002, pp. 98–112.

———. "The Value of Immigrant Life." *Women and Migration in the U.S.-Mexico Borderlands: A Reader*, edited by Denise A. Segura and Patricia Zavella, Duke University Press, 2007, pp. 134–157.

Irvine, Martin. "Work on the Street: Street Art and Visual Culture." *The Handbook of Visual Culture*, edited by Barry Sandywell and Ian Heywood, Berg/Palgrave Macmillan, 2012, pp. 234–278.

Izaguirre, Freddy Jesse. "The Hashtag That Helped Us Survive the War on Migrants." *Level* (blog), 6 Feb. 2020, www.level.medium.com/the-hashtag-that-helped-us-survive-the-war-on-migrants-5a9018414239.

Jagosz, Krystal. "Cache: Don't Be a Chicken." *YouTube*, uploaded by Just2toomuch, 29 Apr. 2010, www.youtube.com/watch?v=bd2Ht6HLnk4.

Jímenez, Lillian. "From the Margin to the Center: Puerto Rican Cinema in New York." *Latin Looks: Images of Latinas and Latinos in U.S. Media*, edited by Clara E. Rodríguez, Westview, 1997, pp. 188–199.

Johnson, David E., and Scott Michaelsen. "Border Secrets: An Introduction." *Border Theory: The Limits of Cultural Politics*, edited by Johnson and Michaelson, University of Minnesota Press, 1997, pp. 1–39.

Kaplan, Amy. "Manifest Domesticity." *Postcolonialisms: An Anthology of Cultural Theory and Criticism*, edited by Gaurav Desai and Supriya Nair, Rutgers University Press, 2005, pp. 479–499.

Kasindorf, Martin. "Guatemalan Native Put Off College to Join Marines." *USA Today*, 24 Mar. 2004.

Kellner, Douglas M., and Meenakshi Gigi Durham, editors. *Media and Cultural Studies: Keyworks*, John Wiley and Sons, 2012.

Kingsolver, Barbara. *The Bean Trees: A Novel*. Harper Perennial, 2013.

Knives Out. Directed by Rian Johnson, Lionsgate, 2019.

Kopan, Tal. "Trump Administration to Turn Away Far More Asylum Seekers at the Border under New Guidance." CNN, 12 July 2018, www.cnn.com/2018/07/11 /politics/border-immigrants-asylum-restrictions/index.html.

La bestia. Directed by Pedro Ultreras, Venevisión International, 2011.

La jaula de oro. Directed by Diego Quemada-Diez, Mexican Film Institute, 2013.

Larsen, Neil. *Reading North by South: On Latin American Literature, Culture, and Politics*. University of Minnesota Press, 1995.

La vida en la vía. Directed by Ricardo Padilla, Cactus Film and Video, 2007.

La vida precoz y breve de Sabina Rivas. Directed by Luis Mandoki, Laguna Productions, Inc., 2012.

Leeson, Michael, creator. *I Married Dora*. Reeves Entertainment Group and Welladay, 1987.

Lennard, Natasha. "Photos of Children Being Teargassed Stoke Outrage—While Playing into Trump's Manufactured Border Crisis." *The Intercept*, 27 Nov. 2018, www.theintercept.com/2018/11/27/us-border-tear-gas/?comments=1.

Lewis, Judith. "Playing the Human Part: Lupe Ontiveros on How Not to Be a Diva." *LA Weekly*, 6 Mar. 2002, www.laweekly.com/playing-the-human-part/.

Lichter, Robert S., and Daniel R. Amundson. "Distorted Reality: Hispanic Characters in TV Entertainment." *Latin Looks: Images of Latinas and Latinos in U.S. Media*, edited by Clara E. Rodríguez, Westview, 1997, pp. 57–79.

Limón, Graciela. *In Search of Bernabé*. Arte Público, 1983.

Lorre, Chuck, and Dottie Dartland Zicklin, creators. *Dharma and Greg*. 20th Century Fox Television, 1997.

Loucky, James, and Marilyn M. Moors, editors. *The Maya Diaspora: Guatemalan Roots, New American Lives*. Temple University Press, 2000.

Lowe, Lisa. *Immigrant Acts: On Asian American Cultural Politics*. Duke University Press, 1996.

Lurie, Joshua. "Taste like Revolution: Local Muralist Cache Spearheads a Chicken-Led Revolution." *New Angeles Monthly*, May 2008, pp. 20–21. *ISSUU*, issuu.com /newangelesmonthly/docs/may2008. Accessed 20 May 2020.

Maher, Kristen Hill, and Jesse Elias. "Docile, Criminal, and Upwardly Mobile? Visual News Framing of Mexican Migrants and the Logics of Neoliberal Multiculturalism." *Latino Studies*, vol. 17, no. 2, 2019, pp. 225–256.

Maid in Manhattan. Directed by Wayne Wang, Revolution Studios, 2002.

María en tierra de nadie. Directed by Marcela Zamora Chamorro, Women Make Movies, 2010.

Mariscal, Jorge. "Homeland Security, Militarism, and the Future of Latinos and Latinas in the United States." *Radical History Review*, no. 93, 2005, pp. 39–52.

Martínez, Demetria. *Mother Tongue*. Ballantine Books, 1994.

Martínez, J. R., and Alexandra Rockey Fleming. *Full of Heart: My Story of Survival, Strength, and Spirit.* Hyperion, 2012.

Martínez, Óscar. *The Beast: Riding the Rails and Dodging Narcos on the Migrant Trail.* Translated by Daniela María Ugaz and John Washington, Verso, 2014.

Mata, Irene. *Domestic Disturbances: Re-imagining Narratives of Gender, Labor, and Immigration.* University of Texas Press, 2014.

Mbembe, Achille. "Necropolitics." Translated by Libby Meintjes, *Public Culture*, vol. 15, no. 1, 2003, pp. 11–40.

Mendez-Hernandez, Raul. *An American Dream.* Self-published, 2014.

Menjívar, Cecilia. "Immigration Law beyond Borders: Externalizing and Internalizing Border Controls in an Era of Securitization." *Annual Review of Law and Social Science*, vol. 10, Nov. 2014, pp. 353–369, doi.org/10.1146/annurev-lawsoc sci-110413-030842.

———. "Liminal Legality: Salvadoran and Guatemalan Immigrants' Lives in the United States." *American Journal of Sociology*, vol. 111, no. 4, 2006, pp. 999–1037. *JSTOR*, jstor.org/stable/10.1086/499509.

Menjívar, Cecilia, and Leisy Abrego. "Legal Violence: Immigration Law and the Lives of Central American Immigrants." *American Journal of Sociology*, vol. 117, no. 5, 2012, pp. 1380–1421. *JSTOR*, jstor.org/stable/10.1086/663575.

Menjívar, Jennifer Gómez, and Gloria E. Chacón. *Indigenous Interfaces: Spaces, Technology, and Social Networks in Mexico and Central America.* University of Arizona Press, 2019.

Messaris, Paul, and Linus Abraham. "The Role of Images in Framing News Stories." *Framing Public Life: Perspectives on Media and Our Understanding of the Social World*, edited by Stephen D. Reese et al., Lawrence Erlbaum Associates, 2001, pp. 215–226.

"Mexico Becoming a 'No-Go Zone' for Migrants as Gruesome Massacre Remains Unresolved Five Years On." Amnesty International, 21 Aug. 2015, www.amnesty .org/en/latest/news/2015/08/mexico-becoming-a-no-go-zone-for-migrants-as -gruesome-massacre-remains-unresolved-five-years-on/.

"Mexico Immigration Detention Profile." Global Detention Project, 2020, www .globaldetentionproject.org/countries/americas/mexico#statistics-data. Accessed 4 Aug. 2020.

"Mid-City: Profile." *Mapping L.A., Los Angeles Times*, maps.latimes.com /neighborhoods/neighborhood/mid-city/. Accessed 13 May 2020.

Mills, Brett. *Television Sitcom.* British Film Institute, 2005.

"Mission and History." Chinese American Museum Los Angeles, www.camla.org /mission-and-history/. Accessed 14 May 2020.

Mitchell, Danielle. "Producing Containment: The Rhetorical Construction of Difference in *Will and Grace*." *Journal of Popular Culture*, vol. 38, no. 6, 2005, pp. 1050–1068.

Mitchell, W. J. T., and Mark B. N. Hansen, editors. *Critical Terms for Media Studies*, University of Chicago Press, 2010.

Monmouth University Polling Institute. "Public Divided on Whether Migrant Caravan Poses Threat." *Monmouth University*, 19 Nov. 2019, www.monmouth.edu /polling-institute/reports/monmouthpoll_us_111918/.

Morgan, Jo-Ann. "Mammy the Huckster: Selling the Old South for the New Century." *American Art*, vol. 9, no. 1, 1995, pp. 86–109.

My Family/Mi Familia. Directed by Gregory Nava, American Playhouse, 1995.

Nazario, Sonia. *Enrique's Journey: The Story of a Boy's Dangerous Odyssey to Reunite with His Mother*. Random House, 2007.

Neuman, W. R., et al. *Common Knowledge: News and the Construction of Political Meaning*. University of Chicago Press, 1992.

Ngai, Mae N. *Impossible Subjects: Illegal Aliens and the Making of Modern America*. Princeton University Press, 2004.

Noe-Bustamante, Luis, et al. "Facts on Hispanics of Salvadoran Origin in the United States, 2017." Pew Research Center, 16 Sept. 2019, www.pewresearch.org /hispanic/fact-sheet/u-s-hispanics-facts-on-salvadoran-origin-latinos/.

Nomad. "United We Stand: The Tragic Story of Marine Jose Gutierrez vs. Trump's Hate-Filled Rhetoric." *Nomadic Politics*, 30 Jul. 2016, https://nomadicpolitics .blogspot.com/2016/07/united-we-stand-tragic-story-of-marine.html.

Noriega, Chon A. "Chicanos in Film." Introduction. *Chicanos and Film: Essays on Chicano Representations and Resistance*, edited by Noriega, Garland, 1992, pp. xi–xxv.

Nuñez, Breena. *From There to Here*. breenache.com/#/from-here-to-there/. Accessed 1 Apr. 2021.

———. *I Exist*. breenache.com/#/the-nib-i-exist/.

"Object of My Rejection." *Will and Grace*, created by David Kohan and Max Mutchnick, season 1, episode 22, Three Sisters Entertainment and NBC Studios, 13 May 1999. NBC, www.nbc.com/will-and-grace-original/video/object-of-my -rejection/3557746.

O'Connor, Allison, et al. "Central American Immigrants in the United States." Migration Policy Institute, 15 Aug. 2019, www.migrationpolicy.org/article /central-american-immigrants-united-states.

Ordoñez, Franco. "Trump Wants to Withdraw Deportation Protections for Families of Active Troops." KUOW, 27 June 2019, www.kuow.org/stories/trump-wants-to -withdraw-deportation-protections-for-families-of-active-troops.

Orlov, Ann, and Reed Ueda. "Central and South Americans." *Harvard Encyclopedia of American Ethnic Groups*, edited by Stephan Thernstrom et al., Harvard University Press, 1980, pp. 210–217.

Padilla, Yajaira M. "Central American Non-belonging: Reading 'El Norte' in Cary Fukunaga's *Sin nombre*." *The Latin American Road Movie*, edited by Jorge Pérez and Verónica Garibotto, Palgrave, 2016, pp. 157–174.

———. "The Central American Transnational Imaginary: Defining the Gendered and Transnational Contours of the Central American Immigrant Experience." *Latino Studies*, vol. 11, no. 2, 2013, pp. 150–166.

———. *Changing Women, Changing Nation: Female Agency, Nationhood, and Identity in Trans-Salvadoran Narratives*. State University of New York Press, 2012.

————. "Domesticating Rosario: Conflicting Representations of the Latina Maid in U.S. Media." *Arizona Journal of Hispanic Cultural Studies*, vol. 13, 2009, pp. 41–59.

————. "Migrant Marías: Troubling Illegibility, Motherhood, and (Im)migration in Marcela Zamora Chamorro's *María en tierra de nadie.*" *Journal of Commonwealth and Postcolonial Studies*, vol. 5, no. 2, 2017, pp. 105–120.

Pazicky, Diana Loercher. *Cultural Orphans in America.* University Press of Mississippi, 2008.

Pérez, Richie. "From Assimilation to Annihilation: Puerto Rican Images in U.S. Films." *Latin Looks: Images of Latinas and Latinos in U.S. Media*, edited by Clara E. Rodríguez, Westview, 1997, pp. 142–163.

Perry, Leah. *The Cultural Politics of U.S. Immigration: Gender, Race, and Media.* New York University Press, 2016.

Podalsky, Laura. *The Politics of Affect and Emotion in Contemporary Latin American Cinema: Argentina, Brazil, and Cuba.* Palgrave Macmillan, 2011.

"Profile of the Unauthorized Population: Los Angeles County, CA." Migration Policy Institute, www.migrationpolicy.org/data/unauthorized-immigrant-population /county/6037. Accessed 13 May 2020.

Quijano, Aníbal. "Coloniality of Power, Eurocentrism, and Latin America." *Nepantla: Views from South*, vol. 1, no. 3, 2000, pp. 533–580.

Ramírez Berg, Charles. *Latino Images in Film: Stereotypes, Subversion, Resistance.* University of Texas Press, 2002.

Reagan, Ronald. "Address to the Nation on United States Policy in Central America." 9 May 1984. National Archives and Records Administration, Ronald Reagan Presidential Library and Museum, www.reaganlibrary.gov/research/speeches/50 984h.

Red Dawn. Directed by John Milius, United Artists, 1984.

Reichman, Daniel. "Honduras: The Perils of Remittance Dependence and Clandestine Migration." Migration Policy Institute, 11 Apr. 2013, www.migrationpolicy .org/article/honduras-perils-remittance-dependence-and-clandestine-migration.

"Remarks by the President on Immigration." The White House: President Barack Obama, 15 June 2012, obamawhitehouse.archives.gov/the-press-office/2012/06 /15/remarks-president-immigration.

Repak, Terry. *Waiting on Washington: Central American Workers in the Nation's Capital.* Temple University Press, 1995.

Rivas, Cecilia M. *Salvadoran Imaginaries: Mediated Identities and Cultures of Consumption.* 1978. Rutgers University Press, 2014.

Rodríguez, Ana P. *Dividing the Isthmus: Central American Transnational Histories, Literatures, and Cultures.* University of Texas Press, 2009.

————. "The Fiction of Solidarity: Transfronterista Feminisms and Anti-imperialist Struggles in Central American Transnational Narratives." *Feminist Studies*, vol. 34, nos. 1–2, 2008, pp. 199–226.

————. "Salvadoran Immigrant Acts and Migration to San Francisco (circa 1960s and 70s)." *U.S. Central Americans: Reconstructing Memories, Struggles, and*

Communities of Resistance, edited by Karina O. Alvarado et al., University of Arizona Press, pp. 41–59.

———. "Toward a Transisthmian Central American Studies." *Latino Studies*, vol. 15, no. 1, 2017, pp. 104–108.

Rodríguez, Clara E. "Introduction." *Latin Looks: Images of Latinas and Latinos in U.S. Media*, edited by Rodríguez, Westview, 1997, pp. 1–12.

Rodríguez, Nestor. "Comparing Mexicans and Central Americans in the Present Wave of U.S. Immigration." *The Other Latinos: Central Americans and South Americans in the United States*, edited by José Luis Falconi and José Antonio Mazzotti, Harvard University Press, 2007, pp. 81–100.

Romero, Mary. *Maid in the U.S.A.* Routledge, 1992.

Rosaldo, Renato. *Culture and Truth: The Remaking of Social Analysis.* Beacon, 1993.

Salvador. Directed by Oliver Stone, Cinema '84, 1986.

Sánchez, Alberto Sandoval. "*West Side Story*: A Puerto Rican Reading of 'America.'" *Latin Looks: Images of Latinas and Latinos in U.S. Media*, edited by Clara E. Rodríguez, Westview, 1997, pp. 164–179.

Santa Ana, Otto. *Brown Tide Rising: Metaphors of Latinos in Contemporary American Public Discourse.* University of Texas Press, 2002.

Scheib, Ronnie. "Dirt." *Variety*, 6 Sept. 2004, www.variety.com/2004/film/reviews /dirt-7-1200531277/.

Schwartzman, Allan. *Street Art.* Bantam Doubleday Dell Publishing Group, 1985.

Seelke, Clare Ribando, and Kristin Finklea. *U.S.-Mexican Security Cooperation: The Mérida Initiative and Beyond.* Report. Congressional Research Service, 29 June 2017, crsreports.congress.gov/product/details?prodcode=R41349. PDF.

Segura, Rosamaría. *Central Americans in Los Angeles.* Arcadia, 2010.

Semple, Kirk. "Trump Transforms Immigrant Caravans in Mexico into Cause Célèbre." *New York Times*, 2 Apr. 2018, www.nytimes.com/2018/04/02/world /americas/caravans-migrants-mexico-trump.html.

Shaw, Deborah. "Migrant Identities in Film: *Sin Nombre* and Migration Films from Mexico and Central America to the United States." *Crossings: Journal of Migration and Culture*, vol. 3, no. 12, 2012, pp. 227–240.

The Short Life of José Antonio Gutiérrez. Directed by Heidi Specogna, Atopia, 2006.

Sin nombre. Directed by Cary Fukunaga, Scion Films, 2009.

Sittig, Ann L., and Martha Florinda González. *The Mayans among Us: Migrant Women and Meatpacking on the Great Plains.* University of Nebraska Press, 2016. *JSTOR*, www.jstor.org/stable/j.ctt1d41ctn. Accessed 10 June 2020.

Skidmore, Thomas E., and Peter H. Smith. *Modern Latin America.* Oxford University Press, 2005.

Sluyter, Andrew, et al., editors. *Hispanic and Latino New Orleans: Immigration and Identity since the Eighteenth Century.* Louisiana State University Press, 2015.

Smaill, Belinda. *The Documentary: Politics, Emotion, Culture.* Palgrave Macmillan, 2010.

Smith, Christian. *Resisting Reagan: The U.S. Central America Peace Movement.* University of Chicago Press, 1996.

Snyder, Gregory J. *Graffiti Lives: Beyond the Tag in New York's Urban Underground.* New York University Press, 2009.

Sontag, Susan. "The Image-World." *A Susan Sontag Reader.* Farrar, Straus, Giroux, 1982, pp. 349–367.

Spanglish. Directed by James L. Brooks, Columbia Pictures Corporation, 2004.

Steimel, Sarah J. "Refugees as People: The Portrayal of Refugees in American Human Interest Stories." *Journal of Refugee Studies,* vol. 23, no. 2, 2010, pp. 219–237.

Storytelling. Directed by Todd Solondz, Good Machine, 2001.

Szpunar, Piotr M. "The Horror at Fort Hood: Disseminating American Exceptionalism." *Media, Culture, and Society,* vol. 35, no. 2, 2013, pp. 182–198.

Torn Apart: Separated at the Border. Directed by Ellen Goosenberg Kent, Talos Films, 2019.

True Love. Directed by Nancy Savoca, J&M Entertainment, 1989.

The 24 Hour Woman. Directed by Nancy Savoca, Dirt Road Productions, 1999.

Under Fire. Directed by Roger Spottiswoode, Lionsgate Films, 1983.

Union Square. Directed by Nancy Savoca, Armian Pictures, 2012.

Valdivia, Angharad N. *A Latina in the Land of Hollywood and Other Essays on Media Culture.* University of Arizona Press, 2000.

Valkenburg, Patti. M., et al. "The Effects of News Frames on Readers Thoughts and Recall." *Communication Research,* vol. 26, no. 5, 1999, pp. 550–569.

Vallen, Mark. "By the Time I Get to Arizona." *Mark Vallen's Art for a Change: Events, Theory, Commentary,* 28 June 2010, www.art-for-a-change.com/blog/2010/06/by -the-time-i-get-to-arizona.html.

Vila, Pablo. "Introduction: Border Ethnographies." *Ethnography on the Border,* edited by Vila, University of Minnesota Press, 2003, pp. ix–xxxv.

Vogt, Wendy A. *Lives in Transit: Violence and Intimacy on the Migrant Journey.* University of California Press, 2018.

Wallace-Sanders, Kimberly. *Mammy: A Century of Race, Gender, and Southern Memory.* University of Michigan Press, 2008.

West Side Story. Directed by Jerome Robbins and Robert Wise, Mirisch Corporation, 1961.

Wetback: The Undocumented Documentary. Directed by Arturo Pérez Torres, National Geographic Video, 2007.

"Will and Grace Scene about Election Special." *YouTube,* uploaded by AllFor You, 27 Sept. 2016, www.youtube.com/watch?v=w_JwOm6sISw.

"What I Did for Love." *Grey's Anatomy,* created by Shonda Rhimes, season 15, episode 23, Shondaland and the Mark Gordon Company, 2 May 2019.

Which Way Home. Directed by Rebecca Cammisa, Docudrama, 2011.

Who Is Dayani Crystal? Directed by Mark Silver, Pulse Films, 2013, www.whois dayanicristal.com. Accessed 23 May 2020.

"The Woman in the Garden." *Bones,* created by Hart Hanson, season 1, episode 13, Farfield Productions, Josephson Entertainment, and 20th Century Fox Television, 15 Feb. 2006. *DailyMotion,* www.dailymotion.com/video/x75s26z. Accessed 15 June 2020.

Women on the Run. The United Nations High Commissioner for Refugees, 2015. UNHCR, www.unhcr.org/en-us/publications/operations/5630f24c6/women -run.html. Accessed 15 May 2019. PDF.

Zamora, Javier. *Unaccompanied*. Copper Canyon, 2017.

Zelazny, Jon. "Neglected Gems of the 1980's: Roger Spottiswoode Remembers *Under Fire*." *The Hollywood Interview*, 9 Apr. 2009, www.thehollywoodinterview.blog spot.com/2009/04/roger-spottiswoode-hollywood-interview.html.

Zentgraf, Kristine M. "Why Women Migrate: Salvadoran and Guatemalan Women in Los Angeles." *Latino L.A.: Transformations, Communities, and Activism*, edited by Enrique C. Ochoa and Gilda L. Ochoa, University of Arizona Press, 2005.

"Zero Tolerance." *Law & Order: Special Victims Unit*, created by Dick Wolf, season 20, episode 3, Wolf Films and Universal Television, 4 Oct. 2018.

Zilberg, Elana. "Fools Banished from the Kingdom: Remapping Geographies of Gang Violence between the Americas (Los Angeles and San Salvador)." *American Quarterly*, vol. 56, no. 3, Sept. 2004, pp. 759–779. *JSTOR*, www.jstor.org/stable /40068242.

———. *Spaces of Detention: The Making of a Transnational Gang Crisis between Los Angeles and El Salvador*. Duke University Press, 2011.

Index

Page numbers followed by f indicate images.

Asian Americans, 12
Asian immigration, 12
Askew, 115
assimilation: and American Dream, 26, 64; and #CentAmStudies, 28; and domestication, 15; and José Gutierrez, 71, 72; and non-belonging, 65; and orphanhood, 86; and stereotypes, 48
asylum: and forever illegals, 40; and José Gutierrez, 78; and Reagan administration, 3, 18; and Sanctuary movement, 34; and Trump administration, 20–21, 83
asylum seekers: and "caravans," 9; feminization of, 7; in human interest stories, 84; and meritocracy, 15, 70; and NACARA, 19; and Reagan administration, 4, 32, 34; and Trump administration, 20–21, 40–42, 142n9; Donald Trump's fixation on, 1

Babel (2006), 46
Bal, Mieke, 123
Banksy, 152n5
Bean Trees (Kingsolver 1988), 33–34, 35
Beast (Martínez 2014), 149n1
Belize, 99, 149n2
belonging: and border spaces, 135; as counternarrative, 14–15; and desire, 27; and José Gutierrez, 68–69; and hegemonic representations, 70; and US Central Americans, 137–138n2; and visibility, 128
Berlant, Lauren, 27, 97
"Betrayal" (Dreier 2018), 70, 83–87, 148n16
Beulah (1950s), 145n9
Biden, Joseph R., 135, 142n10, 143n12
Biden administration, 135–136, 142–143n11
biopower, 100, 135
Biron, Rebecca E., 111

Black Central American migrants, 7
blackness, 132
Bloch, Stefano, 115
Bones (2005–2017), 37–40
border enforcement, 16, 40, 93, 99, 135, 150n10
Borderlands/La Frontera (Anzaldúa 1987), 134
borderlands subjectivities, 13, 16, 134–135
border studies, 134
Boreanaz, David, 37
Brooks, James L., 46
brownness, 77
Brown Tide Rising (Santa Ana 2002), 11
Bush, George W., 81, 147n2, 148n12
Butler, Judith, 8–9
By the Time I Get to Arizona (Mid-City Arts 2010), 114, 119–123, 121f, 128

Cache: art of, 16, 115–119, 116f, 120–125, 127, 152n1; and Central Americanness, 112, 113, 128; family of, 126; identity of, 116–117; and regimes of visibility, 113–114; stance of, 110–111; and street art, 152n3
Cacho, Lisa Marie, 67, 81
CAFTA-DR (Dominican Republic-Central American Free Trade Agreement), 106, 141n4
camp, 56–57, 146n14
Canada, 142n10
caravans, 1, 9, 10, 28, 40
Cárdenas, Maritza E., 118
Casa del Migrante (House of the Migrant), 99
Castañeda, Carlos, 110
Castillo, Ana, 33–34
Catrachos (Guzmán 2020), 130–131
#CentAmStudies, 28
Central America: in film, 32–33; and free trade, 151–152n16; governments of, 149n4; in literary texts, 33–34,

identity politics, 29–30

I Exist (Nuñez), 132

If These Walls Could Talk (1996), 146n20

Illegal Immigration Reform and Immigrant Responsibility Act (IIRIRA), 56, 71, 146n13

illegality: after 9/11, 67; and biopower, 100; and Cache's art, 112, 114; construction of, 11; and Los Angeles Central Americans, 113; and meritocracy, 72; and regimes of visibility, 16; representations of, 40, 42; trope of, 8

images, 74–77, 86–87, 107–108, 141n22, 147n3

"Image-World" (Sontag 1982), 87

I Married Dora (1987), 49

immigrant art, 112, 127–128

immigrant labor: and Chinese Americans, 120; coercion of, 151n14; and coloniality of power, 22; commodification of, 100–101, 106–107, 151n15; and *domésticas*, 46–47, 64–65; domestication of, 15, 51–52; in *El Norte*, 24; exploitation of, 5, 16, 113, 114, 123, 124, 125; gendering of, 59; and IRCA, 141n2; and marginalization, 144n21; and poultry industry, 128; and race, 48–49; representations of, 140n16; and transmigration, 151n14; waves of, 140–141n1

immigrants: and abjection, 30–31; and AEDPA, 147n8; affective constructions of, 27; and art, 112; and Biden administration, 135–136; in *Bones*, 38–40; demographics of, 19; in *El Norte*, 24; as forever illegals, 14; hegemonic depictions of, 9; and IIRIRA, 71–72; and illegality, 42; images of, 41; and IRCA, 18, 36; mainstream depictions of, 6–7; in memoir, 26; and nonbelonging, 5; and nonexistence, 29; quota system for, 138n5; racialization of, 23; and Reagan administration, 3;

studies of, 12; and Trump administration, 20–21; and white privilege, 48; in *Will and Grace*, 46

Immigrants (*Time* magazine 1985), 27

immigrant subjectivities, 47, 52

immigrant youth, 81, 82–87

immigration: and documentaries, 96; and fearmongering, 1; history of, 17; and neoliberalism, 69; and racialized anxieties, 4; waves of, 140–141n1

Immigration and Customs Enforcement (ICE), 84, 153n14

Immigration and Nationality Act of 1965, 3, 11, 138n5

immigration laws, 5, 9, 16, 114, 120–121. *See also specific laws*

immigration policy, 36, 68, 71. *See also specific laws*

Immigration Reform and Control Act (IRCA), 18, 36, 141n2

inclusion: and financial security, 26; and immigrant meritocracy, 15; and neoliberal paradigm, 36; and nonbelonging, 24, 50; and nonexistence, 29; and Reagan administration, 3–4

Inda, Jonathan Xavier, 99–100

"In Death, a Marine Gets His Life Wish" (Crittle 2003), 69

independent cinema, 58

indigeneity, 25, 79

Indigenous groups, 22, 25, 105. *See also specific groups*

Indigenous identities, 67

infantilization, 41, 141n22

In Search of Bernabé (Limón 1993), 34, 36

Intercept, 41

internalized racism, 132

invisibility, 15, 29–30, 43–44, 59, 124, 132–133

Iraq War: and immigrant labor, 15; and J. R. Martínez, 27; and necropower, 81; and veteran deportations, 147n6

Irvine, Martin, 112

Izaguirre, Freddy Jesse, 28

maquiladora industry, 59

Mara Salvatrucha (MS-13): in *Bones*, 37–40; and DACA, 82; images of, 36; and immigrant meritocracy, 15; and immigrant youth, 69–70, 83–87; and Rodney King riots, 10; in *María en tierra de nadie*, 102, 103, 104; and migrant commodification, 101–102, 105; in Javier Zamora's poetry, 43

marginalization: of Black peoples, 22; and coloniality, 23; contestation of, 42; and *domésticas*, 50; and hegemonic representations, 130; and nomenclature, 29; and representations, 30; resistance to, 6, 28, 64; roots of, 5; scholarship on, 17–18

María en tierra de nadie / Mary in No-Man's- Land (2010), 89, 90, 91–92, 96, 97–98, 100, 102, 154n16

Martínez, Demetria, 34, 35

Martínez, J. R., 26–27

Martínez, Óscar, 149n1

Mata, Irene, 46–47, 64

Maya ancestry, 67, 69

Maya people, 23, 24–26, 79, 124, 139n9, 143n14

Mbembe, Achille, 81

McCormack, Eric, 45

media: and belonging, 88; and Central America, 31–32; and human rights, 92; and images, 74; and Latinx peoples, 47; on migrants, 135; and migratory patterns, 49; and transmigration, 89; on Trump administration, 139n12; and US Central Americans, 140n16

media frames, 147n4

Memorandum of Understanding for the Dignified, Orderly, Swift, and Safe Repatriation of Central American Migrants by Land, 150–151n12

Mendez-Hernandez, Raul, 26–27

Menjívar, Cecilia, 18, 21, 99

Mérida Initiative, 99, 150n10

Messaris, Paul, 74

Messing, Debra, 45

mestizaje, 6–7, 22, 132

Mexican Americans, 11–12

Mexican immigration, 11–12

Mexicanization, 55

Mexico: and asylum seekers, 135; as border passage, 98–101, 151n14; and border security, 151n13; and detention centers, 150n9; and forever illegals, 40; and immigration, 4; and immigration law, 150–151n12; and migrant labor, 107; in *Red Dawn*, 32; and transmigration, 15–16, 89–90, 91, 92, 149n2, 149n4

Meza Castro, María Lila, 40–41

Mid-City Arts, 119–120, 121, 153n12

migra-documentaries, 93–94, 97, 98, 100–101, 106, 107–109, 133, 134–135

migrants: and corrupt Mexican officials, 151n13; and documentaries, 94–96; massacre of, 150–151n12

migration: and gang violence, 10; media coverage of, 42; from Mexico, 4; of mothers and children, 62; and Donald Trump, 9; and unaccompanied minors, 7; and US-Mexico border, 16; waves of, 18–19, 63

Migration Protection Protocols, 20

migratory patterns, 49

Milian, Claudia, 22, 23, 25

Milius, John, 32

Miluska, Zaira, 28

Model Immigrants and Undesirable Aliens (Gerken 2013), 71

Morgan, Jo-Ann, 48

Morrison, Shelley (née Rachel Mitrani), 45, 144nn1–2, 146n19

Mother Tongue (Martínez 1994), 34, 35–36

Mullally, Megan, 45

mural moratorium (2002–2013), 111–112

Muslims, 81
My Family/Mi Familia (1995), 36, 49
My Name Is Earl (2005), 49

NAFTA (North American Free Trade Agreement), 146n13, 150n10, 150n11
National Commission of Human Rights in Mexico, 100
nationalism, 71, 72, 133
national security: and asylum seekers, 41; and forever illegals, 30–31; Ronald Reagan on, 2; and SPP, 150n10; Donald Trump on, 1; and US-Mexico interstate regime, 91, 99–100
National Security Entry-Exit Registration System, 81, 148n12
nativism, 82
Nava, Gregory, 24, 49, 89
Nazario, Sonia, 149n1, 154n16
"Necropolitics" (Mbembe 2003), 81
necropower, 81
neoliberalism, 30–31, 36, 52, 70, 72, 86, 88
neoliberal multiculturalism, 77
Nepal, 143n12
New Latin America Cinema, 92, 149n3
New Yorker, 132
New York graffiti movement, 111
New York Magazine, 148n14
Nib, 132
Nicaragua, and asylum, 3; and Contra War, 138n4; and *domésticas*, 49; in film, 33; in *Under Fire*, 33; flag of, 117; history of, 138nn3–4; immigrants from, 138n6; media coverage of, 31–32; and Ronald Reagan, 2–3, 6; and TPS, 143n12; and US media, 31–32
Nicaraguan Adjustment and Central American Relief Act (NACARA), 19–20
9/11 attacks, 148n12
Nolte, Nick, 33

non-belonging: and assimilation, 65; cultural politics of, 136; defined, 17–18, 24; and documentaries, 109; and hegemonic representations, 129–130; and identity, 29–30; and inclusionary possibilities, 43; and transnational affiliations, 28; and US Central Americans, 137–138n2; and US cultural politics, 5
Northern Triangle, 19, 135. *See also specific countries*
Nuñez, Breena, 130, 131–132

Obama, Barack, 9, 20, 115, 125, 139–140n13
Obama administration, 141–142nn6-7
"Object of My Rejection" (*Will and Grace* episode), 53–54
Occupy LA, 110
Oklahoma City bombing, 147n8
Omen, Judd, 32
O'Neal, Ron, 32
Ontiveros, Lupe, 64–65
orphanhood, 77–82, 85, 86
Ortiz, Julieta, 58
otherness, 5–6, 10, 26, 31, 87, 109, 129

Pantoja, Pedro, 102
parody, 54–55
patriotism, 71
"Payday Loan Phenomenology" (Guzmán 2020), 130–131
Pazicky, Diana Loercher, 80
Peña, Elizabeth, 49
Pérez, Louie, 146n21
Perez, Rosie, 146n20
Peric, Suzana, 146n21
Perry, Leah, 11, 36
Personal Responsibility Act and Work Opportunity Reconciliation Act (PRWORA), 146n13, 147n8
Peru, 105

Trump era, 15, 40–41, 52, 69–70, 82–87
24 Hour Woman (1999), 146n20
typecasting, 144n4
Tyson Foods, 128

Ultreras, Pedro, 90, 92
Unaccompanied (Zamora 2017), 42–43
unaccompanied minors: and Biden administration, 142n10; media coverage of, 135, 139n12; and Obama administration, 141–142n6, 142n7; and Trump administration, 83; and US policy, 20; Javier Zamora as, 42–43
Under Fire (1983), 32–33
undocumented immigrants: and biopower, 99–100; and Cache, 111; in *Dirt*, 60; in *El Norte*, 24; and Los Angeles Central Americans, 113; media coverage of, 41–42; in memoir, 26–27; and Mexican law, 150–151n12; and Trump administration, 82, 83; and US domestic labor, 49
Union Square (2012), 146n20
United States-Mexico-Canada Agreement (USMCA), 150n11
USA Patriot Act, 81, 148n12
US Border Patrol, 40–41
US Central Americans: and anti-blackness, 132; and Biden administration, 135–136; communities of, 18–19; defined, 137–138n2; experience of, 12, 13; hegemonic depictions of, 8, 17–18; and identity, 29–30; and invisibility, 132–133; in Los Angeles, 113; and Los Angeles, 117; and marginalization, 5–6; origins of, 138n6; and popular imaginary, 14; studies of, 47; and TPS, 21; and Twitter, 28; and visibility, 118
US Customs and Border Protection Agency, 21

US imperialism, 13, 33, 67, 79, 143–144n17
US intervention, 2, 10–11, 34, 51, 69
US Marine Corps, 138n3
US-Mexico border: Gloria Anzaldúa on, 134; and Biden administration, 142n10; in *Dirt*, 62–63; and family separation, 20, 127, 139n12; interstate regime of, 93, 99–100; and Mexican National Guard, 149n2; and transmigration, 15–16; and Trump administration, 41; Donald Trump on, 1; US focus on, 11–12
US military, 67, 70, 73, 76, 85

Valdivia, Angharad N., 48
"Value of Immigrant Life" (Inda 2002), 99–100
Vega, Paz, 46, 50, 145n6
Veronica's Closet (1997–2000), 49
Vice News Tonight, 139n12
victimization, 42
visibility: and #CentralAmericanTwitter, 28–29; and Cache, 16, 112–114, 117–118, 123, 127–128; in *Dirt*, 52, 60; and *domésticas*, 15, 46–47, 49; and exclusion, 129; and green card soldiers, 67; and marginalization, 30; and Mid-City Arts, 119–121; paradoxes of, 10–12; and representations, 130; and Trump administration, 83; in *Will and Grace*, 55
"Vote Honey" (*Will and Grace* webisode), 45–46

war on terror, 81
Wenders, Wim, 49
Westlake, 113, 117, 118, 153n9
West Side Story (1961), 47–48
Wetback: The Undocumented Documentary (2007), 89, 91–92